Adam Roberts

Critical Essays

Gylphi Contemporary Writers: Critical Essays

Series Editor: Sarah Dillon

Gylphi Contemporary Writers: Critical Essays presents a new approach to the academic study of living authors. The titles in this series are devoted to contemporary British, Irish and American authors whose work is popularly and critically valued but on whom a significant body of academic work has yet to be established. Each of the titles in this series is developed out of the best contributions to an international conference on its author; represents the most intelligent and provocative material in current thinking about that author's work; and, suggests future avenues of thought, comparison and analysis. With each title prefaced by an author foreword, this series embraces the challenges of writing on living authors and provides the foundation stones for future critical work on significant contemporary writers.

Series Titles

David Mitchell: Critical Essays (2011)
Edited by Sarah Dillon. Foreword by David Mitchell.

Maggie Gee: Critical Essays (2015)
Edited by Sarah Dillon and Caroline Edwards. Foreword by Maggie Gee.

China Miéville: Critical Essays (2015)
Edited by Caroline Edwards and Tony Venezia. Foreword by China Miéville.

Adam Roberts: Critical Essays (2016)
Edited by Christos Callow Jr. and Anna McFarlane. Foreword by Adam Roberts.

Rupert Thomson: Critical Essays (2016)
Edited by Rebecca Pohl and Christopher Vardy. Foreword by Rupert Thomson.

Tom McCarthy: Critical Essays (2016)
Edited by Dennis Duncan. Foreword by Tom McCarthy.

Adam Roberts

Critical Essays

edited by

Christos Callow Jr. and Anna McFarlane

Gylphi

A *Gylphi Limited* Book

First published in Great Britain in 2016
by Gylphi Limited

A CIP catalogue record for this book is available from the British Library.

ISBN 978-1-78024-042-8 (pbk)
ISBN 978-1-78024-043-5 (Kindle)
ISBN 978-1-78024-044-2 (EPUB)

Design and typesetting by Gylphi Limited. Printed in the UK by imprintdigital.com, Exeter.

Cover image by Evangelos Callow.

Gylphi Limited
PO Box 993
Canterbury CT1 9EP, UK

Contents

Acknowledgements

The editors would like to thank Caroline Edwards, who, with Christos Callow Jr., co-organized the New Genre Army conference which took place at the University of Lincoln on the 5th of April 2013. Thanks also to all of our contributors for the hard work they have put into this collection. To the series editor of the Gylphi 'Contemporary Writers: Critical Essays' series, Sarah Dillon, we owe a great deal for her thoughtful advice on our manuscript and for supporting us throughout the process, and to Gylphi for working with us to produce a collection that does justice to the hard work of the contributors. We are grateful to Evangelos Callow for designing both the conference poster and the cover of this collection. Thank you to Adam Roberts for his entertaining and thought-provoking participation in the conference and for providing the preface for this collection. Finally, we appreciate our friends and family who have supported us as we worked to bring this collection together.

List of Abbreviations

Abbreviations of works cited by Adam Roberts.

Date of first publication is in parenthesis, followed by details of edition cited throughout (if different from original edition).

AR Roberts, Adam (2013) *Adam Robots: Short Stories*. London: Gollancz.

B Roberts, Adam (2014) *Bête*. London: Gollancz.

BLA Roberts, Adam (2011) *By Light Alone*. London: Gollancz.

G Roberts, Adam (2006) *Gradisil*. London: Gollancz.

HSF Roberts, Adam (2006) *The History of Science Fiction*. Basingstoke: Palgrave Macmillan.

JG Roberts, Adam (2012) *Jack Glass*. London: Gollancz.

LOTH Roberts, Adam (2007) *Land of the Headless*. London: Gollancz.

NMA Roberts, Adam (2010) *New Model Army*. London: Gollancz.

O Roberts, Adam (2001) *On*. London: Gollancz.

P Roberts, Adam (2003) *Polystom*. London: Gollancz.

S Roberts, Adam (2000) *Salt*. London: Gollancz.

SF Roberts, Adam (2000) *Science Fiction*. London: Routledge.

TS Roberts, Adam (2004) *The Snow*. London: Gollancz.

SP Roberts, Adam (2007) *Splinter*. Nottingham: Solaris.

ST Roberts, Adam (2002) *Stone*. London: Gollancz.

SW Roberts, Adam (2008) *Swiftly: A Novel*. London: Gollancz.

YBT Roberts, Adam (2009) *Yellow Blue Tibia: A Novel*. London: Gollancz.

On Being the Object of Critical Scrutiny

Adam Roberts

Writers who become – as I did – the object of academic conferences about their work are liable to say things like 'it's a great honour'. There's a truth in that. It *is* an honour. I am certainly acutely conscious of the honour paid to me, or rather to my writing, when Christos Callow and Caroline Edwards organized New Genre Army, a conference about me. I attended, and was at once gladdened and humbled by the calibre of the papers delivered, the acuity of the critical intelligence bestowed on novels I had once written, the breadth and insight on display. I was, I confess, a little anxious before the event, fearful I suppose that it would be embarrassing to be present at a discussion of my work (embarrassment, of course, is the worst thing imaginable for an Englishman). In the event it was a genuine pleasure.

'Honour' though is a strange, even an archaic quantity to invoke in such a circumstance. We use the phrase *faute de mieux*, as a way of registering the positive social aspect of the occasion. This in turn leads me to wonder if there is a disparity in our vocabulary where this particular mode of positivity is concerned. Think of the reverse case. We might be *shamed* by something; or we might feel *guilty* about something. Since at least Nietzsche, the shift from a predominantly 'shame' culture to a predominantly 'guilt' culture, reflected in among other things the Reformation, the relative atomization of society under the logic of High and then Late Capitalism and so on. Shame is a social and external agony; guilt a personal and internal one. Both have social-prophylactic functions, although each operates very differently to the other. Whether Orestes feels bad or good *in himself* for having murdered his mother is not a relevant question; what matters is what society as a whole thinks of him, and his atonement must happen as a public, external ritual. Contrast Raskolnikov, who could have gotten away with his double-murder if his conscience hadn't prompted him, despite his rational, self-preserving instincts, towards confession. Contrast all those agonized dialogue-of-the-mind-with-itself moderns.

Are there antonymic equivalences for both these terms? Honour, despite its old fashioned semantic-field, functions as a kind of anti-shame, a public iteration of worth, of praise, of merit. What's the antonym for guilt? I'm not sure we have a word that precisely fits the bill; the nearest I can come is the slang phrase 'egoboo', short for 'ego-boost'. That this is a tongue-in-cheek and Internet-only phrase speaks to something significant, I think – to our suspicion that where the honour of anti-shame is a social good, the egoboo of anti-guilt is not, because it borders on vanity, pride, selfishness and naked egoism.

Actually the 'ego' in egoboo is misleading. With guilt we feel bad about ourselves inwardly, perhaps but not necessarily because of some monstrosity of the ego. We can feel guilty for non-ego reasons. And we can feel that sensation's opposite for reasons unconnected with ego, too. Writing is like this. To adapt T. S. Eliot's famous words, good writing is not the expression of ego, but an escape from ego. The best writing is not fuelled by ego but by something the reverse.

The reason I dilate upon this matter is because one thing the conference brought home strongly to me, something re-reading these excellent essays has only enhanced, is the problematic way 'writing', or 'being a writer', straddles precisely this divide, anti-guilt and anti-shame. Publishing a novel is a public act, either shameful or honourable depending on the work. But *writing* a novel is a private act, a guilty or an [insert term here] business. To write a novel is to become intensely self-absorbed. I became a writer because I loved reading so very much, and because I discovered that writing is *like* reading *but more so* – more immersive, more involving, more ego-erasing. The actual writing is the part I enjoy; sitting down with a laptop, a large cup of sugarless black coffee and some headphone music. I've very often had the experience where I start to write, stop to stretch like a cat, thinking that minutes have passed to find that three hours had vanished. Whatever the opposite of guilt is, this is my experience of it in its most intense form.

Of course the inward, personal process must be transformed into an outward public one. We call this metamorphosis 'publication', and it exposes the tender membranes of the writerly consciousness to all manner of harsh buffets and shocks. Bad reviews; poor sales; neglect and abuse. To publish a novel is usually to cross the border into Ignoreland, and that's a hurtful process. Sometimes you're gifted a ticket on the fast train that takes you down to Hostility City, where the grass is green and the women are savagely dismissive of everything you were trying to achieve as an author. So it goes, and we can measure the maturity of an author by the placidity with which he or she encounters such public denigration. That doesn't mean it ever stops hurting, though; and the hurt is a function of precisely this chasm between the private inward impulse, where the writing happens, and the public, shaming-or-honouring world of post-publication.

This means I am all the more aware of the honour done me by the focus of critical attention embodied in this book, and all the more grateful for its sensitivity and penetration. I don't know what I have done to deserve it.

This, in other words, is the vertigo of a book like this, for this particular reader at any rate. Adam Phillips talks somewhere of 'the terrifying mislogic of self-consciousness'. I'm another Adam, and my self-consciousness as a writer extends just far enough to recognize that I don't fully comprehend my own praxis – that, indeed, if I ever found a way of achieving that impossible comprehension it would kill my art. I'm the least-well-placed person to judge my own writing.

Santayana once said (it was in *The Genteel Tradition in American Philosophy*) that 'to understand oneself is the classic form of consolation; to elide oneself is the romantic'. It strikes me that Classic versus Romantic, that old conceptual dogfight, is actually another way of framing this debate. The Classic artist seeks to make her case in public, in the brightness of enlightenment. The Romantic is looking for a more ironic elision of public and private, a configuring of the inward life as the proper matter of public discourse which is, in turn, to make an art that is more elusive. I thought I knew which kind of artist I am; it has taken this concentrated, high-calibre critical attention on my work to make me realize the truth is rather more complicated than I first thought.

New Model Writer

Christos Callow Jr. and Anna McFarlane

When thinking about the career of Adam Roberts there is a tendency to split him into different beasts. There is Adam Roberts, Professor of English Literature and Creative Writing at Royal Holloway, University of London, who holds a PhD in Robert Barrett Browning. Then there is Adam Roberts, science fiction author. There is also Adam Roberts, writer of satirical and comic novels. This polyphony is noted by critics such as Damien Walter, who observes 'there are other original voices in the field, but few as consistently and startlingly original. In a field where most writers can be relied upon to write the same book over and over again, Roberts insists on writing an entirely different book every time' (Walter, 2013). Thus Roberts's books represent unique engagements with science fiction and, indeed, with the history of ideas itself, eschewing the now common contemporary practice in science fiction and fantasy of working in trilogies, though he knows they sell better (Callow, 2013). This makes his work difficult to survey – it is not possible to lump his books together by series, or theme, or sometimes even sub-genre. They must be taken each on their own merits and with due attention paid to their literary progenitors as

Roberts interacts with the genre of science fiction at all possible levels, from offering his own definitions of science fiction to writing it and, finally, to parodying it in his comedy novels. While Roberts is more often classified as a high concept science fiction writer, rather than a writer of 'commercial fiction', he responds to the 'mainstream' through these parodies thereby opening a dialogue with modern pop culture.[1] A writer of such literary variety provides rich material for critical reflection both within and outside academic research.

This is an excellent time to discuss Roberts's work from an academic perspective and within the science fiction community, partly because of his status as an established writer of science fiction: Roberts's novels have always appeared under the Gollancz imprint, home of the SF Masterworks series, and the rise of his reputation over the last few years has taken him from a debut novel recognized on the shortlist for the Arthur C. Clarke Award to his repeated appearance in shortlists almost every year since. In 2013, on the eve of the first academic conference on his work, he finally earned his first major award, the British Science Fiction Association (BSFA) award for *Jack Glass* (2012). Meanwhile, the growing academic interest in science fiction in British academia is evidenced by the increasing number of conferences on the genre, for example: the annual 'Contemporary Research in Speculative Fiction' (CRSF) conference at the University of Liverpool, interdisciplinary conferences such as 'The Fantastika and the Classical World' conference in 2013, the annual 'Stage the Future' conference on science fiction theatre, and the academic programme of the 'World Science Fiction Convention' (or Worldcon), as well as the annual conference of the International Association for the Fantastic in the Arts.

These events demonstrate that science fiction is a hot topic for academic research and, after the David Mitchell, China Miéville and Maggie Gee conferences, the name of Roberts is an important addition to the *Gylphi Contemporary Writers: Critical Essays* series. Roberts as an author has gained high praise from many other significant contemporary science fiction writers and critics since his work has been reviewed in such publications as *Locus, Strange Horizons* and the *Guardian*. Paul Di Filippo (2012) writes in *Locus*: 'his fiction represents some of the best work being done in our 21st-century genre'. Walter (2013) calls him 'the last of the SF writers' while Lavie Tidhar (2011) writes that Roberts 'is both the Fool and Knave of science fiction'. David Barnett (2013) calls him 'the master of the big idea; of high-concept science fiction'. Finally, regarding Roberts's place in contemporary literature, Niall Alexander (2011) writes in *SF Signal*: 'Roberts stands head and shoulders above many of his contemporaries, pushing this and that genre every which way but loose, year in and year out'. The lack of previous academic criticism on the one hand, and the abundance of critical praise on the other – along with the quantity of Roberts's creative and scholarly work – indicate further the demand for academic attention.

Adam Roberts's novels speak to important debates about how science fiction functions as a genre and, more widely, how literature expresses futurist, humanist and posthumanist concerns. Roberts has often used extreme environments to push his characters to the limits of human endurance and to express the impact that material conditions have on human philosophy. His first novel, *Salt* (2000), depicted an inhospitable planet as it is settled by humans for the first time. The planet's surface consists almost entirely of salt and this lethal landscape serves to drive physical barriers between ideologically divided anarchist and militarist communities. In this first novel, Roberts shows many of the themes which resurface in his novels: alienating characters, inhospitable environments and the exploration of ethics and ideology. *On* (2001) is also a novel of extremes, set on an earth that has been through a devastating tragedy with the result that gravity has swung round 90 degrees and turned the world into a wall to which its inhabitants must cling or fall down a never-ending cliff. Meanwhile, in *The Snow* (2004), the disaster facing the earth is a three-mile deep snowfall whose origins may be extraterrestrial. *Gradisil* (2006) combines an exploration of libertarian philosophical positions with a deep engagement with the science fiction canon as Roberts writes about a Heinlein-esque colony on the moon, while *Polystom* (2003) depicts an alternative universe filled with atmosphere, as vacuum is impossible. The title character of *Polystom* searches for the true reality of the universe, only to discover that his world may be a computer simulation. This is a hypothesis which has been suggested by philosophers and explored by scientists, making *Polystom* a strong example of hard science fiction, science fiction with its roots in real science.[2] These novels all, in different ways, investigate humanity's relationship with its environment and explore how a change in the ecosystem, or of physical laws, can affect the ideologies that shape human lives and communities.

Furthermore, in a genre known for privileging technology and setting over character, Roberts has shown an interest in testing the empathy and understanding of the reader to the limit through his alienating protagonists. *Stone* (2002) is a space opera set in a far-future utopia, but the novel tests the limits of such a society through an alienating main character who challenges the reader to construct the plot and an ethical compass from the skewed perspective of a sociopath. *Land of the Headless* (2007) challenges the reader's empathy as the main character is a headless criminal who may or may not be a rapist. He lives in a religious fundamentalist society in which beheading is used as a punishment alongside futuristic technology that can keep the criminal alive, even after their sentence has been carried out. This premise challenges science fiction narratives in which technology is represented as a marker of progress and a savior from irrational or prejudiced ways of life.

Roberts's encyclopedic knowledge of the traditions in which he works has inevitably informed much of his writing, but rather than repeat the formulae of science fictions of the past he reimagines them for his own purposes and in doing so produces a kind of commentary on earlier texts and science fiction sub-genres. In 2007, *Splinter* was published, a reimagining of the Jules Verne book *Hector Servadac* (1877), also known in English as *Off on a Comet.* Roberts found the extant translation outdated and incomplete, so he re-translated Verne's novel into English, leading him to agitate for a complete re-translation and re-appraisal of Verne's work.[3] *Splinter* became a deeply postmodern take on Verne's original, as well as a satire on realist fiction as the main character, Hector Jr., struggles to come to terms with his father's authority and sexual prowess in the days, weeks and months after the end of the world. Roberts's interest in Jules Verne is clearly still with him as he revisits his worlds in *Twenty Trillion Leagues Under the Sea* (2014); however his urge to reimagine science fiction's classic texts is not limited to Jules Verne: 2008's *Swiftly* is a steampunk sequel to Jonathan Swift's *Gulliver's Travels* (1726), in which the empires of the nineteenth century enslave and exploit the races that Gulliver discovered.

Yellow Blue Tibia (2009) and *New Model Army* (2010) use the science fiction toolkit to discuss two different political structures: *Yellow Blue Tibia* satirizes Stalin's authoritarian Communism while *New Model Army* imagines the ultimate participatory democracy through an army that functions as one organism with the help of mobile communications and instant messaging. This political sensibility develops in the two novels that follow as *By Light Alone* (2011) and *Jack Glass* (2012) are increasingly concerned with inequality and poverty. *By Light Alone* is set in a world where human beings have discovered a way to photosynthesize, feeding on sunlight through nanotechnology in their hair. This means that wealthy people who wish to consume conspicuously shave their heads and become fat from solid foods. *Jack Glass* combines the golden age of detective fiction with the golden age of science fiction and its attraction is in the game it plays with genre and language coupled with its interest in inequality, as it depicts a universe divided between the super-rich and powerful and the proletariat who live precarious, violent lives. The murderer in this mystery is revealed in the preface and the book becomes a 'howdunnit' as readers struggle to discover the technological means by which the crime is committed. Finally, this novel represents Roberts's break into mainstream science fiction as it was awarded the BSFA award for best novel and the John W. Campbell Award.[4]

Jack Glass was followed by *Bête* (2014), in which Roberts turns his attention to human–animal relationships. It is worth pausing to think about *Bête* in some detail as the novel, published as this collection was nearing completion, brings together many of the themes that recur throughout Roberts's work and throughout this collection. This combination led Niall Alexander (2014) to proclaim *Bête* 'the best of both worlds – the coming together of all the aspects of Adam Roberts: the author, the professor and the satirist, among others'. The novel follows Graham, a surly meat farmer whose livelihood is taken away when animals are given the power of speech through electronic chips implanted in their brains by animal rights activists. The law considers the speaking animals to be sentient, thereby outlawing Graham's butchery and condemning him to an itinerant life. Like *Swiftly* or *Splinter*, *Bête* can be read as a retelling of an older text: in this case, the story of Oedipus via H. G. Well's *The Island of Dr Moreau* (1896) and C. S. Lewis's *The Lion, the Witch and the Wardrobe* (1950). As well as playing with Roberts's established interest in intertexts, the novel tests the limits of consciousness and humanity through the invention of the electronic chips which attach themselves to the brain stems of the animals allowing them to speak. These loquacious beasts spell the end for the meat industry as we know it, disrupting the food chain and having a huge impact on human relationships in so doing, as in *By Light Alone*. The talking animals also offer a chance to explore the role language and language games (such as the riddles of the Sphinx in the story of Oedipus) play in human culture, a subject Roberts had already begun to explore in his deconstruction of the whodunit in *Jack Glass*. When the relationships between humans and loquacious beasts inevitably break down there are echoes of the philosophy of war, already explored in *New Model Army*, and the interactions between theology and changing scientific possibilities that troubled the protagonist of *Land of the Headless*. The synthesis of these themes in *Bête* shows Roberts's growing mastery of the novel as a mode of expression. The novel captures many of the characteristics that define Roberts's work and, indeed, this collection: the alienating characters that challenge the reader, the political interventions and thought experiments that could map out a better future, the ludic approach of the language game and the intertextual networks that allow Roberts's work to act as a commentary on his literary forebears.

In addition to his science fiction novels, Roberts has written a number of shorter fictions, including parodies and short fiction. His parodies of famous novels and films, such as *The Soddit* (2003), *Star Warped* (2005) and *The Dragon with the Girl Tattoo* (2010) are signed using his pseudonyms; for instance, for *The Soddit* (2003), which parodies J. R. R. Tolkien's *The Hobbit* (1937), he uses the pseudonym A. R. R. R. Roberts, while for the *Star Wars* (1977) parody *Star Warped* (2005) he signs as A3r Roberts. The value of these parodies is in their critical engagement with popular culture, its ideas and aesthetics; furthermore, they are arguably the most linguistically playful of his works, especially when it comes to composing puns, as in the titles of these works. The parodies revel in puns and playing with words, as well as combining genres. For example, in *The Dragon With the Girl Tattoo* we find this passage:

> She hatched an idea. Ideas, you see, are hatched – like dragons. And like dragons, ideas can *burn*. But unlike dragons, ideas are not four-legged scaled creatures that weigh anything from one to forty tonnes. The analogy is not precise in every particular. (Roberts, 2010: 83)

The play on words, combined with the very dragon-like perspective, transforms Stieg Larsson's *The Girl With the Dragon Tattoo* (2005) into a fantastic comedy with traces of Terry Pratchett. Roberts's short stories, many of which are collected in *Adam Robots* (2013), are often specifically concerned with the relationship between scientific innovation and science fiction. His story 'S-Bomb', about a bomb that attacks the superstrings that make up reality, appeared in *Riffing on Strings: Science Fiction and String Theory* (2008) while 'The Chrome Chromosome' describes robots built from chrome DNA and was published in Ken MacLeod's *The Human Genre Project* (2009).

While Roberts has explored science fiction as a writer, he has also contributed to its growing presence in academia. In the year of publication of his debut novel, he also produced his first major academic work on the genre, *Science Fiction* (2000).[5] *Science Fiction*, published as part of Routledge's New Critical Idiom series, provides an overview of science fiction studies for students and scholars alike and is notable for its witty, opinionated tone. He co-edited the *Routledge Companion to Science Fiction* (2009) and provided a chapter on the 'long history' of science fiction for that volume which contains some of the key ideas from his most important work of criticism so far: *The History of Science Fiction* (2006). In this book Roberts foregrounds old world science fiction by finding the beginnings of the genre in the fantastic journeys of Ancient Greek literature, a form he refers to as the *voyages extraordinaire*, using Jules Verne's terminology. He then locates a resurgence in science fiction and its separation from fantasy in the Reformation and the separation of the Protestant and Catholic churches. Roberts argues that this split produced science fiction as a rational narrative, while fantasy would spring from Catholic regions of the world where scientific endeavor was discouraged and treated with suspicion. These different attitudes towards scientific exploration resulted, Roberts argues, in the separate development of the science fiction and the fantastic imaginaries.[6] This long history of science fiction gives far less credit to the so-called 'Golden Age' of American science fiction pulp magazines of the 1930s and 1940s, usually the period understood to have given science fiction its name and to have ushered in the genre by doing so.[7] Roberts's Copernican reassessment of the locus of the science fictional impulse may be at the heart of his importance as a science fiction writer. By seeing the history of science fiction as wrapped up with the history of scientific progress, and the discussion of that progress outside of the Church's bastions of knowledge, Roberts sees it as our journey out of the dark ages through the Enlightenment and connects that history with our current scientific debates and problems. The relevance of contemporary scientific and literary debates in this history mean that the history is left open-ended, perhaps to leave space for the future of science fiction, to be written by Roberts among others. As Andy Sawyer (2011: 181) writes in his review of *The History of Science Fiction*, 'where Roberts stops may well be seen, in further "Histories", as somewhere near the beginning'.

When Christos Callow Jr. and Caroline Edwards organized the 'New Genre Army' conference at the University of Lincoln in April 2013 it was with the goal of analyzing the work of a writer who had been the subject of no previous academic research, with the exception of a conference paper by Anna McFarlane, delivered at the 2011 CRSF conference. New Genre Army was organized to address this deficit, but it seemed that even the presence of the author himself could not resolve the quantum uncertainty between his different roles as writer, critic, and satirist. He is a critical literary mind at one moment and, at another, a creative writer musing about the ethics of a photosynthesizing humanity. Perhaps that flexibility is part of the pleasure for academics engaging with Roberts's work which resists being forced into one box or another through the power of our observations; rather we hope to uncover the plurality of his work through the chapters that follow.

Farah Mendlesohn opens this collection with 'The Disassociated Hero', an insightful introduction to Roberts's work in which she diagnoses the main protagonists in almost all of his novels with dissociative personality disorder. In doing so, Mendlesohn positions Roberts's work as a diagnostic tool in itself, finding sociopathic tendencies in a genre that is famed for its love of setting and the privileging of hardware over character. Particularly focusing on *Gradisil* and *Jack Glass*, Mendlesohn shows that the 'character problem' in science fiction – its obsession with setting and technology over characterization – allows the conditions for these twisted, alienating protagonists. Mendlesohn uses children's literature to distinguish between the use of extrinsic character (character shaped by circumstances) and intrinsic character (character as relatively fixed and innate), a distinction which emphasizes the ideological nature of the reader position, one that is crucial to the character problem in science fiction, and in the novels of Adam Roberts.

Michelle Yost also hones in on the alienating nature of many of Roberts's characters and this leads her to consider his novels as contemporary examples of Menippean satire. She particularly focuses on his portrayal of radical theocracies in *Salt, Land of the Headless* and *Snow,* thereby showing how Roberts uses science fiction as a satirical thought experiment in her chapter 'Pax Per Tyrannis: Religious and Political Extremism Exposed via Menippean Satire in the Novels of Adam Roberts'. Yost argues that these novels show the untenability of such theocracies through hyperbolic examples that satirize contemporary fundamentalist societies by drawing attention to their logical inconsistencies and their moral failures. These alienating characters have had an impact on the reader reception of Roberts's work, as shown by Niall Harrison in 'New Model Readers: Changing Critical and Popular Receptions of the Science Fiction of Adam Roberts'. Through rigorous analysis, Harrison looks at the new model readers – science fiction fans who at first found Roberts's characters (and indeed, his novels on the whole) somewhat alienating but have learned to read and enjoy Roberts's style by using *Yellow Blue Tibia* as something of a Rosetta stone, a key to approaching the rest of his oeuvre.

Anna McFarlane begins looking at Roberts's work through a political lens by approaching *Jack Glass* through one of its intertexts. In 'Breaking the Cycle of the Golden Age: *Jack Glass* and Isaac Asimov's *Foundation* Trilogy', McFarlane focuses on the ways in which the novel overcomes the conventions of Golden Age science fiction by reading *Jack Glass* alongside Asimov's *Foundation* novels to show that the move from Asimov's Foundation to Jack Glass's galaxy is a move from Newtonian physics to chaos theory, a move which demands attention be paid to small phenomenon, such as individual humans rather than 'the masses'. McFarlane argues that this move produces a more democratic view of the galaxy, one that demands revolution to escape the exploitative hierarches under which Jack Glass lives.

In her chapter 'On the Topic of Plenty: Sunshine and Ice-Cream Mountains in *By Light Alone*', Catherine Parry investigates the connection between food and dehumanization in *By Light Alone*'s post-scarcity society. Parry highlights the importance of food to Roberts's work in both *By Light Alone* and *Bête* before examining *By Light Alone*'s use of food as a marker of economic inequality. While recognizing the serious consideration of ecojustice, Parry also shows that *By Light Alone* revels in the intertextuality so central to his work through his use of the Homeric narrative structures and characters.

Thomas Wellmann's 'Nation-State 2.0: Visions of Europe in Adam Roberts's *New Model Army*' argues for the importance of the European landscape, nations and nationality in *New Model Army*; he shows that the ongoing arguments over the legitimacy of the European Union's power are a part of the novel's satirical target and are skillfully negotiated through the novel's structure-theme interaction. The novel's evocation of a 'true democracy' invites questions about the relationship between the individual and their community, or the relationship between single nation states and the European community, between warring nations and (ideally) peaceful union.

The next section of the book consists of two ludic approaches which reflect Roberts's playful style through their form as well as their content. First, Paul Graham Raven looks at *New Model Army* from a different angle; he takes an experimental approach to Adam Roberts's use of intertextuality as bricolage by constructing a response to an imaginary text, Graeme P. Crow's *Thunder and Consolation: New Model Army as Ephemeral Anarchist Utopia* (2013) and considers how Burroughsian cut-up methods and bricolage can be used to engage with *New Model Army*'s networked milieu. Following Raven is Andrew M. Butler who explores the plurality of 'Roberts the author' and the tensions inherent in approaching a body of work via the author and via the genre. The first assumes an individual creative genie while the latter treats the work as engaging in a collective project. Butler approaches Roberts as a polymath in order to walk the line between the two approaches, exploring the lives and works of various authors by the name of 'Adam Roberts' and conflating them in order to draw the reader's attention to the impact that the author's name and biography have on our interpretation of the text. Butler uses this intertextuality of the authorial persona to approach the intertextuality in Roberts's writing, drawing attention to the ways in which his novels act as meta-commentaries on (among others) Jules Verne's *voyages extraordinaires,* crime fiction, Golden Age science fiction and Swiftian satire in order to push generic boundaries. Based on Andrew M. Butler's keynote speech to the New Genre Army conference, the chapter is a lively, satirical investigation into the role of the living, present author.

The final section of our collection specifically analyses the intertextuality so central to Roberts's oeuvre. Glyn Morgan begins with 'Beyond Brobdingnagians and Bolsheviks: Extra-Textual Readings of *Swiftly* and *Yellow Blue Tibia*'. Using the theory of Gérard Genette, Morgan analyses the paratexts, intertexts and metatextual practices used in Roberts's fiction. He begins by exploring *Swiftly*'s relationship to *Gulliver's Travels* (1726) and the genre of alternate history. Morgan argues that *Swiftly* occupies multiple positions as a sequel, an alternate history and a steampunk novel, none of which completely capture its genre. He goes on to discuss the importance of metatextuality in *Yellow Blue Tibia* as the main protagonist is a science fiction writer who has worked on Robert Barret Browning, just like Adam Roberts. Through exploring these different textual layers Morgan finds that

Roberts's work demands an intertextual reading and thereby draws attention to the intertextuality of science fiction more generally. In 'Rule of Law: Reiterating Genre in *Jack Glass*', Paul March-Russell continues analyzing Roberts's use of intertextuality as *Jack Glass* subverts the Golden Age of detective fiction, an act that March-Russell identifies as an act of doubling. Reading the novel alongside Golden Age crime fictions by Agatha Christie and Dorothy L. Sayers, among others, March-Russell argues that this subversion allows *Jack Glass* to uncover moral, ethical and political content in detective fiction that would otherwise be overlooked.

Each chapter in this collection explores the challenge posed to science fiction, literary fiction and contemporary ideas through Roberts's novels. His use of the science fiction toolkit combined with his sharp and sometimes lyrical prose blurs the distinction that some would wish to maintain between science fiction and mainstream literature. This challenge was recognized by Kim Stanley Robinson who suggested that the literary establishment was turning its back on a new golden age of British science fiction and it should have awarded Roberts the Booker Prize for *Yellow Blue Tibia* (Robinson, 2009). Roberts also tests the boundaries of genre by inhabiting and repeating traditional formulae but with a self-aware tone, a wit that comes from his deep knowledge of his subject and its relationship to the wider historical context. He challenges the rigidity of academic styles by bringing his wit to his sometimes playful criticism, while producing work that is astoundingly broad in scope and richly researched, like *The History of Science Fiction*. These contradictions, challenges and tributes to the genre, are some of the tangles that *Adam Roberts: Critical Essays* addresses. The contributions to this collection come from science fiction scholars and critics. Perhaps our aim here is not to collapse the quantum wave form of uncertainty into specific labels, to pin down the Adam Roberts's new model writing, but to understand the multiple possibilities and the many alternate futures that Roberts's work represents for science fiction and for science fiction studies.

Notes

1 Roberts has been named a 'high concept' SF author on Tor.com in an article entitled 'Meet Adam Roberts: the King of High Concept' (Anders, 2009).

2 The suggestion that the world might be a computer simulation was put forward by Nick Bostrom (2003) and tested in 2012 by a team of scientists led by Silas R. Beane (2012).

3 As Roberts explains in 'Jules Verne Deserves a Better Translation Service' (2007).

4 For a more detailed description of Adam Roberts's novels, see his entry in the *Encyclopedia of Science Fiction* (Clute, 2014).

5 While this was Roberts's first major work of science fiction criticism, he had already shown signs of interest in writing about science fictional topics academically through such articles as 'DH Lawrence and Wells' Future Men' (1993) and 'Keats's "Attic Shape": Ode on a Grecian Urn and Non-Euclidian Geometry' (1995).

6 He explains that, 'to a Protestant imagination ... the cosmos expands before the probing inquiries of empirical science through the seventeenth and eighteenth centuries and the imaginative-speculative exploration of that universe expands with it. This is the science fiction imagination, and it becomes increasingly a function of western Protestant culture. From this SF develops as an imaginatively expansive and (crucially) materialist mode of literature, as opposed to the magical-fantastic, fundamentally religious mode that comes to be known as Fantasy' (*HSF*: x).

7 For example, in Gary Westfahl's *The Mechanics of Wonder* (1998).

Works Cited

Alexander, Niall (2011) 'Niall Alexander on *By Light Alone* by Adam Roberts', *SF Signal*, 14 November, URL (consulted March 2014): http://www.sfsignal.com/archives/2011/11/guest_review_niall_alexander_on_by_light_alone_by_adam_roberts/

Alexander, Niall (2014) 'Eternal Treblinka of the Spotless Soul: *Bête* by Adam Roberts', *Tor.com*, 24 September, URL (consulted August 2015): http://www.tor.com/2014/09/24/book-review-bete-adam-roberts/

Anders, Lou (2009) 'Meet Adam Roberts: the King of High Concept', *Tor.com*, 4 February, URL (consulted March 2014): http://www.tor.com/blogs/2009/02/meet-adam-roberts

Barnett, David (2013) '*By Light Alone,* By Adam Roberts', *The Independent,* 14 August, URL (consulted March 2014): http://www.independent.co.uk/arts-entertainment/books/reviews/by-light-alone-by-adam-roberts-2337172.html

Beane, Silas R. (2012) 'Constraints on the Universe as a Numerical Simulation', Cornell University Library, 9 November, URL (consulted August 2015): http://arxiv.org/pdf/1210.1847v2.pdf

Bostrom, Nick (2003) 'Are You Living in a Simulation?', *Philosophical Quarterly* 53(211): 243–55.

Callow, Christos, Jr. (2013) 'Irony, Man: An Interview with Adam Roberts', *Strange Horizons,* 25 March, URL (consulted March 2014): http://www.strangehorizons.com/2013/20130325/2roberts-a.shtml

Clute, John (2014) 'Roberts, Adam' in John Clute, David Langford, Peter Nicholls and Graham Sleight (eds) *The Encyclopedia of Science Fiction,* 8 September, URL (consulted September 2014): http://www.sf-encyclopedia.com/entry/roberts_adam

Di Filippo, Paul (2012) 'Paul Di Filippo Reviews Adam Roberts', *Locus Online,* 24 August, URL (consulted March 2014): http://www.locusmag.com/Reviews/2012/08/paul-di-filippo-reviews-adam-roberts/

Roberts, Adam (1993) 'D. H. Lawrence and Wells' Future Men', *Notes and Queries* 40: 67–8.

Roberts, Adam (1995) 'Keats's "Attic Shape": Ode on a Grecian Urn and Non-Euclidian Geometry', *Keats-Shelley Review* 9: 1–14.

Roberts, Adam (2007) 'Jules Verne Deserves a Better Translation Service', *Guardian,* 11 September, URL (consulted March 2014): http://www.theguardian.com/books/booksblog/2007/sep/11/julesvernedeservesabetter

Roberts, Adam (2010) *The Dragon With the Girl Tattoo.* London: Gollancz.

Robinson, Kim Stanley (2009) 'Science Fiction: The Stories of Now', *New Scientist,* 16 September, Issue 2726, URL (consulted March 2014): http://www.newscientist.com/article/mg20327263.200-why-isnt-science-fiction-winning-any-literary-awards.html

Sawyer, Andy (2011) 'Review: *The History of Science Fiction* by Adam Roberts', *Utopian Studies,* 22(1): 177–81.

Tidhar, Lavie (2011) 'Shall I Tell You The Problem With Adam Roberts?', *Lavie Tidhar Wordpress,* 14 December, URL (consulted March 2014): http://lavietidhar.wordpress.com/tag/stone/

Walter, Damien (2013) 'Adam Roberts: Last of the SF Writers', *Guardian*, 15 February, URL (consulted March 2014): http://www.guardian.co.uk/books/booksblog/2013/feb/15/adam-roberts-last-sci-fi-writer
Westfahl, Gary (1998) *The Mechanics of Wonder: The Creation of the Idea of Science Fiction*. Liverpool: University of Liverpool Press.

Part I

Alienating Characters

THE DISASSOCIATED HERO

Farah Mendlesohn

For some time now, I have been fascinated by the ways in which a text positions a reader, and what that does to the reading of the text. In *Rhetorics of Fantasy* (2008), I was concerned with the ways the reader position shaped the nature of the fantastic world constructed, and how it politicized that text, positioning the reader as insider or outsider, as critic or consensualist. When I moved on to work on children's science fiction, and more recently children's fantasy, the sense that the reader position was essentially a political or ideological position was intensified. Whereas in fantasy different reader positions appeared to exist more or less in parallel across the genre, in fiction for children there was and is a very clear sense that reader positions have changed dramatically across the past two hundred years, and that this change is firmly linked to understandings of 'the child' (a construction used far too frequently in the field) and to a belief in what the young reader should take from a text.

The history of the child reader's position with regards to the text is necessarily too complex to discuss in full here, but a short version of this can be drawn as follows: eighteenth- and early nineteenth-century fiction positions children outside the text as spectators.[1] The relationship constructed between child and protagonist is often distant but intense, for the major purpose of such fiction is to operate as a warning to the child. It is the consequences of the activities of the protagonist, rather than the protagonist him/herself, which are the focus of the tale, as the bad child is punished, the good rewarded. As this period of literature represents personality as coherent and unchanging, character sketches are drawn in such a way that the character is intrinsic to itself, an actor upon the world, rather than a function of societal pressures (see, for example, the characters in either Dickens's work for children, or that of Thackeray, or Kingsley). This intensifies the distance, and the emphasis on the outcome and consequences of actions taken.

By the end of the nineteenth century, in such texts as Louisa May Alcott's *Little Women* (1868), or Rudyard Kipling's *Stalky and Co.* (1899), and well into the 1940s and 1950s, a new reader position was being constructed, one which still positioned the child as the outsider (the third person narrative position will do that) but which focalized the reader on the character's experience of events and the consequences *on their character*, rather than disassociating the two. This construction of the reader position is aimed at fostering admiration and respect for the main protagonists. The child characters here are models to emulate even when, or especially when, as with Jo March, their struggle to *be good* is long and difficult. This particular model was endemic in the boys' book of the nineteenth century, constructed in Frederic William Farrar's *Eric, Or Little By Little* (1858) a transitional text that deploys both fear for dreadful consequences, and admiration for those who can resist temptation. This approach bedded down in Thomas Hughes's *Tom Brown's Schooldays* (1857) and was mocked mercilessly in *Stalky & Co.*

As children's fiction moved into the twentieth century a shift emerged that we could already see in *Little Women*, from admiration to a requirement to identify, to see the child protagonist as oneself and explore or apply their choices to *what you would have done*. This is most explicitly stated at the very end of Noel Streatfeild's *Ballet Shoes* (1936: 235). Which of the three Fossil sisters – Posy the dancer,

Pauline the actress, or Petrova the engineer and auxiliary pilot – *would you want to be*?[2]

What we see is a growing trajectory of intimacy with the characters in the text, and an increasing sense that it is the character and the development of character that is at stake, rather than the adventure per se, so that in *The Lion, the Witch and the Wardrobe* (1950), the major driver of the story is the character of Edmund and how he is formed and reshaped – a trope that recurs even more vividly in *The Voyage of the Dawn Treader* (1952). The reader's gaze is drawn into an intimacy with the protagonist. For all that the story is meant to be an adventure and allegory of Christ's passion, it is Judas who walks away with our sympathy, although not yet, I suspect, our identification. In much teen fiction of the 1950s, particularly the career books, a muted form of this mode was carried over: the protagonist's failures, as well as his or her successes, were part of a learning curve that the reader was expected to share. Increasingly the trajectory of experience rather than the outcome was the focus of the story (see for example Judy Blume's *Are You There God? It's Me, Margaret* [1970] whose story is unmemorable, while the stations of her Calgary are distinct). You can see this in modern fantasy sequences, where the growing into grace of godhood or prophecy is the bulk of the story, or in science fiction for teens where there is either an adult mentor or a school, as in David Eddings's Belgariad sequence (1982–4), Kathleen Duey's *Skin Hunger* (2007), much of Bruce 's work or even Suzanne Collins's *The Hunger Games* (2008), which could be understood as a futuristic version of Thomas Hughes's Rugby from *Tom Brown's School Days*.

The real move towards identification with the character as the primary ideal position of the reader comes with the rise and rise of the first person in fiction for children. We see the first person as early as Robert Louis Stevenson's *Treasure Island* (1883) and *Kidnapped* (1886), and it has, for better or worse, come to dominate what is labelled Young Adult (YA) fiction.[3] It is a position which when delivered 'honestly' is constructed as impermeable and sealed. By this I do not mean that the narrator cannot be unreliable or the text deconstructed, but that the assumption which it wants the reader to adopt is an intimacy and identification with that character. Even where first person is not the choice of the author, this concept of *identification* with the character now runs through the review columns and children's book reports, and is a given within the many bibliographies available to advise you on buying for your children. Inevitably, this now influences the reporting and contextualization of fiction for adults, and is, I suspect, what people increasingly mean when they discuss the quality of characterization in a text.

The ideological nature of the reader-protagonist relationship

The construction of this reader–protagonist relationship is at the heart of what is regarded as 'the character problem' in science fiction: as I have written in *The Cambridge Companion to Science Fiction* (2003: 10), one reason science fiction 'falls down' on characterization for non-SF critics can be because the reader is looking in the wrong direction, at human beings, rather than the planet; for one-to-one relationships, rather than the relationship of person to polis. There is certainly a case to be made that the rather stiff and self-declared rational characters (something I will be exploring in a moment) with which Roberts peoples his novels are far less interesting than the worlds he creates: *Salt* (2000), *On* (2001), *Stone* (2002) and even, to a degree, *Polystom* (2010), are all picaresques (novels in which an individual moves through a world, having only loosely connected adventures which neither promote character growth nor cohere as plot), or planetary romances, in which the intensity of the emotional connection between individuals never matches the intensity of relationships between individual and world. This is perhaps most vivid in *On*, where Tighe's survival is precisely dependent on that intensity. In a world in which gravity is vertical, clinging to people in the world of *On* is a lot less important than clinging to a ledge or to the social structures of your community (and there may be a truth in that which should be more widely acknowledged).

However, what I want to propose here, is that 'the character problem' is also linked to the choice made by many within the genre to eschew the 'identification with' position that has become the default in much mainstream literature (although I do recognize, not all such literature). Science fiction, like the thriller, has continued to make use of the more distant position in which the protagonist explores on our behalf the physical and moral landscape of the situation. We are not expected to identify with this exploration, but to ride along as a companion. The degree to which this companionate role is collaborative or antagonistic varies enormously, but I would contend that for much science fiction (if not fantasy, where the discourse has shifted dramatically in the past twenty years, as discussed in *Rhetorics of Fantasy*), the position 'this protagonist is like me, and therefore someone with whom I am comfortable to explore the world' is far less important. This opens up some very real possibilities that I think Adam Roberts has deliberately positioned himself to exploit.

The ideological nature of the reader position is crucial to understanding the work of Adam Roberts, because the more of it one reads with this in mind the clearer it becomes that it is not simply that his protagonists are unlikeable, or that they seem for the most part very flat, but that these protagonists are radically disassociated both from the models of reader–protagonist relationship that I have described and, for the most part, from the character-context that literature has come to take for granted ever since the mainstream moved from an idea of intrinsic character to consequent character. Intrinsic character is common to nineteenth-century literature; it assumes that people begin good or bad, and that this position shapes the effect of the world upon them. Most nineteenth-century novels are stories of intrinsic character overcoming the pressures of the world – thus, in a mid-twentieth-century holdover, Edmund is saved both because of Aslan's sacrifice, but also because he had 'gone wrong' without it fundamentally changing who he was underneath. This is made even more vivid in the peeling away of Eustace's dragon nature in *The Voyage of the Dawn Treader*. There is never any hint that the White Witch could be redeemed. In contrast, modern fiction tends towards the representation of consequential character. Here, what happens in the world profoundly affects the individual, who may grow into or away from grace. In Roberts, we read over and over again of the Fall of Man (and occasionally woman),[4] but I intend to argue that the men and women

Roberts creates are, with only a few exceptions, understood as having *intrinsic* character which is revealed by the decline of their worlds, rather than extrinsic characters which are shaped by them.

One issue to consider in understanding the protagonists of a Roberts novel is the degree to which the worlds Roberts creates are marginal: not one of the societies he builds offers space for the careless. The world of Salt only just qualifies to be in the 'Goldilocks zone'; to live on earth in *On* is to cling like a puffin to a ledge, as one false move is a death sentence; in *Gradisil* (2006) the uplands are utterly marginal, and rendered more marginal by the libertarian philosophy.[5] In most of Roberts's fiction, the world is dispassionately out to kill the protagonist – frequently helped by the other characters, of course.

I have now made three points that I want to bring together:

1 that Roberts maintains the reader in an external relationship with the protagonist, one in which admiration or identification is not required.

2 that the characters Roberts creates have fundamentally stronger relationships with the worlds they are in, than with the people with whom they interact. And,

3 that the characters are essentially intrinsic; they come with character intact and the trajectory of the text is to 'reveal' rather than shape.

Combine all of these together, and as a result of reading all thirteen novels currently in print in consecutive order, I came to the conclusion that the protagonist in an Adam Roberts text is, with one exception, diagnosable with one of the non-treatable personality disorders – to wit, sociopathy, disassociation, or narcissism – and that this is a rather more revealing lens through which to see these texts than to simply remark on the general unlikeability of a Roberts protagonist.[6]

The World Health Organization no longer uses the term sociopath, but 'dissocial personality disorder'.[7] Dissocial personality disorder is characterized by at least three of the following:

1 Callous unconcern for the feelings of others

2 Gross and persistent attitude of irresponsibility and disregard for social norms, rules, and obligations

3 Incapacity to maintain enduring relationships though having no difficulty in establishing them

4 Very low tolerance to frustration and a low threshold for discharge of violence
5 Incapacity to experience guilt or to profit from experience, particularly punishment
6 Markedly prone to blame others, or to offer plausible rationalizations for the behaviour that has brought the person into conflict with society.

Roberts deploys characters who fit comfortably into this category in almost all of his work: in *Salt, Polystom, On, Stone,* and *Jack Glass* (2012). I am less comfortable placing *Land of the Headless* (2007) and *New Model Army* (2010) into this category because both protagonists seem to fit as easily (perhaps more easily) into the clinical definitions of narcissistic personality disorder, in which the individual is described as being excessively pre-occupied with issues of personal adequacy, power, prestige and vanity.

Not every character in Roberts's fiction seems to be constructed as an intrinsic sociopath. At least two of the sociopathic protagonists have extrinsic, consequential characters. Tighe in *On* has clearly defined relationships with his parents and his family, and it is only as the traumatic processional of his picaresque proceeds that he appears to be increasingly unable to maintain relationships, although he retains the skill of establishing them; the further Tighe travels, the less the people around him seem like people, and the more they resemble landscape distinguished from the architecture only by being a little less interesting. Polystom is a member of a sociopathic society: as in the ante-bellum American South sociopathy has been embedded in the culture by legitimating all the above characteristics when applied to a class of persons understood to be non-people. Polystom's uncle rapes slaves but sees them as toys; revolt cannot have motives, it just is, and is rationalized through scientific discourse; there can be no profiting from experience because there can be no acknowledgement of others of this class as actors; the failure of a relationship must therefore be the fault of the other, and not the fault of the institution or one's collaboration with this institution. In *Polystom,* the protagonist's love of poetry becomes (rather cleverly) not the chink through which empathy enters, disrupting the pathological society, but the wall he builds around himself; its artificiality becomes a distancing device, a display of culture and a metaphor for the falsity of the world.

Intrinsic sociopathy, which I think I find more interesting as a device, is vivid in *Salt, Stone, Jack Glass,* and *New Model Army*. What I noticed in the consecutive reading I undertook is that many of Roberts's novels can be paired, as he returns to issues he wants to explore. *Stone* and *Jack Glass* is one such pairing, *Salt* and *New Model Army* is another.

In *Stone* and the first novella of *Jack Glass*, 'In the Box', we are presented with the classic sociopath: both protagonists, Ae in *Stone* and Jack Glass in 'In the Box', appear relentlessly normal and pleasant. Both are people we are inclined to like, although in *Stone* we know from the beginning that the character is a murderer; in *Jack Glass*, we are situated rather differently. The use of the name Jac, without a surname, creates an ambiguity in this most literalist of genres. Jac may be Jack, but we cannot be absolutely sure: his presentation as a disabled, legless man, guilty of a non-violent crime, is, excuse the joke, *disarming*.[8] Both characters turn out to have no sense of allegiance to those around them, and to be able to contemplate levels of violence alien to even the violent characters with whom Jack Glass is incarcerated. However the structure of their sociopathy is rather different with Ae (*Stone*) a passive sociopath who looks to blame others, and Jack Glass an active, but even less associated character. This difference shapes both their function and the stories told.

The main character in *Stone*, Ae, is an experimental sociopath. Although lacking empathy there is an intensity of engagement with her subjects that renders her fascinating and attractive. Ae wants to know what happens if.... She is the toddler who pulls the lead on the lamp while watching her parents watch what she does. She is that person who wonders idly how long a spider plant can last without water, or how much she has to bate a dog before it will bite. Ae can learn, but her learning is not correctly categorized, a lesson from one experience is not extrapolated to her position in the world: *murdering X is wrong, but perhaps murdering Y won't be?* The isolating punishment of her prison therefore, is in part the absence of objects/personalities she can tease, and *in addition* the absence of the parental disapproval that is part of the structure of her sociopathy. The trajectory of the story entirely depends on this position of the character, and the sympathy it engenders in us – because it is hard to hate the childlike. Otherwise the story is riddled with what I have been known to call 'the stupid': twists and turns that anyone who understands narrative would question. Over and over again Ae trusts the orders she is given, the clues she is offered, to follow a paper chase of a story in which she will eventually be betrayed. That the novel as a whole does not trigger 'the stupid' response is precisely because the sociopathy of this character renders her actions plausible. The structure of the rescue and the mission relieves her from responsibility for her own actions – a responsibility she has already disowned in her understandings of the murders she committed, which were neither crimes of passion nor motive, but always of impulse or curiosity. The mission bates her curiosity – *what happens if I follow this clue* – and panders to the invisible *how will the parents/authority react if I do this?* Similarly, Ae's innate likeableness – there is nothing vicious, she is actually rather gentle between murders – facilitates her moving through the worlds that Roberts has set up. This explains *why* the picaresque mode: in the picaresque, first, one is always leaving people behind just as they get to know you, second, you leave behind your mess for someone else to clear up – although the park keepers may chase after you – and third, you yourself make no more attachment to people than tourists do to the people who clear their bed chambers. The picaresque, in its structure – always going forward, never looking back – is itself a sociopathic form.

The protagonist of the novella 'In the Box' is a rather different mode of sociopath, and indeed, can only be kept in this category as long as we do not read into the next two novellas: the back story of Jack Glass will turn out to be that of a determined ideologue (which itself tends to require at least a hint of sociopathy) but this is invisible here. When we meet Jack Glass he is the second most vulnerable member of a team of convicts dropped on an asteroid: they have enough tools and food to survive *if* they cooperate and if they hollow out the asteroid and render it habitable for a future settler. Refusing either of these activities will result in death. Although at first necessity seems to drive the team to collaborate, a true cooperation never emerges, with several members of the team playing a continually changing power game in which each considers themselves the leader, while creating a predator prey relationship between themselves and the two weakest members of the group: Jack Glass, or 'Jac', who has no legs, and Gordius, a timid and obese man. Both are picked out for abuse and rape. Gordius quickly crumbles. Jac disassociates: from the beginning he steps back mentally and acts as the observer and the narrative voice is distanced, describing his internal feelings from an external position. We know he is terrified, not of the people with whom he is incarcerated, but that the police force who have incarcerated him will discover who he truly is. The result is several manifestations of disassociation which appear at first to be extrinsic, linked to his situation.

Although the story is told in third person, the focalization of the story is solidly with Jac, it is his perception we receive, and the third person acts to compound the disassociation which is such a feature of the novella.

Jac's descriptions of his companions is essentially anthropological:

> Day followed day. Jac kept his eye on them all. Marit had a cruel streak, no question; but Jac figured Davide was more immediately dangerous, for his frustration was working alchemically upon his rage ... Lwon and E-d-C were too focused on manoeuvering for position in the group as a whole to divert energy towards persecuting Gordius or Jac. No: Mo and Marit were the most immediate threat. (*JG*: 43)

The tone is cold and even though we understand as readers that these are Jac's observations, they are indirect, disassociated from him. The thread of Jac's narrative is, throughout, disengaged: he is disengaged from the dominance games, from the abuse, and even from his own physical activity. He spends much of his time polishing a piece of glass. When challenged, he presents this endless polishing of the glass as something to pass the time.

Jac's position as observer rather than actor in the political interaction within the group seems to be utterly justified by his need to escape, rather than to survive. It is noticeable that the only other character who even thinks of escape is Gordius, and that this is based on his experience with his cell mates. But Jac's disassociation is reinforced in the way the repeated rapes are described. First, they are understood as symptomatic of the group's politics, a reflection of power, not lust or pleasure:

> The hierarchy was made most manifest in the group's sexual arrangements. Gordius got the worst of this, unluckily for him, with everyone but Jac taking humiliating advantage of his body in various ways. To begin with he wept openly at his cruel usage, complained, begged them to leave him be. But after a while he seemed to become habituated to it, in a glum sort of way. The other men would often discuss him as a sexual object, combining many taunts at his obesity with more admiring observations that his extra weight at least gave him a feminine quality, at least from certain angles. With respect to Jac their comments were more dismissive: his deformity was, all agreed, a repulsive thing. It meant that they left his rear-end alone, although all five of them did insist upon other ways in which he could gratify them. Jac seemed to take these indignities with a quiet stoicism; but then it was hard to tell what he was really thinking. He kept his thoughts to himself. (*JG*: 35)

Gordius is the emoter, positioned as the feminine both in usage and response. Jac is impassive, 'taking it like a man' to deploy a cliché, but also exempt from the most feminizing form of abuse, more exempt than the two members of the group, Mo and Marit, who occupy a middling position. 'Sometimes they were treated as *de facto* alphas ... But sometimes, without warning, the top three would treat Marit and Mo as betas ... This was mostly a question of penetrative sex ... ' (*JG*: 35). Read closely, it suggests that under some circumstances Jac occupies a higher or at least less touchable position in the hierarchy, a point reinforced when Roberts adds that it is more likely to be Gordius whom Mo hurts in turn. This structure, fragile though it may be, is underscored because Jac takes no part in the usage of Gordius.

The choice *not* to exploit Gordius, or to kick the cat further down the line, positions us to regard Jac as nicer, more civilized, someone who does not prey on his fellow, nor kick the next person down the line. Jac is positioned in this moment as Gentle Jesus Meek and Mild. The actual key set of words is 'it was hard to tell what he was really thinking'. In reality these descriptive scenes will not be evidence of Jac's empathy with Gordius – as Gordius hopes – but evidence of Jac's disassociation from the group, his continual apartness from their concerns. Similarly, it is not evidence of his acceptance that he is at the bottom of the hierarchy, but instead it is retrospective evidence that he is simply not in the game. At moments of conflict or dominance games Jac disappears into the background, he disassociates. Where Gordius makes his presence felt even in whimpers, Jac quietly slides into grey. All of this is reinforced by the cool, descriptive voice of the third person, the voice of the 'disinterested' narrator.

Towards the end of the story, Gordius attacks Jac, and we hear Jac's reasoning as to what he will and will not do:

> The options slotted into place beside him. To strike repeatedly at the body, or the neck, or perhaps at the face. That would surely encourage Gordius to cease his attack, but it would surely open wounds in the skin. (*JG*: 65)

When the fight, such as it is, is over, Jac offers a little tender loving care, worried that 'a cut might very easily become infected. And once infection took hold, who knows where it might go – it could suppurate, whole patches of skin could become open sores. Gordius might die in agony. Jac didn't want that' (*JG*: 67). Over and over again Jac's sociopathy is disguised in apparent sympathy, even empathy, with Gordius, which is why the final section, in which Jac turns Gordius into a space suit, is both shocking and moving. The section begins with the most intimate of manoeuvres, a kiss. As Jac forces a kiss on Mo he uses it to silence him, cutting him open with his sharpened shard of glass. There is an intimacy to Jac's actions, and for the first time an openness to his motivations that we have not seen before. As he skins Gordius and prepares his body, every action is described. His only utterance, 'What can I tell you? ... This is the truth on which space settlement is founded. Energy is valuable, and raw materials are precious, but human beings are mere resources to be exploited' (*JG*: 92). And with that the text returns to the careful, disassociated description of engineering the body suit, of a type *absolutely congruent with the expectations of the genre*. And that is crucial. This is not the horror of the gothic. The ending of 'In the Box' is horrific because it reveals something about the nature of a genre in which fine descriptions of engineering have generally been prized above fine descriptions of people; where the environment and how an individual relates to the environment is considered more important than how individuals relate to each other. 'In the Box' homes in on this: it is not a perversion to say that the others die because they are more concerned with their relationships with each other, than they are with their relationship with the asteroid. Jac succeeds because he follows the rules of genre, not because he is subversive, and in doing so reveals that the genre as a whole is sociopathic to the core. That is where the real shock lies in this story.

The idea that the genre might be sociopathic to the core, is clearest in three stories: *Gradisil,* and two novels I intend to pair, *Salt* and *New Model Army*. In *Gradisil,* Roberts offers a neat reversal, telling the story of Jesus from the point of view of Judas. It is a tale of narcissism, but there is always a question over *whose* narcissism, and whose sociopathy is at stake. The first part of *Gradisil* is a not untypical tale of libertarian colonialism in which rather a lot of incorrect assumptions about 'how the west was won' are transported to space. A bunch of dreamers, drifters and very wealthy no-hopers establish a foothold in the Lagrange territories, and then seek to fight off the government (the USA) and seek independence. This is a very twentieth-century interpretation of how western expansion, or even the founding of America, worked: a more accurate picture runs, government provides means and licenses for settlement and piracy; people collaborate to survive or die; and they get pissed off with government and shoot for independence when the services they want from the government are refused ... everything from help clearing out the natives, to roads or power. The belief that colonial (and other expansionist) enterprises are the actions of individuals resisting the state, is a form of institutionalized sociopathy that has infected the American body politic and the genre of science fiction. In order to bring together these people, in the second part of the book the titular character Gradisil (granddaughter of the earliest protagonist) plays on their isolation, creating a network of those who eschew the benefits of statism.

The last part of *Gradisil* openly acknowledges this: telling the story of the titular character through the eyes of a man who knows his role is to 'play wife' to the dignitary – by which I mean both offering the stability and support great roles seem to demand, and providing camouflage for his wife's other activities. This deliberately draws attention to the sociopathy at the heart of both Gradisil and the colonization project. Gradisil and the other colonizers all have far stronger relationships to their surroundings than they ever do to people; the focus is always on what is built, and what is created. Most live isolated lives; even those who live in groups remain isolated within those groups and from other communities. Gradisil herself rejects the companionship of marriage and family in any sense that we would recognize: her children are appeasement to her husband, to keep him happy and occupied: her decision to sacrifice the only pregnancy to which he is genetically connected is not a 'sacrifice' in the usual sense of the word: it is, as Paul realizes, a strategic ploy in which a pregnancy was generated in order to mislead the strategists of the USA. That Gradisil does not calculate the impression that this strategy will make on Paul is a symptom of her assumption, shaped in part by the kind of people she is trying to organize, that everyone makes the same calculations that she does, and that her husband is as invested in the project as she; or, if not her political project, the project of family. She misreads his investment in *her* because for all of her calculation of the emotional response around her to the cause, this kind of person to person calculation is unrecognizable to her.

Gradisil's story is told from the outside in that, while it is Paul's internal narrative, he is positioned as observer to someone else's story, not as the centre of his own, while *Salt* and *New Model Army* are told from the inside. In both cases we are dealing with the *intrinsic* sociopath, people who are utterly divorced from the common connections of the world but, in both cases, do not necessarily understand themselves this way. Once again, this position, if accepted, turns both novels into critiques of a kind of sociopathy endemic to science fiction.

In *Salt*, we are presented with two protagonists, one authoritarian, one anarchist: I am assuming that a modern audience will be inclined to sympathize with the anarchic character (although I am not convinced that would always have been the case: Harry Harrison's *The Stainless Steel Rat* is a genuinely subversive figure when he first appears in 1961). Both protagonists begin the novel ensconced within the moral culture of their communities and *both* – and this is important – think of themselves as good people. Petja, the Alsist, sees himself as a cell within a larger organism in which whatever he does is for the good of himself and, by extension, of his community. Barlei, leader of the Senaar, sees himself as a cell within a larger organism which must be led. Both talk in terms of nature, and of what is natural or inevitable. Both deteriorate morally not by deviating from their core beliefs – although Petja is eventually excluded from a relationship and from relationships with some of his colleagues because he is seen as a 'rigidist', an obsessive in matters of love, work and ideology – but because they become ever more entrenched in the exquisite purity of their belief as something separate from the people: this rapidly leads to what Ken MacLeod once summed up for me in conversation as 'the wrong kind of people' problem. Once ideology becomes the ruler of the people rather than its servant you are half way down the road to a society which by its nature produces sociopaths, more in love with the beauties of the world they describe than either its reality or its people. Crucially, by the end of the book both characters, who feel themselves so distinct, have fallen prey to the same delusion; that they know what is right for everyone and that they themselves are part of a wider movement. It is these two points that pair this book with *New Model Army*.

The multiple narrative positions of *Salt* allow us to judge and contexualize: it is fairly transparent that Barlei's paternalism has gone toxic, that 'for' the people has become meaningless; Petja's anarchism has become unhinged isolation. The more Petja moves away from the collective the less contextualized his anarchism, and the less he seems to be fighting a war, and the more to be locked into nihilism. What is intended to be narratively ambiguous ends up too conclusive with an enormous sense of loss as Petja (more than Barlei) loses the thing he thinks he is fighting for.

This is where the first person narrative of *New Model Army* has a very real strength: as readers, locked into the head of a narrator we cannot easily judge reliable or unreliable, we must be conscious that the story we are invited to believe in is utterly dependent on the reliability or otherwise of the narrator protagonist. Either he is a part of a distributed army, set on recreating the thirty years war in England's Green and Pleasant Land, or he is a delusional sociopath/psychopath who is creating mayhem within a recognized structure of terror. There is also, however, a middle road in which the sociopath becomes the perfect soldier in a distributed army, precisely because it is his disassociation that allows the character to fight with people he has never met and to whom he feels no collective loyalty (something that armies are usually keen to inculcate); it allows him to move in and out of the civilian population; to regard his ex-lover's house as an ideal billet.

All of the novels I have considered here, and several that I have not, have a trajectory that begins with a conventional reader position of identification: Petja and Gradisil are engaged in colonizing projects familiar to and welcomed by the SF reader; Jac is incarcerated with a gang of bloodthirsty criminals; Polystom is a poet; Ae is terribly sweet and our Soldier is a good old boy. However, as the novels proceed we are increasingly estranged from them, not because they are changed by their adventures, but because they become progressively more themselves. Their adventures strip away the artifice of culture and justification constructed by the character but perhaps more significantly strip away the justifications accreted by genre expectation. In focusing precisely on what happens when a character's relationship with the environment or world is stronger than his or her relationships with people, Roberts reveals a delusion at the heart of the genre.

Notes

1 For more on the history of the child reader's position see Beverly Lyon Clark's *Kiddie Lit* (2004) or Maria Nikolajeva's *Power, Voice and Subjectivity in Literature for Young Readers* (2012).

2 I wanted to be Petrova, was far more like Pauline, and have turned out to be Dr. Jakes.

3 Young Adult fiction is directed at teens and is as much an ideological construction of what teenagers want as it is a marketing label.

4 As is common in writing by men in science fiction, there are not enough women in most of Roberts's books for population to be sustained. However, in most of his texts there are reasons for a sexual imbalance, and many of the populations are sustained only by migration, or are shrinking, so he gets a pass.

5 One political issue I have with most SF, and Roberts's in particular, is that historically communalist societies are better at surviving.

6 The exception is the protagonist of *Yellow Blue Tibia* (2009), who is quite clearly suffering from PTSD, but otherwise seems quite normal and connected to people for a Roberts protagonist.

7 The ICD-10 Classification of Mental and Behavioural Disorders Diagnostic criteria for research, 1993, F60.

8 In the two succeeding novellas, Jack Glass is reimagined as a revolutionary; once he is given motive, he is actually a functionally weakened character.

Works Cited

Clarke, Beverly Lyon (2004) *Kiddie Lit: The Cultural Construction of Children's Literature in America*. Baltimore, MD: Johns Hopkins University Press.

James, Edward and Farah Mendlesohn (eds) (2003) *The Cambridge Companion to Science Fiction*. Cambridge: Cambridge University Press.

Mendlesohn, Farah (2008) *Rhetorics of Fantasy*. Westport, CT: Wesleyan University Press.

Nikolajeva, Maria (2012) *Power, Voice and Subjectivity in Literature for Young Readers*. London: Routledge.

Streatfeild, Noel (1935/ 2011) *Ballet Shoes*. London: Puffin.

Pax Per Tyrannis

Religious and Political Extremism Exposed via Menippean Satire in the Novels of Adam Roberts

Michelle Yost

> My enemies tell me that many stayed away in protest of my handling of the war, at the fact of the war at all! Mendacity. How easily cancer breaks into the body politic. But I can still see that littering of pale bodies along the route, an insult to a great man. There were so few of them bothered to turn up, and those that did wore such ragged clothing, and seemed to be protesting and preaching sedition with the very boniness of their arms and legs, the very drawn and skull-visible faces. The people are the limb of my body. I will not have it.
>
> *Salt* (224)

How does a dictator justify their actions? How does a political terrorist? From his earliest work, Adam Roberts has employed political and religious extremism in his narratives, from warring ideology in *Salt* (2000) to beheading for adultery in *Land of the Headless* (2007), and the rise of the conservative New United States of America in *The Snow* (2004). When reading many of Roberts's novels, there is a sense of a certain cultural and institutional irreverence, and in some cases, this irreverence is carried over into the more ancient genre of Menippean satire.[1] These narrative constructs are built upon the hypocrisies and anxieties readers may sense in contemporary socio-political and religious institutions, the flaws of which are magnified by Roberts in satiric hyperbole. Science fiction serves as a vehicle for Roberts's exploration of extremist perceptions of religious and political necessity; his satirical *gedankenexperiments* are about the truths, lies and shades of grey that people use to justify their actions, whether it is the exploitation of the poor or the bombing of a public place.[2]

Northrop Frye provides a useful definition of the Menippean satire that seems to best encompass Roberts's work:

> The Menippean satire deals less with people as such than with mental attitudes. Pedants, bigots, cranks, parvenus, virtuosi, enthusiasts, rapacious and incompetent professional men of all kinds, are handled in terms of their occupational approach to life as distinct from their social behaviour. The Menippean satire thus resembles the confession in its ability to handle abstract ideas and theories, and differs from the novel in its characterization, which is stylised rather than naturalistic, and presents people as mouthpieces of the ideas they represent. (Frye, 1957: 309)

Roberts fills the pages of his narratives with characters who often appear as caricatures of religious fundamentalism, political extremism, and homicidal compulsion. The competing narrators of Barlei and Petja in *Salt* both use the language of religious and political necessity to justify their acts of violence. The poet Jon Cavala in *Land of the Headless* loses his head (but not his life) in strict accordance with religious interpretations of punishment for extra-marital sex. Tira is essentially forced into a loveless marriage in *The Snow* by the New USA to stabilize and rebuild the remnants of humanity. Where there has been some criticism of Roberts's novels being severely estranged from traditional storytelling (Kincaid, 2011), it should be considered that this is perhaps because readers are not capable of reconciling their paradigms for human action with the radicalized visions Roberts has generated; his characters are not people so much as they are the avatars of ideas that reach into the absurd and the uncomfortable; they are the Panglosses and Pantagruels of modern dogmas. This chapter aims to present a working thesis arguing that some of Roberts's works operate as portraits of extremist theocracy (the blending of political and religious practice) under which his characters and their society suffer, showing these contexts as untenable states of being for human existence. By presenting this state of affairs as satire, Roberts is tacitly acknowledging the hyperbole of his thought experiments (rather than attempting to induce fear) and simultaneously ridiculing institutions that would embrace radical religio-political practice.

In his informative article, 'Learning to read Adam Roberts', Paul Kincaid first proposed the interpretation of Roberts's novels as Menippean satire. Kincaid, however, viewed works such as *Swiftly* (2004) and *Yellow Blue Tibia* (2010) as satires of science fiction itself (Kincaid, 2011). He does not address the overarching satire that permeates Roberts's work, criticizing non-democratic institutions of religion, government, and the military as oppressive and detrimental to the average individual excluded by a hierarchy of power. The violence exercised by these institutions in the name of maintaining the institution is justified in myriad ways that would strike any but the institutional zealot as bordering on the insane. But in the Menippean satire, making sense of the subject being satirized is not the point: exposing the subjects as the flawed products of flawed philosophies is.

Consider Bakhtin's definition of Menippean satire:

> The most important characteristic of the menippea as a genre is the fact that its bold and unrestrained use of the fantastic and adventure is internally motivated, justified by and devoted to a purely ideational and philosophical end: the creation of *extraordinary situations* for the provoking and testing of a philosophical idea, a discourse, a *truth*, embodied in the image of a wise man, a seeker of truth. (Bakhtin, 1994: 189)

The central character of Roberts's novels – be they presented to us in first or third person – is the wise man/wise woman in extraordinary situations seeking truth in a world that seems turned on its head by philosophical extremism. To this end, we will use *Salt* to identify the 'wise man', *Land of the Headless* to explore the 'extraordinary situation', and *The Snow* to uncover the 'truth'. In each, the necessity of the violence employed in the narratives is explored, and the hypocrisy of *pax per tyrannis* ('peace through tyranny') exposed as a dangerous path for humanity. A unifying setting to all three novels is the deserts in which Roberts places these narratives: a desert of salt, a desert of sand, and a desert of snow; extreme environments provoking extreme reaction, the barrenness of the land creating a blank space to bring to the forefront the human mind and test its philosophical limits.

The Wise Man

Salt, Adam Roberts's first SF novel, presents two narrators: the free wise man, Petja, and the autocratic despot, Barlei. Both represent opposing religious and political views on the new colony world of Salt. The opening quote from the beginning of this chapter comes from Barlei, leader of the Senaar settlement in the south, whose first-person narrative is given over to the justification of his actions that lead to violent confrontation for everyone on the planet. He perceives 'enemies' in anyone who does not agree with him, and sedition in the appearance of an emaciated populace that is starving because of his policies. Barlei interprets the failure of his policies not as any fault on his part, but as 'cancer' (*S*: 224), projecting his own moral and political shortcomings onto those forced to endure his failings as a leader. What also helps to establish Barlei as a caricature is the hyperbolic, paranoid language, and the fact that we have no other internal view of the Senaar than Barlei until the last chapter (which comes from an average, non-political individual). Moreover, Barlei's reliability as a narrator decreases with each appearance of his voice.

Barlei's voice is contrasted with that of Petja, from the northern Als settlement, in every way the polar opposite (politically, religiously, geographically), whose position as the reasonable, peaceable member of an anarchist group gradually deteriorates, turning him into everything he never wanted to be: a war leader and a terrorist. Because Barlei's account of the conflict between Senaar and Als is written with loaded language and questionable motives, Petja, in turn, must be our wise man seeking truth, even as his actions come to resemble those of a terrorist (targeting not just the Senaaran military, but its civilian population and public works as well) rather than the pacifist he used to be. 'The testing of a wise man is a test of his philosophical position in the world,' Bakhtin says, 'not a test of any other features of his character independent of that position' (Bakhtin, 1994: 189). Petja – and the Alsists as a whole – fail to sustain their philosophy of equality without hierarchy, freedom without legal compulsion, faith without dogma. They fail to do so, not because they are wrong, but because the implied malignance that is Senaar's totalitarian plutocracy/theocracy is too strong. The 'truth' that Petja finds is that giving himself wholly to the cause of warring against Senaar is the only freedom which remains to him, and is an ultimately fatal choice.

Roberts excoriates the theocracy, which uses wealth and violence to subdue its own population and bring others into its sphere of rule. Barlei seeks to make Senaar the hegemony of Salt in violation of the colonization agreements. He is the obfuscator of truth, and Petja's account of the war is as close to the truth as we can get, but it must be filtered through a mentality radically different from our own. He is the Alsist ideal, the utopian ideal, an extension of Le Guin's anarchist 'utopia' in *The Dispossessed*. Petja shows us a civilization where everyone is responsible for themselves and free to do as they choose, without legal ramifications, worship the Divine as it best suits them, enter and leave relationships at leisure, existing in a balance of mere contentedness. To be called a 'rigidist' is an insult, meaning you are possessive and lacking in social flexibility, perhaps even going so far as to establish hierarchy, all sins to the Alsist.

This stands in contrast to Senaar, where wealth buys votes and political power, women are subservient to men, and where there is rampant hierarchical capitalism in all aspects of life, from marriage to healthcare. The society Roberts describes via Barlei is not subtle in its satirical tone, especially when it comes to the position of Barlei's new home on Salt:

> It might have looked as if I was hiding under the protection of the dome, as if I was afraid to brave the dangers of radiation like my peo-

> ple. Worse (in political terms) it associated me with the weak, the sick and the children. So I chose a site on a raised plateau, five metres above sea-level, overlooking the Galilee (enemy propaganda suggests I had the police evict two families to vacate this space, but this is not true; both families were very happy to give the ground over to me). (*S*: 48)

Barlei repeatedly makes reference to 'enemies' and 'propaganda', ensuring that future readers on Salt understand that his record of the settlement of Salt, and the ensuing war between Senaar and Als, is the most truthful, the most divine. But by his character protesting too much, Roberts leads us to understand Barlei's narrative to be the most false. He is the pedant and parvenu which Frye cites as a target of the Menippean satire.

At times, the society Petja describes may seem crude and undesirable, but Roberts is simply exposing the occasionally silly practices that we engage in every day: forcing ourselves out of politeness to remain part of a conversation in which we have no interest; being coy and discrete about sexual interest instead of open and honest; trying to claim others as our property (via marriage, birth or political hierarchy); employing a complex legal system that exists to perpetuate itself rather than letting human nature, through either a fistfight or hunger, control behaviour. Worst of all, claiming to have an all-knowing 'truth' about God's divine will, and how others should live their lives – this is the source of the great conflict between Als and Senaar. The latter simply cannot accept that the former would choose to live as they do, rather than the Senaaran way. Als is not really perfect, and Petja is not a saint, but he moves from naiveté to the 'wise man' who finally knows the human world through Senaar and Barlei; it is not a good world, but he knows it now. Petja realizes how the Senaar organize their society, and as a 'wise man', does not want such a political structure in his life.

In the case of both narrators, however, their tales appear to be seeking the legalistic and moral Defence of Necessity. According to English Common Law the use of the Necessity Defence (breaking the law due to immediate need) means that the defender faced an unjustified threat, the defender's interests are stronger than the attacker's, the response must be proportional to the threat, and the force exercised must be necessary to avoid the threat (Lazar, 2012: 3–4). The conflict between Senaar and Als begins with men among the Senarrans fathering children with Als women; the Senaarans are a patriarchal society, and though the Alsists recognize no '-archy' form of government, 'parenting is of the mother' (*S*: 145) and no Alsist would dream of coming between a woman and her child. Though Barlei insists that the fathers only want visiting rights to their children, no father ever shows up. Instead, troops are sent to physically take the children, killing several Alsists in the process, and starting a war. This was done to prevent the children from becoming 'warped by the culture of Als' (*S*: 55); to be clear, there was no physical threat to the children of the people of Senaar; the Senaarans simply objected to the Alsist lifestyle.

Barlei goes on to list the *casus belli* (provocations of war) to further establish his Defence of Necessity:

> [T]he trail of events leading to war implicates Als as the criminals. It was they who wickedly imprisoned the children, they who resisted a lawful operation of seizure (supported by the courts) with murderous force, and they who exacted a terrorist revenge on the civilians of our nation. At each stage we, the nation of Senaar (of whom you can feel genuine pride) responded with strength and restraint. (*S*: 161)

These are exaggerations, of course, and stand in contrast to Petja's account of events, but this is the satire. *Who* Barlei and Petja are as individuals is not as important as the philosophical ideas they represent. Readers must recognize Barlei as a crank and an incompetent leader, and through this recognition of defective character prevent such individuals from manifesting power in the real world. In a post-9/11 world (and it must be remembered that *Salt* was published the year before) it is not politically correct to empathize with or even endeavour to understand the terrorist; but it was the actions of Barlei that brought terrorism on his people, and had he been a more competent, sympathetic leader not bent on global dominance, individuals like Petja would not have brought terrorism to Salt. But this is the embodiment of Menippean satire, 'its concern with current and topical issues' (Bakhtin, 1994: 192), a millennia-old method of raising the mirror for society's review.

The Extraordinary Situation

The setting for any of Roberts's Menippean *gedankenexperiments* is one of Bakhtin's 'extraordinary situations', employing the fantastic 'not for the positive *embodiment* of truth, but as a mode for searching after truth, provoking it, and, more important, *testing* it.' (Bakhtin, 1994: 189). Reviews of *Land of the Headless* use words such as 'absurd' (*The Times*), 'grotesque' (*Starburst*), and 'burlesque' (*Locus*), reinforcing the absurdist situation in which the characters find themselves (Roberts, 2007). These settings and events that are meant to provoke the incredulity of readers, to touch something within us that rebels at living in such a world of extremes.

Like Voltaire's naive Candide, Roberts's Jon Cavala is the victim of a world that never seems to finish grinding him under foot; he is a poet no one has ever heard of, potentially a rapist, a reluctant soldier, prisoner, impoverished labourer, and a man without a head. *Land of the Headless* is another theocracy, based upon Roberts's invented meshing of Islamic-Christian values, dictated by the 'Bibliqu'rân', where out-of-wedlock fornication is punishable by the ancient practice of beheading. But because those values also stress the importance of mercy and forgiveness, the headless are kept alive by technology, and forced to live on in a world where their headlessness forever marks them as criminals, to be further punished and abused at will by any of the headed without legal recourse. Jon Cavala's situation is further complicated by the fact that his 'victim' (who recanted the sex being consensual, thus leaving her partner to face the charge of rape) was the daughter of a prominent citizen, and after being arrested once more by a friend of that prominent citizen (and once more accused of rape), Cavala is forced into the military, a trade as far from his former occupation as humanly imaginable. Many of the headless are pressed into military service for lack of any other economic option, their condition necessitating a regular supply of replacement hormones, having lost the various glands normally located in the head. The military as last-resort-for-the-poor is little changed between Roberts's imagined world and the circumstances for many in this world.

In order to save the head of the woman Siuzan Delage, who had befriended Jon after his 'execution', he tries to confess to his superior officer that he raped Siuzan, knowing that a second offence will result in a more permanent execution. Without a trace of irony, the officer tells Jon that this crime is inconsequential: 'You are new. But you will soon learn that the least infraction of military orders – let us say, stepping accidentally upon a newly watered lawn, or failing to address an officer as "Superior" – is infinitely more serious than rape, murder and heresy in the civilian world. That's always been the way in armies' (*LOTH*: 100). This satirical view of military law as separate and above civil law is as much commentary upon the present as the future.

Beheadings for adultery, blasphemy and murder, which leave the 'criminal' still living, are not the extraordinary situation here, but the very existence of this fundamentalist world: that is the focus of the satire. This is not Earth; humanity has expanded into the universe, and yet the world of Pluse uses a medieval penal code. The contradictory nature of this is highlighted in a discussion between headless soldiers about spaceflight and the 'God Particle' (that is, the Higgs Boson):

> 'If our spaceship is not powered by the God particles pouring from its nose,' said Syrophoenician, evidently in an argumentative mood, 'then perhaps you may explain to me, *sieur* soldier, how it is that only the godly may travel this way?'
>
> 'Another fallacy,' retorted Geza.
>
> 'You assert that the ungodly travel through space?'
>
> 'Indeed they do.'
>
> 'But not *faster than light* – only faith in the All'God permits travel that is faster than light.'
>
> 'You are wrong.'
>
> 'Soldier!' barked Syrophoenician, in imitation of a superior, with a metallic and sneering edge to his words. 'Your words are rotten and decayed, because your mind is rotten and decayed. Everybody knows that only the godly may travel faster than light.'

> 'A popular fallacy,' said Geza knowingly, 'is still a fallacy, for all its popularity.' (*LOTH*: 138)

Worlds not ruled by the All'God theology are 'Devil worlds' and nearly incomprehensible for the faithful to the point that the laws of physics do not apply to the secular. This is a hyperbolic construction by Roberts that illustrates the unbalanced nature of extreme beliefs. The exchange between the soldiers takes the extraordinary situation of space travel and employs it as a mirror for unquestioning faith (Frye's pedants and cranks) that misuses science for false conclusions.

Headless Jon Cavala is technically blind and deaf but for his mechanical appendages feeding grainy sight and tinny sounds to his ordinator (the device which has replaced his brain); and yet when it comes to the examination of philosophy he sees and hears more clearly than the headed (and many of his fellow headless). This is surely one of the supreme ironies of the novel; Cavala's satirical remarks pass over the 'heads' of nearly everyone, while they repeat the same mantras and asinine philosophies without ever hearing Cavala or considering his words:

> 'The divine We is who we are. Our religion is the spinal cord of our civilisation. Without the All'God all its richness would crumble.'
>
> 'It seems to me,' I said, after a silence. 'that the worship of God evolves over time, as cultures evolve. Is it heresy to say so?'
>
> 'Many scholars,' said Siuzan, 'and many theologians have argued the point. It can hardly be called heresy to discuss it…'
>
> 'Yet a man was beheaded last year for insisting the practice of decapitation be discontinued!' I said. 'It is heresy to oppose the beheadings, and heresy results in beheading…'
>
> 'The All'God's law,' she said again, 'is the All'God's law.'
>
> […]
>
> 'Though we speak to one another, you and I, perhaps,' I said, 'are having different conversations.' (*LOTH*: 11).

Speaking without really listening to each other is a feature found in many of Roberts's novels. This discussion of theocracy and theology between Jon and Siuzan is an example of the classic Menippean dialogue, where 'the dramatic interest is in a conflict of ideas rather than of character' (Frye: 310). For all of the fantastic action in *Land of the Headless*, it is still primarily a satire of ideas.

Even the progression of the novel appears to follow Bakhtin's outline of the Menippean satire as a 'three-planed construction', moving between Earth, Olympus (heaven) and the nether world (Bakhtin, 1994: 190). Beginning on Earth – or Pluse, in this case – Jon Cavala is forced by extraordinary circumstance (the loss of his head and the punitive arrest by a local police chief) to descend into hell: the army. He is tortured and starved along with the rest of the headless soldiers, called 'carcasses', to make him fight without regard for self. Sent to the world Athena to fight in the Sugar War, Cavala is treated to a vision while unconscious on the battlefield, what Bakhin calls 'dialogues of the dead' (Bakhtin, 1994: 190), in which truth is revealed to him. At the end of the war, Cavala makes his way back to Pluse – our metaphorical stand-in for Earth – where the final revelation of the lies that forced him into the military are revealed, and he is allowed to ascend to Olympus/heaven, a town called Montmorillon, the so-called 'Land of the Headless'. Nothing has changed on Pluse; the medieval legal system is still in place, Jon Cavala's head is not restored, but our protagonist has tested the philosophies and beliefs of his planet, and they have been found wanting. Cavala, however, is now wiser, and has found some semblance of happiness (with the minimum of vengeance) and that is the most that can be expected in a Menippean satire.

There is really no defence given for the necessity of beheading criminals, short of it being written in an ancient religious text. There is no defence given for the torture of headless soldiers who are considered nothing more than cannon fodder. There is no defence given for the continued persecution of the headless even as they occupy the bottom rungs of society. This is the satire Roberts has presented; a violent world that practises violence without necessity, merely at will. The reason Pluse is at war with Athena is because Athena does not want to trade with a world that practices such barbarism.

The Truth

Three miles of snow covering the Earth is an extraordinary situation, indeed, but by placing his novel *The Snow* on Earth – unlike our previous examples – Roberts brings his quest for truth closer to home. *The Snow* does not read as an overt satire like the previous two novels discussed because its characters are not as far flung from Earth. But the spirit of Mennipus is found in the irony that oozes between narrative segments. The Truth Roberts and his readers are in search of is not just an explanation for the Snow (as it is always referred to with a capital 'S'), but the truth of memory and how the mind can twist events in extraordinary situations. Tira is our 'wise man' – or woman, in this instance – who is testing our philosophies during her journey from beneath the Snow into the post-Snow world dominated by the American military. Why has Roberts chosen a woman, and a minority, to be the truth seeker? As he says in an interview with Alec Ash, 'The really big social questions of the 20th century were ... problems of encountering otherness: Race, gender, sexual orientation.' (Ash, 2011) By being neither white nor American, racially, Tira stands out in a world dominated by white snow and white survivors who take control of her life. The 'Truth' of what happened to the world, and Tira's unwitting role in uncovering it, is the driving force of the plot.

Tira's autobiography is presented as a series of documents (her survivor's account, a confession, further testimony and a coda) interspersed with other government documents, mimicking the epistolary novel. This gives Roberts the chance to highlight government censorship and misinformation, an essential part of truth-seeking in the satire; several documents start with '[Warning: this is an Illegal Document under the Texts (Restricted) Act ...]' (*TS*: 57) and for us, the readers, to be reading them is a crime, a violation of government injunction. But in *The Snow,* we are never entirely certain about the truth, because of incomplete, censored and contradictory testimony. The larger Truth to be garnered from this, as readers, is that a totalitarian military dictatorship – which is essentially what the New USA (NUSA – 'noose-ah', like a hangman's rope) is, despite all of its claims to being a democracy – will keep the truth from people;

it is comical that the state-run newspaper is called *Truth*, 'a sort-of-*Pravda*' according to Tira (*TS*: 94). The terrorist who becomes her lover reveals that *Truth* is run by family members of Liberty's mayor (*TS*: 151), that there is no free press in this new world order. In a somewhat comical statement that would likely make more sense to American readers than British, Tira states that in NUSA the only two political parties are the Republicans and the Free Republicans because mostly military and military-connected people survived the Snow, leaving few Democrats: 'the policy differences were tiny, really. Tiny.' (*TS*: 118–9). It is a subtle cultural reference to the predominance of conservative, Republican-affiliated American armed forces, and survivalist-minded individuals, many of whom do not trust the government. It is not just satirical but *ironic* that Roberts establishes a conservative, totalitarian government constructed from surviving American Republicans in his novel, turning the new government into a force American conservatives would oppose in our present reality.

When Tira is rescued from her confinement beneath the Snow, she is taken to a survivors' city called Liberty, one of several in the 'Free World' – a term Roberts is obviously using ironically. Despite the extraordinary circumstances and rarity of survivors, Tira still needs a sponsor to immigrate to Liberty (just as the impoverished labourers in *Salt* could be sponsored to move to Senaar for work) and it is suggested that because she is an attractive young woman, this will be easy (*TS*: 62–3). Tira does not want to go to the informal meet-and-greet which is really intended to find her a husband, but her interviewer suggests that while she can do what she likes – 'it's a free world, after all' (*TS*: 63) – without a sponsor (that is, a man, a husband) she will not be able to get a job or money. Women in this new world have been reverted to the old status of wife and procreator, auctioned to the highest bidder ('Crow' being the winner of Tira's hand in this instance) as we learn during the little 'party' thrown for Tira to meet several prominent members of Liberty. This is a Truth, however, that will never be spoken out loud, only implied, because it runs counter to everything for which this 'free world' *should* stand.

After her incarceration for associating with a known terrorist, 'Fred', and subsequently being infected by the alien Snow (an organism in the lungs that is not fatal, but is feared because of its permanence) Tira has her first open and honest conversation with the husband she felt forced upon her. When his statements about the nature of their relationship challenge her own, Tira begins to question the version of events told up to this point. Perhaps the Truth was *not* that her husband was racist and ceased marital relations when he found she was not white, pushing her into the arms of another lover, but that when she found another lover, he ceased marital relations. Tira is forced to question herself after Crow's revelation: 'the plain confidence with which he spoke unsettled my thoughts. Was I wrong? Had I misremembered the sequence of events? Because it is easy to do that, isn't it: to think *A* happened before *B* when in fact it happened after' (*TS*: 286). Reversing the order of events changes the context of their relationship from one of racial tensions to sexual tensions. Tira admits that it is possible she misunderstood her husband and their relationship the entire time because of past experiences clouding her emotions. The Truth is not just about politics, NUSA, and the Snow, but about Tira herself.

The Snow is the *force majeure* that has given the surviving military nearly unlimited powers, an Emergency 'with a big, pronged, capital "E"' (*TS*: 95) that justifies any necessity in the government's eyes. Tira highlights the suffering caused by military mismanagement, while at the same time admitting that she 'didn't suffer the way plenty of people in the city did' due to her highly connected military marriage (*TS*: 95). Roberts, in classical Menippean satirical form, is channelling contemporary observations into his novel, specifically that militaries make bad governments – not that traditional governments are really any better according to the characters in the novel.

In addition to Tira's voice, we have 'Fred' and his confession to terrorist activities both before and after the arrival of the Snow. He does not channel satire, but the abbreviated, broken-down 'Reader's Digest' version of the Truth: 'Authority Abuses. That's what Authority does, it's in its nature, it can't help it' (*TS*: 212–3). Fred is not, to say the least, a neuronormative individual, having indulged in heavy drug use before the Snow. He claims to have been abducted by aliens as a child, and is infected with the Snow later – his testimony about events and the corruption of the government is, at best, questionable. Tira often refers to him as being 'paranoid' and 'insane', so his view of events must be balanced against hers.

During one exchange with Tira, after the bombings of Liberty begin, she refers to Fred's proclamations as a 'justificatory dialectic' (*TS*: 151), revealing both her distaste for Fred's activities, and the very nature of both terrorist and dictatorial defensive statements: it is about justifying actions, on both sides. People like Tira, caught in the middle, only want to be left in peace and are swayed by neither side. Tira is the voice that was missing from *Salt*; had it been written in the vein of that novel, *The Snow* would have been constructed of narratives from Crow (the totalitarian) and Fred (the anarchist), two sides of the socio-political divide. Tira is the third voice, the middle road, looking for the Truth about the Snow and about herself. Roberts gives her this power not necessarily because she is female, but because she belongs to neither political faction; her failings are personal, not political.

Names are all listed as [Blank] and expletives as [*expletive deleted*] in an almost childish attempt to shield readers from any painful truths or offensive language. It is comical to read about the various [Blank]s in Tira's narrative, using context to discern which [Blank] she is referring to, while using one's imagination to fill in the appropriate [*expletive deleted*]. In her coda, written twenty years later, Tira remarks that 'it seems nowadays foolish and over-sensitive to blank out all the names' but that it was 'so redolent of its era' (*TS*: 291). Besides providing readers with some semblance of closure to the story and a finishing off of the Truth we have been seeking, the coda also reassures us that the dictatorial government has eased its hold on society, and that its attitudes have become a source of disdain. Release comes with Truth about the Others (the aliens which caused the Snow) and the terror which gripped Liberty. There is no restoration of the old Earth, but there is continuation of humanity and some semblance of peace.

Conclusion

What is the truth Adam Roberts is trying to tell his readers? It seems almost invariable from novel to novel: extremism in the form of government and/or faith that results in violence and suffering is immoral and an unsustainable method of existence; they result in dystopian nightmares. None of the novels discussed here are cheerful, and Roberts admitted in an interview to writing 'gloomy' stories: 'Certainly, some of my earlier works are very dour and very grim. But I like to think that they're dour and grim in an ironic way' (Callow, 2013). Irony, the heart of satire, is central to Roberts's philosophy on science fiction. Not necessarily amusing in a humorous way, the irony is meant to awaken the reader's sense of the absurd, even in the face of the depressing. Frye cautions that the Menippean satire constructed from a single intellectual idea 'makes for violent dislocations in the customary logic of narrative, though the appearance of carelessness that results reflects only the carelessness of the reader or his tendency to judge by a novel-centered conception of fiction' (Frye, 1957: 310).

The terrorist characters in Roberts's fiction are neither entirely evil nor fully justified in their actions, because it is almost always something in the nature of an oppressive society that pushes seemingly ordinary men to the extremes of human behaviour. Just as Voltaire's *Candide* is a 'fiercely relentless attack ... against the evils of religious fanaticism, war, colonialism, slavery and mass atrocities' (May, 2003: xx), the novels of Adam Roberts serve as serio-comic, ironic glimpses into our own present, satiric parables that may escape the notice of the naïve and uninitiated. Reading him as a modern Menippean satirist may help readers to digest the somewhat stilted, dissonant characters they encounter, but it is difficult to know if Roberts himself would be pleased by such a designation. He cites Robert Graves's *The White Goddess* as one of 'the core books' of his life (Roberts, 2004) and the writing of *The Snow* as his tribute to Graves; yet Graves states that in poetical history, satirists were considered 'destructive or noxious' and writers of 'left-handed poetry' (Graves, 1948: 444–5) – which was a deep insult. Roberts, though, will hopefully appreciate a more modern assessment of his satire as in the tradition of Voltaire and Twain, highlighting those absurd aspects of everyday life that threaten to drag us into rigid self-righteousness and political strife.

Notes

1 A third-century BC Greek satirist, all the works of Mennipus have been lost, but his method of ridiculing serious subjects – and the brand of satire named for him – survives in later Greek and Roman writers. The satires of Lucian are among the most famous, and Menippus appears as a character in Lucian's *Dialogues of the Dead*.

2 *Gedankenexperiment*, from the German, is 'thought' + 'experiment', an experiment with preset conditions carried out only in the mind.

Works Cited

Ash, Alec (2011) 'Adam Roberts on Science Fiction Classics', *Five Books*, 22 November, URL (consulted March 2012): http://fivebooks.com/interviews/adam-roberts-on-science-fiction-classics

Bakhtin, M. M. (1981) *The Dialogic Imagination*. Michael Holquist (ed.), Caryl Emerson and Michael Holquist (trans.). Austin, TX: University of Texas Press.

Bakhtin, M. M. (1994) 'Literature as Ideological Form', in Pam Morris (ed.) *The Bakhtin Reader: Selected Writings of Bakhtin, Medvedev and Voloshinov*, pp. 123–193. London: Edward Arnold.

Callow, Christos, Jr. (2013) 'Irony, Man: An Interview with Adam Roberts', *Strange Horizons*, 25 March, URL (consulted October 2013): http://www.strangehorizons.com/2013/20130325/2roberts-a.shtml

Frye, Northrop (1957) *Anatomy of Criticism*. London: Penguin Books.

Graves, Robert (1948) *The White Goddess: A Historical Grammar of Poetic Myth*. New York: Farrar, Straus and Giroux.

Kincaid, Paul (2011) 'Learning to read Adam Roberts', *Big Other*, 5 March, URL (consulted March 2012): http://bigother.com/2011/03/05/learning-to-read-adam-roberts/

Lazar, Seth (2012) 'Necessity in Self-Defense and War', *Philosophy & Public Affairs*. 40(1): 3–44.

May, Gita (2003) 'Introduction', *Candide*, Voltaire. New York: Barnes & Noble Classics: xiii–xxv.

Roberts, Adam (2004) 'The Snow', *AdamRoberts.com*, 11 November, URL (consulted March 2012): http://www.adamroberts.com/2004/11/11/the-snow/

Roberts, Adam (2007) 'Land of the Headless: Reviews', URL (consulted April 2015): http://www.adamroberts.com/writing/land-of-the-headless/

Roberts, Adam (2008) 'Vector on Headless', *AdamRoberts.com*, 27 January, URL (consulted March 2012): http://www.adamroberts.com/2008/01/27/headless-in-vector/

NEW MODEL READERS

CHANGING CRITICAL AND POPULAR RECEPTIONS OF THE SCIENCE FICTION OF ADAM ROBERTS

Niall Harrison

Introduction

In March 2013, in an interview published by *Strange Horizons*, Adam Roberts commented on the reception of his work by the science-fiction reading community:

> I think there is something idiosyncratic or eccentric about my relationship with science fiction that isn't shared by the large majority of science fiction fans. I think what they get out of science fiction doesn't map exactly onto what I get out of science fiction. It means that the kind of science fiction I write doesn't necessarily chime with what a large readership finds interesting or appealing. *Or* I just write shit. It's hard to know. It's one of the two, certainly. (Callow Jr., 2013)

This was not the first time Roberts had voiced such sentiments (Adascalitei, 2009b; Baki, 2010). But it may turn out to be the last. Less than a week after the *Strange Horizons* interview appeared, Roberts's idiosyncrasies were finally legitimized, when *Jack Glass* (2012), his thirteenth novel, won the British Science Fiction Association Award for Best Novel. A few months later it also picked up the John W. Campbell Memorial Award. Receipt of two major awards in the same year is the sort of thing that indicates a new stature in the field.[1]

In truth, the shift has been underway for several years. Arguably the turning point came in 2009. In the 16 September issue of *New Scientist* (a science fiction special), Kim Stanley Robinson stated that 'three or four of the last 10 Booker prizes should have gone to science fiction novels [...] Indeed this year the prize should probably go to a science fiction comedy called *Yellow Blue Tibia*, by Adam Roberts' (Robinson, 2009). The issue appeared the week after that year's Man Booker Prize shortlist had been announced – the right time to pick up a little general media attention, and a lot of SF community discussion. The following year, *Yellow Blue Tibia* was shortlisted for three awards. Indeed, at the time of writing there are 18 nominations for novel awards listed for Roberts's work in the SF Awards Database; of these 14 are for *Yellow Blue Tibia* or more recent books (Kelly, 2016).

One question this chapter attempts to answer is how this turning point should be understood. To what extent can it be attributed to *Yellow Blue Tibia* itself (that is, the qualities of the novel), and to what extent to Robinson's intervention (and the associated attention)? More generally: how has the science fiction field received and contextualized Adam Roberts, and how has that changed over time? As a starting point, I look at reviews and discussions of three of Roberts's novels: *The Snow* (2004), regarded as one of his less successful books; *Gradisil* (2006), which received a couple of award nominations and remains his only novel to be published in the US (at the time of writing); and *Yellow Blue Tibia*, which as noted above can be seen as his breakthrough book.[2] I conclude with a brief discussion of the reception of *New Model Army* (2010), as an example of a post-breakthrough novel.

Some recurring approaches are obvious. The most long-lasting originates with Jon Courtenay Grimwood's review of Roberts's third novel, *Stone* (2002), for the *Guardian* (Grimwood, 2002). In a capsule review, Grimwood provides a lens through which many subsequent Roberts novels have been analysed, perhaps not least because a version of his introductory assessment – 'Adam Roberts has always been king of the high concept' – appeared as a cover blurb for the next five years.[3] Kim Stanley Robinson's comments, meanwhile, offer two alternative lenses for *Yellow Blue Tibia*: as a Booker contender (which among other things I take to be a proxy for 'a novel whose literary craft is worth paying attention to'), and as a comedy. A fourth lens is less common in blurbs, but appears in reviews and is acknowledged by Roberts in interviews: 'almost everything I write is in dialogue with the backlist [...] what I'm trying to do is to deconstruct or ironically engage with [...] the stuff that's gone before' (Callow Jr., 2013). These alternative lenses have become more popular in recent reviews.

My aim is not to argue that contemporary reviews were 'wrong' or 'right', but to explore how Roberts's novels were read on publication, and consider what other readings might be more obvious today. This is clearly a partial analysis; but it will be sufficient, I hope, for a preliminary discussion of how the reception of Roberts's work has evolved in tandem with the work itself, and to raise some larger questions about how the science fiction field handles idiosyncrasy.

The Snow (2004)

The protagonist of Adam Roberts's fifth novel is Tira Bojani Sahai: daughter of an immigrant and mother of an estranged daughter. She is living in London when, one September 6th, it begins to snow. Months later, it shows no sign of stopping. The initial chapters describe the scrabble for survival as the snow accumulates and essential services shut down; Tira ends up living in a snow cave at the bottom of a buried office block. Eventually, she is rescued by Americans and carried up to their new military settlement, Liberty, where she is told that the world has been covered to a depth of several miles. The event is now known, with capitalization, as the Snow. Once in Liberty, Tira becomes involved with a high-ranking official, and subsequently with a dissident and potential terrorist, leading to her internment and interrogation; there is a clear engagement with the post-9/11 security state in these passages. Following an escape attempt, Tira has an encounter with what appears to be an alien, out on the snow, and intuits that what appeared to be a natural or human-made disaster was in fact invasive terraforming. All of this is told through a complex structure: *The Snow* is composed of a series of found documents originating with the post-Snow society. The lengthiest are Tira's written testimony; others include an interview with a scientist who claims to know that the Snow was a scientific experiment gone wrong, a confession/pre-Snow memoir by Tira's dissident partner, and a few short adverts and informational documents from the post-Snow society. Most have been classified and censored, with many names and some other details redacted.

The Snow was not a critical darling. Of nine reviews identified in research for this chapter only three were positive. Most infamously, Christopher Priest concluded in the *Guardian* that it 'shows every sign of being a hasty first draft; it does its author no credit at all and is a significant disappointment' (Priest, 2004). In *Locus,* Nick Gevers evaluated *The Snow* as a failure in SF terms. He opened by linking Grimwood's 'high-concept' blurb to 'the Ballardian disaster story', but identified a core problem of 'muffled unsubtlety' springing from 'obvious satire' and a protagonist with a 'curiously directionless and sterile' voice (Gevers, 2004: 27). Finally, Gevers found that the Snow itself is asked to stand for too much, represent too many qualities, and concluded that 'such flailing multivalency is ultimately very unenlightening'. Put another way, Gevers diagnosed failure in three of the four lenses noted earlier: the high-concept is asked to bear too much weight, the literary style is misjudged, and the humour is overobvious.

Other reviewers may have disagreed with Gevers, but the lenses they applied were similar; and the 'high-concept' and 'literary' lenses were almost universal. Paul di Filippo in *Asimov's* – by far the most enthusiastic reviewer of this novel – in fact praised the multivalency of the high concept precisely *because* he felt the literary style was successful: 'Roberts also utilizes snow [...] in many metaphorical ways [...] This literary flair is typical of Roberts's finely crafted prose'

(Di Filippo, 2006). However, while most reviews drew comparisons between the novel's opening movement and the work of Ballard and Wyndham, none mentioned the equally prominent intertexts referenced by the novel's ending. Indeed Gevers suggests that the introduction of aliens in the novel's final third 'seems merely gratuitous'.

It is worth, therefore, looking a bit more closely at how the novel's intertexts develop. The similarities to Ballard and Wyndham are clear enough from the abstract and totalizing nature of the catastrophe, and the small privileged survivalist community that follows it, respectively.[4] But even early on, Tira raises the possibility of sentience when speculating about the causes of the Snow:

> That evening, as the light faded, I stood on the roof with my head back, just looking up. [...] I found myself thinking silly things. I wondered, for instance, whether the cloud might be sentient – a cloud-brain, stretched over the whole globe. (*TS*: 8)

This foreshadows her conclusion about the aliens – or, as they are meaningfully labelled, the Others – at the end of the book: 'I believe they are the snow' (*TS*: 295). However, the aliens cannot be fully understood within the novel's early catastrophe frame. The introduction of a non-human sentience triggers a new and crucial intertext: when she learns of the Others, Tira's reaction is 'that sounds more like *War of the Worlds*' (*TS*: 245). A page later, Tira's informant invokes the critique of colonialism in Wells's novel:

> 'It's like the British invade India, they steamroller over India, and force every Indian into British schools and the British army and the British way of life. And then, having committed that force majeur, they start themselves wearing turbans and saris and riding elephants.' He threw up his hands, shaking his head. 'Is that the way imperialisation happens?' (*TS*: 246)

A few pages later, the connection between the snow and imperialism is repeated: 'What we have to do [...] is understand the imperial mindset. Now that's not a straightforward thing' (*TS*: 249).

This equivalence with the imperialist actions of (white) humans is challenged later. Characters question whether the Others 'have the same relationship to motive, to notions of responsibility, guilt, shame, that we do' (*TS*: 277). Indeed the precise nature of the Others remains subject to debate, with some arguing that they are merely mass hallucinations (*TS*: 290). But that the equivalence is drawn at all is significant. In the context of *The Snow*'s early war-on-terror satire, the obvious real-world parallel raised in the reader's mind is not in fact the British in India, but imperial America in the early twenty-first century; this establishes a link between the libertarian and postcolonial concerns of the novel, and crucially positions the imperialists, rather than the subjects of imperialism, as the Other.[5]

How can we reconcile these changing intertexts? A model recently advanced by Brian Attebery identifies common science-fictional narrative structures as 'parabolas': 'more concrete than themes, more complex than motifs, parabolas are combinations of meaningful setting, character, and action that lend themselves to endless redefinition and jazzlike improvisation' (Attebery and Hollinger, 2013: vii). Parabolas are an emergent feature of SF as a genre whose works are in conversation with one another; Attebery uses the generation starship tale as a prototypical example, tracing its history and variation through works by Robert Heinlein, Gene Wolfe, Ursula K. Le Guin, and Molly Gloss, among others. Importantly, 'having evoked a parabola such as the generation starship, a writer can rely on readers to supply information from the megatext' (Attebery, 2013: 13).

Approaching *The Snow* with this framework in mind, we can see a story that begins in one parabola (apocalypse) and ends in another (invasion), and which in doing so invites a reader to reflect on how the two patterns interact: the way in which invasions are apocalyptic for those on the receiving end, for example. Moreover, having identified this architecture, we can see that other Roberts novels enact similar shifts. Among others, *Polystom* (2003) moves from Bob Shaw-esque alternate physics to Greg Egan-esque reality simulation, while *New Model Army* begins as near-future military SF and ends as a satire of singularity fiction. A critical lens only highlighted by Roberts in recent years (Callow Jr., 2013) – the intertextuality of Roberts's fiction – thus leads to insights into both early and more recent novels.

Gradisil (2006)

Roberts's sixth novel received wider attention than *The Snow*. A total of 21 reviews were identified in research for this chapter, of which only one was strongly negative; 10 were positive and 10 were mixed. *Gradisil* was also shortlisted for the Philip K. Dick Award and the Arthur C. Clarke Award, and it became the first (and so far, only) of Roberts's novels to be published in the US, with an edition from Pyr in 2007.

It is probably not a coincidence that *Gradisil* is, at least superficially, one of Roberts's most conventional novels in genre-SF terms; it features spaceships, and even includes a timeline for its future. Opening in the mid-21st century, *Gradisil* describes the founding and growth of the Uplands, a proto-nation of individuals wealthy enough to have their own 'house' in near-Earth orbit, as seen by three generations of the Gyeroffy family. First we meet Klara Gyeroffy, whose memoir relates her experiences as a young woman, when her father was an early pioneer of the Uplands; he was eventually killed by a US agent, and Klara swore vengeance. Second, at the turn of the twenty-second century comes the story of the first US-Uplands war and of Klara's daughter Gradisil, steely politician and inspirational leader, as seen through the eyes of her husband Paul Caunes and by a US colonel, David Slater. This story ends in another betrayal, with Paul arranging for Gradisil's capture by the US. Finally, after another few decades have passed, we follow Gradisil's children, Hope and Sol, and their competing visions for the future of the Uplands – and for how to live in the shadow of their father's actions. The novel's parabola remains consistent: *Gradisil* begins as a near-future space-colonization future history, and that is how it concludes.

Perhaps because its most obvious intertexts fall within the mainline of American genre SF history, reviewers seemed more eager to identify them; or at least to identify a kinship with that area of SF. In *Locus*, Nick Gevers positioned *Gradisil* as in dialogue with 'Heinleinian SF' (Gevers, 2006: 56); for the *SF Site*, Greg L. Johnson heard 'echoes […] of Arthur C. Clarke's *Islands in the Sky*, Poul Anderson's *Tales of the Flying Mountains* and, of course, Robert A. Heinlein's *The Moon is a Harsh Mistress*' (Johnson, 2007); and Farah Mendlesohn identified a similarity to the works of Joe Haldeman (Mendlesohn, 2007). Others found reference-points beyond the genre. Nic Clarke, writing at *Eve's Alexandria,* diagnosed the novel as an '*Oresteia*-in-Space' (Clarke and Hoyle, 2007); and Ed Park, in the *LA Times,* highlighted several direct references to the work of Vladimir Nabokov, including a mention of 'Charles Kinbote' in the acknowledgments (Park, 2007).

A transatlantic divide was visible in the other lenses used. In particular, no US reviewers engaged with *Gradisil* as a 'high-concept' novel (that blurb was not used on the cover of the US edition, although Lou Anders, editor at Pyr, did subsequently wheel it out for a post promoting Roberts at the US-based site *Tor.com* a few years later [Anders, 2009]). In the UK however, a notable engagement with this lens came from John Clute, who suggested that Roberts is:

> ... a creator of worlds in particular, stripped down worlds, worlds baldly illustrative of thesis; he is a writer whose books work as strobes, illuminating (or not illuminating) extremely narrow avenues of conjecture or vision. He carries to an extremity a way of shaping thought and presentation common to sf writers as a cohort: that familiar (and indeed necessary) propensity of sf writers to think of the world as a case to be argued. (Clute, 2009)

For Clute, *Gradisil*'s application of this methodology to Earth's near future was near-fatally flawed, producing a 'starved' world unable to properly critique the politics of the Upland movement; improbable in its elisions of computing/information technology and of climate change; and unconvincing in its depiction of geopolitics, too similar to the present in which it was written.

Reviewers' attempts to identify elements of critique or satire in *Gradisil* could be seen as evidence that this is indeed a flawed approach to doing SF. Only five reviews (three UK, two US) discussed *Gradisil* as at all satiric, and most pointed to specific satiric *elements,* such as the portrayal of the USA and its military. The larger architecture of the novel was widely accepted as sincere, if perhaps not completely coherent; but the novel can also be seen as more generally satiric with respect to the SF traditions it is engaging.[6]

Klara's narrative begins with her father, 'the sort of man who flew into the Uplands as a hobby' (*G*: 3), a pioneer and audodidact with little patience for the 'wasteful' (*G*: 6) technologies supported by NASA (and, by implication, government-sponsored spaceflight in general). The Uplands itself is described as a place of freedom, freedom defined as 'no government, no taxes' (*G*: 18). So, as many reviewers correctly noted, the stage is set with Libertarian, neo-Heinleinian furniture. More strikingly, the uplanders are SF fans. Klara describes the early uplanders as, 'men of moderate or comfortable means who had grown up watching SF screenshows and reading SF stories' (*G*: 27). Yet this techno-optimism is by no means uncomplicated. The Uplands, it is made clear, is both elitist, in the sense that it is only accessible to the wealthy, and parasitic, in the sense that its inhabitants remain dependent on Earth's resources.

Its inhabitants are also incompetent to administer any sort of social contract, precisely because of the characteristics that made them become uplanders. Fairly early in the novel, teenage Klara runs away to live with Jon, a man old enough to be her grandfather. When (inevitably) their relationship breaks down, Jon is devastated and, unable to deal with his emotions, attacks and breaches a habitat with Klara inside. A meeting is convened to decide how the incident should be dealt with: there is a sense that this is seen as exciting, and there is much pedantic arguing about what form a potential legal system should take. Jon, stricken with remorse, suggests that he exile himself to the moon. The reaction of the uplanders is telling:

> What happened next was that this new plan of Jon's squeezed out the pretence that we were a constituted court of law. The primary interest of uplanders (which is to say, the fascination with technical aspects of space flight, problem-solving and science-fiction dreams) came to the fore instead. 'How will you power the flight?' (*G*: 59)

Nerding trumps justice, and no punishment is levied against Jon. Indeed, he becomes a kind of hero when his moonflight is a success. Similarly, when Klara's farther is murdered, the juvenile obsessiveness of the uplanders precludes any fair resolution. For all these events, Klara is the narrator. She is her father's daughter – and she loves the country of the Uplands, the tangible qualities of its space and light, which Roberts describes in striking terms throughout the novel – but as an old woman recalling events of her youth, she is not a typical SF protagonist. She thus encourages us to view what is a typical SF scenario from a distance, and to see its flaws. Through her, we can see the human cost of frontier/military SF's common emphasis on problem-solving and technical accomplishment (by men), but the context is darkly absurd – 'How will you power the flight?' – rather than straightforwardly humorous.

Similar arguments can be made about the second and third sections of *Gradisil*'s narrative. In part two – the section which contains the US lampoonery noted in reviews – the key again is the choice of narrator. Paul Caunes, Gradisil's husband, is a depressed and self-absorbed man, the antithesis of a conventional hard SF protagonist and, like Klara, positioned at a remove from the narrative action. In part three, our viewpoint is Paul and Gradisil's son Hope, who at first appears to be more familiar: he is a man with a grand planetary-engineering scheme that would enable the Uplands to become a truly independent state. But it transpires that this scheme is in fact a displacement activity, doing significant harm to his emotional health. In fact, it is so implausible that the only person who wants to fund it is a crackpot trillionaire who believes it will impress the aliens who must be living on Venus. With Hope, we are within the Uplands perspective at last, but obsessive technological grandiosity – a narrowness of perspective – in itself becomes a critique. *Gradisil* is attempting to render an earlier generation's SF with as much psychological plausibility as possible and, as a result, an argument that the 'reality' of those earlier narratives would be broken societies populated by damaged citizens.

Yellow Blue Tibia (2009)

For the novels immediately following *Gradisil*, Adam Roberts's reputation continued to be mixed. Rich Horton's verdict on *Splinter* (2007), in a review for the *SF Site*, could stand for many:

> This is rather an impressive novel, but not quite one I could love. It's well-imagined, and well-written. The main character is thoroughly believable. Only, he's not terribly interesting, and not terribly nice, without being in any sense evil. All of this makes sense, and works quite well in working out the novel's themes. Yet it held me at a distance from the book – and left me respecting Roberts's achievement, but no more. (Horton, 2007)

However, *Yellow Blue Tibia* – an alien-invasion novel, of a kind, set primarily in 1980s Russia – met with more favourable attention on its publication, and has continued to enjoy a good reputation since. Of 14 reviews identified between January and August 2009, nine were positive-to-glowing, and none were entirely negative. Mixed notices appeared in *Locus* and *Strange Horizons*, but nevertheless represent an interesting contrast to the Horton review quoted above, and its ilk. For Adrienne Martini, the narrator's 'mix of bitterness and heart makes him an engaging character' (Martini, 2009) while Michael Froggatt noted that, 'fortunately, the one character who is fully-rounded, plausible, and entertaining throughout is Skvorecky himself' (Froggatt and Nussbaum, 2009). Adjectives such as 'fun', 'engaging' and even 'hilarious' make appearances: almost unheard of descriptions for a Roberts novel.

At the same time, however, Roberts was becoming more widely known as a critic – and that work, published primarily in *Strange Horizons*, the *Guardian*, and on his blog *Punkadiddle*, was often deemed to be funny in a way that his fiction usually was not. It still divided opinions, however; in particular, he published an open letter at *Punkadiddle* regarding the ballot for that year's Hugo Awards: 'Dear Science Fiction Fandom [...] your shortlists aren't very good' (Roberts, 2009). There are probably many SF readers, particularly in the US, who have not read any of Roberts's novels but know his name from the discussion that followed, which included over three hundred comments on the original post alone, agreements and disagreements united at least in their vehemence. Enter, stage left, Kim Stanley Robinson, with praise perfectly timed and framed to grab the attention of the UK literary media; coverage in the *Guardian* and a segment on *Newsnight Review* followed (Flood, 2009; Whitfield,

2009). In 2010, *Yellow Blue Tibia* was shortlisted for the BSFA Award, the Arthur C. Clarke Award, and the John W. Campbell Memorial Award. All of this ensured further attention for *Yellow Blue Tibia*. In addition to the 14 reviews mentioned above, a further 15 were identified between September 2009 and January 2011, once again mostly positive.

So it seems very likely external factors contributed to *Yellow Blue Tibia*'s success. Equally, the novel clearly struck a stronger chord with many readers than had any of Roberts's previous books.[7] In contrast to coverage of *The Snow* and *Gradisil*, there was almost no discussion of *Yellow Blue Tibia* as high-concept; instead reviews focused on the novel's comedic and intertextual qualities, specifically receiving it as a comedy *about* science fiction. *Yellow Blue Tibia*, by articulating the particular view of science fiction that it does in the particular way that it does, not only makes its own themes readily accessible to an SF readership, but acts as a kind of Rosetta Stone for Roberts's fiction in general.

The first crucial element is the narrative voice. *Yellow Blue Tibia* opens shortly after the Second World War. Konstantin Skvorecky, along with other Russian science fiction writers, is recruited by Stalin to write an alien invasion narrative that can be used to give the Soviet populace an enemy to unite against. The project barely gets off the ground before it is shut down. Forty years later, Skvorecky starts to encounter evidence that the story he worked on might be coming true. Despite this biography, there are similarities between Skvorecky and Roberts. Most noticeable are habits of voice visible both here and in Roberts's non-fiction writing: the use of colons and semicolons to focus attention; the use of emphasis to convey a sense of authorial *fussiness*; the love of wordplay and puns; and the use of one- or two-word sub-clauses to, I would suggest, draw out a thought.[8] Skvorecky mentions that he has translated some work by Robert Browning, on whom Roberts did his PhD (*YBT*: 68). And perhaps most notable is the following exchange – quoted in several reviews – in which one of Skvorecky's fellow SF writers diagnoses his core flaw:

> 'One thing I hate in this world and you are fucking *it*. You are an ironist.'
>
> 'An ironist?'
>
> 'Fundamentally, you take nothing seriously. You believe it is all a game. It was the same in your novels; they were never serious. They had no heart.' (*YBT*: 122)

A lack of heart is one of the core flaws identified in Roberts's earlier novels by Horton and other reviewers; linking this 'lack' to an ironic sensibility may inflect subsequent reading of those novels.

The second element to consider is the structure. *Yellow Blue Tibia* is one of the most straightforward of Roberts's novels in that regard, being a single, consistent, first-person narrative by a character at the heart of the action. The found documents and textual games of *The Snow* and *Gradisil* are absent. Skvorecky addresses the issue of narratorial reliability head-on – 'I am not trying to trick you' (*YBT*: 35) – and he is broadly true to his word. There is no parabolic twist, and the novel concludes with a long conversation in which the various improbable events of the plot are explained as consequences of manipulating the quantum-mechanical multiverse. For example, at one point Skvorecky is caught in a grenade blast in a nuclear reactor; not only does he suffer no serious injuries, but a fragment of irradiated shrapnel lodges in his brain in just the right place to kill a developing tumour. The reason things worked out this way, we are told, is that Skvorecky is loved by Dora, a woman who is a 'reality catalyst' (*YBT*: 306), able to make the highly implausible timelines in which Skvorecky survives more likely than the ones in which he dies. Thus *Yellow Blue Tibia* provides a clear science-fictional justification for its Hollywood action narrative logic, and in doing so highlights how Roberts has shaped the larger architecture of his novel as a comment on a particular generic form. As with the voice, this recognition encourages reflection on Roberts's earlier novels. A similar project can be identified in *Gradisil*, as noted earlier.

Finally, there is the matter of science fiction itself. *Yellow Blue Tibia* argues that science-fictionality is a mode, a way of seeing the world.[9] At a very literal level, Skvorecky deploys SF descriptions throughout: streetlights are 'a line of alien eyes, glowering down upon the road' (*YBT*: 63); a character is described as having 'triffid-thick legs' (*YBT*: 142); a sunset paints the sky 'Jupiter-oranges' (*YBT*: 163); water in the spent fuel pools in a nuclear reactor is 'like the water that might fill the lakes of a distant planet in a science fiction magazine's cover illustration' (*YBT*: 185); when being reunited with Dora is for Skvorecky like having a Keatsian planet 'swim into [his] ken', he ponders whether his relationship to that planet is imperialist, 'dropping interplanetary troopers onto the surface' (*YBT*: 259); and so forth. More self-referentially, at various points the novel touches on how SF *misrepresents* the world, for instance in its tendency to casual planet-exploding genocide, and the moral implications of that, or the sexist, boys-own stereotypes it can perpetuate. This is a novel that treats the idea that SF has had a broad cultural impact seriously, even if it is not the impact the genre might hope for. Important characters are Scientologists, and the 'problem' of Ufology is much-discussed: on the one hand, UFOs obviously do not exist; and on the other hand, millions of people are certain that they have encountered them. What is true for Ufology is, the novel argues, true for SF as a whole: SF's imagining of things that do not exist has had an enormous impact on the cultural landscape. The elegance of *Yellow Blue Tibia* is that it makes this a self-evident truth, but in fact to think about and accept this argument is to become aware of the *artifice* of SF: to become, for a moment, like Skvorecky, like his author, an ironist.

Conclusions: New model readers?

There is no sign of Jon Courtenay Grimwood's blurb on the paperback edition of *Jack Glass*. Instead, we are told that *The Times* places Adam Roberts 'in the tradition of Swift, Orwell and Atwood' (*JG*: cover). The high concept is played down; the literary and satiric qualities of Roberts's writing are played up. The same shift is visible in the critical discussion around Roberts's work. From novel to novel the balance of attention shifts but, in the broadest terms, the field's sense of what is represented by 'an Adam Roberts novel' is different now than it was a decade ago. At the same time, Roberts's popularity – at least as tracked by such metrics as award nominations and volume of reviews – has increased.

What all this tells us about the work itself is open to debate. In her critical study of Diana Wynne Jones, Farah Mendlesohn argues that Jones's novels can be understood as manuals, training a generation of critical readers – and training them, in part, to read Jones (Mendlesohn, 2008). It is tempting to suggest that something similar is true of Adam Roberts's novels, in particular a book like *Yellow Blue Tibia*. It is a milestone in Roberts's career for reasons inherent to the text as well as the circumstances of its reception, yet it is not *as* different to what came before as some discussions of Roberts's work would have you believe. It is simply more explicit about the ways in which Roberts structures his novels to interrogate the assumptions of particular narrative patterns.

So it is not a coincidence that the most sustained bout of reviewerly theorizing about Roberts can be found in the discussion of *New Model Army*, the novel that immediately followed *Yellow Blue Tibia*. Set in the near future, in a disunited Britain riven by civil war, it is narrated by a soldier in a networked army-for-hire – the new model army of the title – explicitly an atom in a larger structure, part of a kind of distributed consciousness. Among other themes the novel deals with democracy, war, male sexuality and identity, and the techno-utopian vision of the 'singularity'. It was also the occasion for an essay by Paul Kincaid, 'Learning to Read Adam Roberts' (2011), that sparked a certain amount of discussion. In the essay, Kincaid acknowledges that he has had a 'blind spot' with respect to Roberts's novels, but notes that he has been driven to re-engage with them by the acclaim of others. He goes on to argue that Roberts's novels can be read as examples of Menippean Satire, as defined by Northrop Frye, 'a vision of the world in terms of a single intellectual pattern […] makes for violent dislocations in the customary logic of narrative' (Frye, 2000). For Kincaid, this explains many of the characteristics he has previously seen as flaws, and still sees as flaws in *New Model Army*: the characters seem inconsistent or contradictory, but, 'take them out of the novel and consider them not as characters but as roles, as functions, and they work perfectly well'. More specifically:

> ... if you remove that issue of character, you see not a novelistic plot but a satirical structure. In a novel the impetus is to find a plot that will tell the story of the novel's subject, and since the more a reader believes in the story the more likely she is to be convinced by the subject, so story becomes central to what the fiction is doing. For a Menippean Satire, the subject remains central and the story is less important. (Kincaid, 2011)

In one sense this is an extension of the structural artifice revealed by *Yellow Blue Tibia*; in another it is a version of Grimwood's 'high concept' and Clute's 'worlds baldly illustrative of thesis', suggesting that in Roberts's fiction it is the structure – the *argument* of the narrative – that is paramount, and all other aspects are subordinate. Where Kincaid develops this lens is in identifying a single purpose running through Roberts's novels: 'Roberts is satirizing science fiction'.

In a response to Kincaid, Rich Puchalsky argued that, 'the concept of Menippean satire comes with a lot of baggage that doesn't seem to apply, and doesn't include a good deal of what I see as being there' (Puchalsky, 2011). I agree. Kincaid's model does not fully account for how Roberts handles character. A Roberts protagonist is not cartoonish, bouncing from situation to situation as required; within a given situation, they are often fully rounded. It is precisely that effort to provide coherence that produces *Gradisil*'s distorted souls. But Kincaid is right that a Roberts protagonist is often not coherent over the length of a novel, that there will be gaps, or unexpected choices. For Puchalsky, those gaps are part of the point:

> Roberts's works seem to me to be best described as experimental [...] His novels seem to me to be characterized by a high degree of formal structure coupled with underdetermination of what that structure means. [...] They are writerly artifacts, and while some of them work as satires – Roberts writes what he knows, and what he knows is SF – they do not seem to me to pick out a direction and then set out to guide the reader along it. (Puchalsky, 2011)

This is certainly true of a novel like *The Snow*, with its 'flailing multivalency' as identified by Nick Gevers: it offers the snow in metaphor after metaphor, as a blank canvas for lost souls to rewrite their lives, as scientific hubris, as emptiness, as smothering white supremacy, as a drug, as life. It is a rationale for the parabolic twists in some of Roberts's novels, upending the table and letting the pieces fall into a new configuration. And yet here too there is an insufficiency; Puchalsky's suggestion cannot quite account for a novel like *Yellow Blue Tibia* that encodes a much more conclusive argument.

One way to close the gap is to consider Roberts's works as structured by a tension between sincerity and insincerity that can express itself in different ways. In many of his novels, in particular those of the last five years or so, the tension is visible at a micro level, as in *Yellow Blue Tibia*, with its fussing about language and precision of understanding. It can also be discerned at the macro level: the way that a novel such as *Gradisil* is *structurally* insincere. Or the way that many of Roberts's novels return to certain common themes of human experience – in particular love and war – as though seeking a way to authorize its readers to experience deep emotion, without fully relinquishing their ironic distance. This tension is part of the reason it has taken over a decade for the distributed consciousness of the SF field to feel that it understands 'the Adam Roberts novel', because it is uncomfortable: contemporary genre science fiction is predominantly a sincere, even *earnest* form, both politically and stylistically.

Any understanding of any working writer should be provisional, however, and I suspect grand unified theories of Adam Roberts in particular are doomed to fail. The evolving response to his work can, perhaps, be seen as a demonstration that the SF field is not quite as self-aware about this as it should be. A critical culture that attempts to *solve* a writer (Roberts writes high-concept novels; Roberts writes SF satire) can reify patterns into rules. The former are useful interpretive tools, but are changed by each new datapoint. The latter represent an elision of specificity, an attempt to constrain idiosyncrasy that goes against everything Roberts's fiction – so far! – has stood for.

Notes

1 As, of course, is an academic conference devoted to a specific author – not a common occurrence for working SF writers – such as the New Genre Army conference on 5 April 2013 that led to the present volume.

2 Reviews were identified through Google searches and specific review of the archives of the following publications: *Foundation, Infinity Plus, Interzone, Locus, The New York Review of Science Fiction, SFX, The SF Site, Strange Horizons,* and *Vector*. Reviews appearing more than 24 months after the first edition of the novel were excluded. In total, nine reviews were identified for *The Snow*, 21 for *Gradisil*, and 29 for *Yellow Blue Tibia*. The full list of reviews can be seen in 'New Model Readers – reviews of Adam Roberts' (Harrison, 2014).

3 Roberts's covers during this period reinforced the blurb's prominence by featuring austerely abstract designs, reminiscent of the covers given to Greg Egan – himself a famously high-concept writer – around the same time. See the covers for *Polystom, The Snow, Gradisil* and *Land of the Headless* in the *Encyclopedia of Science Fiction* gallery for Adam Roberts (Clute, 2014a) (*Salt, On* and *Stone* were reissued in the same style); and covers for *Luminous, Schild's Ladder* and *Teranesia* in the *Encyclopedia of Science Fiction* gallery for Greg Egan (Clute, 2014b). *Axiomatic, Distress, Diaspora, Quarantine* and *Permutation City* were reissued in the same style.

4 For example, one might compare it to Ballard's *The Drowned World* (1962) or Wyndham's *The Kraken Wakes* (1953).

5 Which is not to say the exploration of this link is entirely successful. The portrayal of Tira as a woman of colour, specifically of Indian descent, strikes some false notes, such as her internal agonizing over the extent of her post-Snow husband's racism: 'Clearly there was some racist component in his make-up, but racism – or homophobia, or hatred of women (again, all of which accusations I threw at Crow from time to time) – cannot make up a whole person' (*TS*: 78). This reads more like an authorial attempt to create complexity than the natural pathway of Tira's thoughts; it has a theoretical, lecturing air that is at odds with her characterization elsewhere.

6 An example of this sort of discussion took place at *More Words, Deeper Hole*, the LiveJournal of Hugo-winning fan writer James Nicoll; Nicoll and his commenters took exception to the suggestion that *Gradisil* may be considered hard SF (Nicoll, 2007).

7 The most notable exception to *Yellow Blue Tibia*'s generally positive reception is Catherynne M. Valente's review, in which she identified numerous errors in the representation of Soviet culture and history (Valente, 2010). It is interesting to compare Valente's review with that by Mihai Adascalite, a Romanian reviewer who reports that 'the first thing that struck me [...] is how realistic is described the Communism times of that period. Well, there are small differences with what happened in my country, but the general line is quite the same' (Adascalite, 2009). These interpretations – a broadly 'authentic' atmosphere, but many errors of detail – are not contradictory, and are both consistent with the novel's form and project.

8 I am engaging in my own minor parody here. Consider the following quotes as supporting evidence. From Roberts's academic monograph *Riddles of the Hobbit*: 'At any rate, I take it that a mode that prizes invention and ingenuity is best discussed *ingeniously*. A reader may ask: "ah, but is what you are arguing here *true*?" That is a valid and important question, but it is not, I submit, a *simple* question' (Roberts, 2013: 15). And in Skvorecky's voice, early in *Yellow Blue Tibia*: 'I am writing it to record the most profound change in my life; nothing less than a translation from one manner of existence into another, from something grossly physical into something – let us say, *spiritual*' (*YBT*: 35). And the puns? I refer you to the author's Twitter account, @arrroberts.

9 For examples of this contention in SF criticism rather than SF novels, see Mendlesohn (2003) and Csicsery-Ronay (2008).

Works Cited

Adascalitei, Mihai (2009a) 'Yellow Blue Tibia by Adam Roberts', *Dark Wolf's Fantasy Reviews*, 21 May, URL (consulted January 2016): http://darkwolfsfantasyreviews.blogspot.co.uk/2009/05/yellow-blue-tibia-by-adam-roberts.html

Adascalitei, Mihai (2009b) 'Interview – Adam Roberts', *Dark Wolf's Fantasy Reviews*, 22 June, URL (consulted January 2016): http://darkwolfsfantasyreviews.blogspot.co.uk/2009/06/interview-adam-roberts.html

Anders, Lou (2009) 'Meet Adam Roberts: the King of High Concept', *Tor.com*, 4 February, URL (consulted January 2016): http://www.tor.com/blogs/2009/02/meet-adam-roberts

Attebery, Brian and Veronica Hollinger (2013) 'Parabolas of Science Fiction', in Brian Attebery and Veronica Hollinger (eds) *Parabolas of Science Fiction*, p. vii. Middletown: Wesleyan University Press.

Attebery, Brian (2013) 'Science Fictional Parabolas: Jazz, Geometry, and Generation Starships' in Brian Attebery and Veronica Hollinger (eds) *Parabolas of Science Fiction*, pp. 3–23. Middletown: Wesleyan University Press.

Baki, Jason (2010) 'Adam Roberts: Author Interview', *Kamivision*, 19 April, URL (consulted January 2016): https://web.archive.org/web/20101016204557/http://kamvision.blogspot.com/2010/04/adam-roberts-interview.html

Callow, Christos, Jr. (2013) 'Irony, Man: An Interview with Adam Roberts', *Strange Horizons*, 25 March, URL (consulted January 2016): http://www.strangehorizons.com/2013/20130325/2roberts-a.shtml

Clarke, Nic and Victoria Hoyle (2007) 'Tin Can Land', *Eve's Alexandria*, 24 April, URL (consulted January 2016): http://evesalexandria.typepad.com/eves_alexandria/2007/04/tin_can_land.html

Clute, John (2009) 'A Clanking of Motor Homunculi', in *Canary Fever: Reviews*, pp. 245–55. Harold Wood: Beccon.

Clute, John, (ed.) (2014a) 'Adam Roberts – Gallery', *The Encyclopedia of Science Fiction*, URL (consulted January 2016): http://sf-encyclopedia.co.uk/gallery.php?filter=adam%20roberts&slide=1

Clute, John, (ed.) (2014b) 'Greg Egan: Gallery', *The Encyclopedia of Science Fiction*, URL (consulted September 2016): http://sf-encyclopedia.co.uk/gallery.php?filter=greg%20egan&slide=1

Csicsery-Ronay, Istvan, Jr. (2008) *The Seven Beauties of Science Fiction*. Middletown: Wesleyan University Press.

Di Filippo, Paul (2006) 'On Books', *Asimov's Science Fiction Magazine*, March, URL (consulted January 2016): https://web.archive.org/web/20060208215740/http://www.asimovs.com/_issue_0603/onbooks.shtml

Flood, Alison (2009) 'Science fiction author hits out at Booker judges' *Guardian*, 18 September, URL (consulted January 2016): http://www.theguardian.com/books/2009/sep/18/science-fiction-booker-prize

Froggatt, Michael and Nussbaum, Abigail (2009) 'Two Views: *Yellow Blue Tibia*', *Strange Horizons*, 9 March, URL (consulted January 2016): http://www.strangehorizons.com/reviews/2009/03/two_views_yello-comments.shtml

Frye, Northrop (2000) *Anatomy of Criticism*. Princeton: Princeton University Press. URL (consulted January 2016): http://northropfrye-theanatomyofcriticism.blogspot.co.uk/

Gevers, Nick (2004) 'Reviews by Nick Gevers', *Locus,* October 525; 53(4): 27.

Gevers, Nick (2006) 'Locus Looks at Books: Nick Gevers', *Locus,* May 544; 56(5): 25.

Grimwood, Jon Courtenay (2002) 'The return of Philip K. Dick', *Guardian,* 31 August, URL (consulted January 2016): http://www.theguardian.com/books/2002/aug/31/sciencefictionfantasyandhorror.philipkdick

Harrison, Niall (2014) 'New Model Readers: reviews of Adam Roberts', *Google Docs,* January, URL (consulted January 2016): http://goo.gl/NHZsIZ

Horton, Rich (2007) 'Splinter', *SF Site,* November, URL (consulted January 2016): http://www.sfsite.com/11a/sp259.htm

Johnson, Greg L. (2007) 'Gradisil – review', *SF Site,* May, URL (consulted January 2016): http://www.sfsite.com/05a/gr247.htm

Kelly, Mark R. (2014) 'Adam Roberts', *Science Fiction Awards Database,* URL (consulted January 2016): http://www.sfadb.com/Adam_Roberts

Kincaid, Paul (2011) 'Learning to Read Adam Roberts', *Big Other,* 5 March, URL (consulted January 2016): http://bigother.com/2011/03/05/learning-to-read-adam-roberts/

Martini, Adrienne (2009) 'Locus Looks at Books: *Yellow Blue Tibia*', *Locus* 62(4): 23, URL (consulted January 2016): http://www.locusmag.com/Features/2009/04/adrienne-martini-reviews-adam-roberts.html

Mendlesohn, Farah (2003) 'Introduction: Reading Science Fiction', in Edward James and Farah Mendlesohn (eds), *The Cambridge Companion to Science Fiction,* pp. 1–14. Cambridge: Cambridge University Press.

Mendlesohn, Farah (2007) 'The 2007 Arthur C. Clarke Award Shortlist', *Strange Horizons,* 16 April, URL (consulted January 2016): http://www.strangehorizons.com/reviews/2007/04/the_2007_arthur.shtml

Mendlesohn, Farah (2008) *Diana Wynne Jones: Children's Literature and the Fantastic Tradition.* London: Routledge.

Nicoll, James (2007) 'Cue Historical Laughter', *More Words, Deeper Hole,* 25 February, URL (consulted January 2016): http://james-nicoll.livejournal.com/711630.html

Park, Ed (2007). 'Astral Weeks: Kinbote in Space', *Los Angeles Times,* January. URL for archived text (consulted January 2016): http://theunarchivable.blogspot.co.uk/2007/12/review-of-adam-robertss-gradisil.html

Priest, Christopher (2004). 'The White Stuff', *Guardian,* 21 August, URL (consulted January 2016): http://www.theguardian.com/books/2004/aug/21/featuresreviews.guardianreview11

Puchalsky, Rich (2011). 'On learning to read Adam Roberts', *Rich Puchalsky's blog*, 8 March, URL (consulted January 2016): http://rpuchalsky.blogspot.co.uk/2011/03/on-learning-to-read-adam-roberts.html

Roberts, Adam (2009) 'Hugos 2009', *Punkadiddle*, 17 July, URL (consulted January 2016): https://web.archive.org/web/20101015043910/http://punkadiddle.blogspot.com/2009/07/hugos-2009.html

Roberts, Adam (2013) *The Riddles of the Hobbit*. Basingstoke: Palgrave Macmillan.

Robinson, Kim Stanley (2009) 'Science fiction: the stories of now', *New Scientist*, 16 September, URL (consulted 2016): http://www.newscientist.com/article/mg20327263.200-why-isnt-science-fiction-winning-any-literary-awards.html

Valente, Catherynne M (2010) 'Yellow Blue OH MY GOD NO', *Rules for Anchorites*, 26 February, URL (consulted January 2016): http://catvalente.livejournal.com/569516.html

Whitfield, Kit (2009) 'So do I think there's a problem with the readership?', *Kit Whitfield's blog*, 12 October, URL (consulted January 2016): http://kitwhitfield.blogspot.co.uk/2009/10/so-do-i-think-theres-problem-with.html

Part II

Political Interventions

Breaking the Cycle of the Golden Age
Jack Glass and Isaac Asimov's *Foundation* Trilogy

Anna McFarlane

The feminist science fiction author Angela Carter (1983: 69) once wrote, 'reading is just as creative an activity as writing, and most intellectual development depends upon new readings of old texts. I am all for putting new wine in old bottles, especially if the pressure of the new wine makes the old bottles explode'. This kind of reading and writing is crucial to the development of a genre like science fiction, so consciously intertextual, and so considerate of its past while at the same time imagining the really new and futuristic. Adam Roberts has been putting 'new wine into old bottles' since his first novel, *Salt* (2000), and continues to do so with each addition to his oeuvre as he continues his quest to write fiction in every subgenre of science fiction.[1]

Jack Glass (2012) is no exception. It has two subtitles: *The Story of a Murderer* and *A Golden Age Story*. These two subtitles clarify in advance the old bottles Roberts has his sights on: first and foremost, the traditions of Golden Age detective fiction;[2] second, the tradition of Golden Age science fiction. Damien Walter describes *Jack Glass* as 'a science fiction novel about our nostalgia for science fiction novels, replete with the favourite devices of Golden Age SF' (Walter, 2013). These devices include Faster Than Light (FTL) travel, spaceships, and something the Golden Age magazines might have referred to as 'psy powers' but that modern readers are more likely to identify as neurally-implanted iPhone – known as 'bId' (biolink iData) – communications systems. However, Roberts manipulates these devices and uses them to create a universe that differs from Golden Age models in significant and challenging ways. His anti-hero, Jack Glass, serial killer and master criminal, says:

> Once we are free… once we have evolved beyond the old medieval power structures and the medieval internecine violence they create, *then* we'll be able to use the technology responsibly. Everything depends on that. Have I killed people? – I have. But only in the service of that higher cause. (*JG*: 357)

In this speech, it could be Roberts himself talking about his own writing project. Roberts fights against the clichés and stereotypes that became entrenched in the Golden Age of science fiction and, in doing so, he kills the heroes of that era, leaving the science fiction fan with a character like Jack Glass, who cannot be pinned down, or cheered on, or relied upon. Jack Glass exposes 'medieval power structures', just as Roberts exposes some of the dated structures of Golden Age science fiction. Jack Glass also seeks to achieve freedom; this can be read as freedom from the political systems that control the galaxy of *Jack Glass,* as well as freedom from the generic structures, left over from the past, that sometimes constrain science fiction's contemporary evolution.

In this chapter, I will show how Roberts moves away from the cyclical historical model used in Golden Age science fiction by reading *Jack Glass* alongside Isaac Asimov's *Foundation* series. Instead of the cyclical conception of history that Asimov uses in *Foundation,* Roberts shows history and time taking place in a quantum and chaotic paradigm. Quantum physics and chaos theory combine to render linear or cyclical conceptions of history impossible and to challenge simplistic notions of historical authority. Roberts breaks the cycle, thereby giving his characters, and especially the proletariat, agency within this system in a way that was not possible within Golden Age science fiction's elitist valourization of technocrats and lone inventors, foregrounded at the expense of the 'mob', or society at large.[3] He humanizes these characters by inscribing clear distinctions between human and non-human, reliant on metaphors inspired by quantum physics. If the human brain has the power to make a 'quantum leap' from one level of understanding to the next then the possibility of a circular history that sees the same human actions repeated over and over again is ruled out. Roberts draws attention to the breaking of this cycle through his use of a typical Golden Age device, the robot, which he adapts and changes, disrupting the reader's (and, especially, the science fiction fan's) expectations of repeated history and a cyclical model of history and progress.

In breaking this cycle, Roberts captures the impact that chaotic and quantum paradigms must have on our understanding of temporality, which no longer occurs in predictable cycles or relies on historical necessity. This change carries a political dimension as the novel's use of chaotic history opens a space for a revolutionary future. The narrative structure and the characterization of *Jack Glass* reinforce the sense of a break from the Golden Age past and amount to a challenge to the readership, rather than the comforting reassurance that made much of Golden Age science fiction so popular. This challenge has proved exciting to the readership, as shown by the book's critical and popular success, and I argue that this suggests an audience hungry for art that offers change through the plurality of the future, rather than the return of the status quo that Depression-era readers of Asimov sought out.[4] This engagement with the present is essential to all science fiction. As Roberts writes in his introduction to the genre, *Science Fiction* (2000), 'SF does not project us into the future; it relates to us stories about our present, and more importantly about the past that has led to this present. Counter-intuitively, SF is a *historiographic* mode, a means of symbolically writing about history' (*SF*: 35–6). This awareness leads to a novel about history and nostalgia which intensely engages with our contemporary historical moment by exploring the role of the contemporary precariat through different representations of servitude: the duplicitous servant, the silent droid and the freed-woman who challenges historical necessity through creating her own narrative. These historical challenges are clarified through the novel's use of history, one that is in stark contrast to that of the *Foundation* trilogy.

The Golden Age, Asimov, and *Foundation*

Isaac Asimov was a prolific writer with almost 500 non-fiction titles, anthologies and novels to his name but, as Roberts writes in *A History of Science Fiction* (2006: 197), 'it was the work [Asimov] created during the 1940s and the early 1950s, at the very heart, chronologically and culturally, of Golden Age SF that has sustained his reputation'. The *Foundation* stories were published between 1942 and 1953, serialized in the magazine *Astounding Science-Fiction* under the editorship of John W. Campbell before their publication in paperback. They are, therefore, quintessentially 'Golden Age' as the consensus is to define the Golden Age as synonymous with the time Campbell spent at the helm of *Astounding*, with due credit given to the groundwork done by Hugo Gernsback and his magazine *Amazing Stories*.[5] These serialized *Foundation* stories were later collected into three novels, known as the *Foundation* trilogy.[6] The trilogy consists of *Foundation* (1951/1994), *Foundation and Empire* (1952) and *Second Foundation* (1953) and takes place as a Galactic Empire is about to fall, leading to 30,000 years of barbarism. This fall is predicted by a 'psycho-historian', Hari Seldon. Through psycho-history, the statistical analysis of various probabilities of mass human behaviour, he can predict the fall of the empire and seeks to form a plan that will see it restored in a far shorter time, a mere millennium. The key to his plan is the establishment of two 'foundations': two planets where the skills of the empire will be concealed and maintained. The first foundation is the custodian of the empire's powers of physics; they hold the secrets to atomic energy and various associated technologies. The second foundation holds the power of psychology and of psycho-history itself. These plans run smoothly until the Mule, a mutant whose genetic mutation could not be foreseen by the Seldon plan, comes to power and disturbs the smooth path of, what the novel refers to as, psycho-historical necessity. Some of the themes of the novel, such as the struggle to save the universe writ large onto an epic, generation-spanning canvas were already common storylines in the pulp magazines at the time, particularly in E. E. Smith's *Lensman* series.[7] However, the idea of psycho-historical necessity, of a social, 'hard' science, was new to science fiction and would quickly become extremely popular.

'Psycho-historical necessity' means that human actions are taken within a historical and psychological context that can determine the outcome of those actions. In this sense, it resembles the theoretical approach of historical materialism formulated by Karl Marx and best summarized in *The Eighteenth Brumaire of Louis Bonaparte* (1852):

> Men make their own history, but they do not make it just as they please; they do not make it under circumstances chosen by themselves, but under circumstances directly encountered, given and transmitted from the past. The tradition of all the dead generations weighs like a nightmare on the brain of the living. (Marx, 1852/1979: 103)

Marx emphasizes the contingency of human action. He does not deny the existence of free will, but highlights that it must happen within a socio-political context shaped by the past. Psycho-history also acts as a challenge to an unfettered belief in free will but, rather than pitting the present against the past, Asimov pits the 'mob' against the individual. Psycho-history is described, in *Foundation and Empire,* in the following way:

> Psycho-history dealt not with man, but with man-masses. It was the science of mobs; mobs in their billions. It could forecast reactions to stimuli with something of the accuracy that a lesser science could bring to the forecast of a rebound of a billiard ball. The reaction of one man could be forecast by no known mathematics; the reaction of a billion is something else again. (Asimov, 1952/1996: 7)

The 'science' of psycho-history pays lip service to the materialist principles of much Golden Age science fiction.[8] The Newtonian description of its workings – human 'reactions to stimuli' compared to 'the rebound of a billiard ball' – gives the theory an impression of scientific rigour. However, the description also engenders an elitist attitude as the predictable mobs are contrasted with the individual. This was a common trope in the American pulp magazines, which created heroes in the image of Thomas Edison, a lone genius improving life for humanity with only a faith in science to guide (inevitably) him. The intention of many of the stories was to educate the reader about the scientific practice in question. This involved glorifying science, and therefore scientists. Stories such as Robert A. Heinlein's 'The Roads Must Roll' (1940) proclaimed a belief that objective, rational technology would lead to the correct course of action, while personifying that objectivity in the figure of the scientist. Technocracy was valourized, and those who held its secrets were represented as superior and capable. While this belief in technology was supposed to promote an objective, scientific and utilitarian approach to human problems, in Asimov's hands Seldon becomes a god. This is reflected in the language the characters use to talk about their relationship to the legend of Seldon. Seldon 'helps those who help themselves' (Asimov, 1952/1996: 108) they say.

Seldon's god-like position, his ability to predict human actions and political outcomes, leads him to have power over history itself. He masters history and plans the future of the galaxy but the future relies on 'psycho-historical necessity' which assumes that history is cyclical and repeats itself, just with different window-dressing.[9] This belief in the cyclic nature of history is embedded in the novels through Asimov's use of Edward Gibbon's *History of the Decline and Fall of the Roman Empire* (1776–81) as source material. By reimagining the rise and fall of empire in a distant future, Asimov assumes a cyclical conception of history, one that Marx would reject in favour of a teleological model, based on progression to a communist society.[10] This cyclical conception of history proves contradictory to the materialist commitment that Golden Age science fiction had undertaken. If humans adapt to advances in technology then they should change their characters and their very destiny, not just repeat the same old mistakes in the same way and end up back where they started.[11] Asimov does not depict any adaptation in the face of new technologies, but portrays a universal and unchanging human nature. This obscures the workings of psycho-historical necessity that guide the populace without their knowledge, in such a way that they do not know when they are acting in accordance with the plan, and with historical determinism, or to what extent they have free will. Ducem Barr, an expert on psycho-history, says in *Foundation and Empire*, 'there's nothing to *do*. It's all already *done*. It's proceeding now. Because you don't hear the wheels turning and the gongs beating doesn't mean it's any the less certain' (Asimov, 1952/1996: 70). Psycho-history is not just difficult to understand, it is impossible for the populace to understand it if the Seldon plan is to work:

> The laws of Psychohistory are statistical in nature and are rendered invalid if the actions of individual men are not random in nature. If a sizable group of human beings learned of key details of the Plan, their actions would be governed by that knowledge and would no longer be random in the meaning of the axioms of Psychohistory. In other words, they would no longer be perfectly predictable. (Asimov, 1953/1995: 116)

This means that the people of the Galaxy are largely objectified as they react to forces over which they have no control. The masses are not spoken of respectfully in the *Foundation* novels, but treated as if they, en masse, follow the path of historical necessity blindly and stupidly:

> The larger groups; the billions that occupied planets; the trillions that occupied Sectors; the quadrillions that occupied the whole Galaxy, became, not simply human beings, but gigantic forces amenable to statistical treatment – so that to Hari Seldon, the future became clear and inevitable, and the Plan could be set up. (Asimov, 1953/1995: 109)

This disrespect for the masses is elitist and patronizing as those in power, whilst ignorant of the details of psychohistory, can claim superiority over the common man through their theoretical understanding of the process. This allows them to patronize members of the proletariat. For example, Salvor Hardin the mayor of Terminus explains the behaviour of a native of a neighbouring, more backwards, planet: 'He's merely the product of his environment. He doesn't understand much except that "I got a gun and you ain't"' (Asimov, 1951/1994: 56). This dismissive attitude, and the class distinction between the rulers and the ruled that is obvious in the novels, shows the elitism of the galaxy of the *Foundation* novels.[12]

Jack Glass: A Golden Age Story

The *Foundation* trilogy resonates thematically with *Jack Glass*; both texts are concerned with the future of the Galaxy and of humanity itself, as well as with the course of history and how it is formed. In *The History of Science Fiction,* Roberts explains that the scientific culture of the twenty-first century, particularly the discovery of chaos theory, has dated the *Foundation* novels while, in turn, creating new themes and challenges for SF:

> [The big ideas of the *Foundation* novels] have much less purchase today than they did in the 1940s and 1950s; not because history has ceased to matter, but because the development of Chaos Theory in the 1980s has finally put to rest the old Positivist philosophical chimera of a science so comprehensive that it can wholly predict the future. History evidently is a chaotic system. (*HSF*: 197–8)[13]

Like the *Foundation* trilogy, *Jack Glass* shows a society in crisis, but it does so with this chaotic model of history in mind. In *Jack Glass,* the galaxy is ruled by an oligarchy, known as the Ulanovs, who run the galaxy with a corporatist philosophy. The law of the universe, the Lex Ulanova, is designed to protect market interests above all else, and to crush the collective power of the sumpolloi, the majority of the galaxy who live in poverty.[14] The priorities of the Lex Ulanova reduce human life to a resource – and a cheap one in a highly overpopulated galaxy. In both the *Foundation* novels and *Jack Glass* the masses are guided by strong forces that are external to them. However, rather than reducing humanity to a blind mass of predictable objects, Adam Roberts makes the problem of ethics in a massively over-populated galaxy one of the main concerns of the novel. This is foregrounded by the novel's structure. It consists of three short stories, each representing a different subgenre of detective fiction. With each story, the scope of the novel becomes wider, exploring the galaxy on a different scale with each new story. The first takes place among a small group of people imprisoned in an asteroid. The second follows Diana and Eva Argent, two wealthy teenagers who will one day inherit great galactic power. This story begins to explore the social structures of the galaxy as Diana investigates the death of a servant. In the third story, Diana must escape assassination and, in doing so, leave the safety of her privileged bubble to go out into the galaxy with Jack Glass himself, who has been cunningly disguised as her butler until her life is endangered.

The three stories of which the novel consists serve to broaden its scope from the interpersonal (the people in the asteroid) to the political (the wealthy teenage daughters of the political elite) until finally depicting the socio-political interconnections that define and confine life in the galaxy. This broadening of the reader's perspective is reflected and reinforced by the different subgenres represented by each story. We are told in the preface that each part of the novel can be seen as a prison story, a 'regular whodunit', or a locked-room mystery – unless the reader decides that each story is all three at once (*JG*: 1). This means that, when the setting of a story is among prisoners sentenced to inhabit an asteroid for 11 years we assume that we are reading the prison story – but then realize that this could as easily be a locked room mystery, and that the story hinges on the past crimes of all the inhabitants, and is therefore a 'regular whodunit'. A locked room mystery involving the death of a servant can just as easily be considered a prison mystery when all the servants are dosed with a drug to induce loyalty to their master. In this sense, all the servants are imprisoned. Each story overturns the reader's assumptions about which subgenre they are reading, about the constraints of crime and punishment, until the whole galaxy becomes a prison that must be wholly reformed, or escaped. Jack Glass explains: 'I'm happy to agree the Solar System is, in the largest sense, a prison' (*JG*: 296). He claims this to be so because the galaxy is trapped in the matrix of corporatist, Ulanov, rule. As he says, 'Only when the guards of Ulanov tyranny have been eliminated, and the prison of poverty itself dismantled, can humanity achieve its potential. *Then* we'll be ready for the stars – not before!' (*JG*: 357).

In leaving the safety of her privileged world and finding herself in the home of the sumpolloi, known as the 'Sump', Diana becomes conscious of the scale of human existence in the galaxy and how that existence has been affected by the power games of her wealthy and privileged class. Through Diana, the faceless masses become a primary concern of the novel:

> [Diana] thought of the multitude. Trillions of human beings, wrapped like a fog about their home star. The mind collapsed at the scale and the numbers. But if ethics meant anything at all, it meant not letting the largeness of the human population overwhelm our moral knowledge that life is lived individually, and that even when agglomerated into billions and trillions individual human beings deserve better than being used as tools. That the overwhelming majority of this vast mass of humanity was poor, living precarious and subsistence lives in leaky shanty bubbles, eating ghunk and drinking recycled water – this made this more, not less, true. These were the people least able to help themselves. They should be helped, not exploited. (*JG*: 239)

This ethical focus on the masses is in stark contrast to their portrayal as a mindless mob in the *Foundation* novels and it is *Jack Glass*'s foregrounding of the economics that leads to their exploitation and poverty which gives the novel this ethical focus. In the *Foundation* novels the mobs are ruled by forces that are necessarily beyond their understanding, the forces of psycho-history. The trillions of Asimov's galaxy are not to be understood, but merely objectified as atoms of a larger organism, or cogs in a machine. In drawing attention to the individuality of the trillions and how their living conditions are shaped by the economic and political structure of their galaxy, Roberts gives them back their humanity and, in doing so, grounds the narrative tension of *Jack Glass* in a galaxy full of human characters whose lives must be weighed in the balance by those seeking to change the power structures.

The importance of the recognition of humanity in creating change is emphasized through the exceptionalism of human beings and their differentiation from artificial intelligence. In part two, 'The FTL Murders', we meet Diana and Eva Argent, on their first trip to earth. Diana is skilled in psychology and in solving human problems. Through this training she has acquired a love of solving murder mysteries. Diana reflects on the importance of sleep and dreams to her thought processes:

> Dreams! Any old AI can crunch data, draw hypotheses and spot patterns. But there are no AIs, and very few *human* minds, that can intuit solutions from interacting chaotic systems... dreams iterate and test mental schemas, discarding the maladaptive to return the adaptive to the slush to be reworked. Dreams are emotional preparations for solving problems... dreams intoxicate the individual out of reliance on common sense and preconception, and tempt her into the orbit of private logic. (*JG*: 119)

This recognition of history as a chaotic system, of existence being made up of several interacting chaotic systems, means that a linear approach, a simple chain of causes and effects, no longer applies and one must reach outside of the known patterns in order to arrive at answers – one must create these connections through interpretation, and without the inhibitions of Newtonian consequences that might limit these effects. It is only the human mind that can achieve this, to make a 'quantum leap' to another level of understanding, an 'orbit of private logic'.

The theme of the orbit also appears in the first story, 'In the Box', when Jack is trapped on his asteroid prison: 'He was inside a box: the box was made of stone, and it was passing around the sun at a distance of many hundreds of millions of miles. Its path was a perverted circle' (*JG*: 56). At first glance, this mention of the orbit might be seen as a metaphor for a cyclical pattern of history, as we have already seen in the *Foundation* novels, a repeating circle only perverted by slight superficial differences. However, once we reach the end of the story (or earlier, if the reader guesses the outcome in advance) we realize that Jack intends to escape this circle by leaving the asteroid in a quantum leap of his own. The cycle of historical repetition that Asimov supposes does not hold here. Rather than a Newtonian understanding of the movement of planetary bodies in orbit, repetitive and cyclical, Roberts reminds us of the orbit of electrons in quantum physics – not merely moving in 'perverted circles', but also occasionally leaping improbably in response to bursts of energy, like Diana's mind moving into a 'private orbit of logic' through the creative energy of her dreams.

The novel's focus on quantum, rather than Newtonian, physics can also be seen in its second part, 'The FTL Murders'. This title brings together two things that are essentially impossible – the discovery of faster-than-light travel, and the murders and escapes that we read about in the novel. Our narrator, in the book's preface, writes, 'FTL! We all know it is impossible, we know every one of us that the laws of physics disallow it. But still!' (*JG*: 1). This 'But still!' is at the heart of not only science fiction, but detective fiction as well – we know that the murder or the technology is impossible, but still we want to find out how it happened, how, for some reason, it became possible for however brief an instant. Eva and Diana are visited by an agent of the Lex Ulanova who warns them that Jack Glass may be in the area. She says, '*one* of the remarkable things about Mr Glass is the knack he has for *making the impossible happen*' (*JG*: 137; emphasis in original). This applies to the murders, or to the acquisition of faster than light travel. There is the sense that the 'impossible' can happen and, in *Jack Glass,* this is a force for change, for intellectual excitement and for hope. The laws of physics themselves, through the interplay of Newtonian and quantum conceptions of time, or the relationship between cause and effect, are exposed as systems of knowledge, and thereby denaturalized. Through showing the laws of physics as complex and chaotic, *Jack Glass* denaturalizes systems of power. This extends to the political systems in power over the galaxy which he shows as unnatural and contingent. The impossible – the revolution – becomes possible. The power of imagining the impossible in challenging these power structures is recognized by Diana as she intuitively realizes the importance of FTL technology, whether it truly exists or not:

> 'If there really were an FTL technology then people could use it to flee the system... couldn't they? They could use it to escape the Lex Ulanova altogether... The point is that the idea of it could become a symbol, a flag. A banner. A rallying point for revolution.' (*JG*: 145)

Imagining the impossible offers a way out of the prison of the galaxy, the prison of Ulanov rule and the inequality on which it relies. As physical laws can be subverted with surprising results (for example, through FTL technology), so political rule can be unexpectedly subverted through an impossible dream.

Breaking the Cycle

Isaac Asimov's *Foundation* novels did not attempt to design a blueprint for a new world; they remained trapped in old patterns, in old cycles.[15] However, the stories and novels were hugely popular and Brian Aldiss argues that this was because of, rather than despite, their conservatism. In his history of science fiction, *Billion Year Spree* (Aldiss, 1973: 238), he writes, 'the pulps gave a whole stratum of the American public, hit by the Depression and other economic evils, a sort of unified viewpoint'. Unified viewpoints are hard to come by in twenty-first century literature, partly due to the influence of postmodern techniques, and *Jack Glass* is no exception.[16] But yet, it has been more popular than any other Roberts novel, winning both the BSFA Award and the John W. Campbell Award. This might be surprising, given that the book has been released into a British society struggling with a modern Depression and concerned with inequality and poverty. Perhaps *Jack Glass* finds a society asking itself how it can change, rather than asking how it can stay the same. It has become popular because it resonates with the unrest in Western democracies, and particularly with the tension between the establishment (banks, neo-liberal governments, capitalism in general) and the rhizomatic groups, such as Anonymous and Occupy, which act as a challenge to these systems. The discussion of (not often *with*) these groups has centred on their silence, or the lack of cohesion in their demands – a plurality that is necessarily a part of their horizontal organization.[17]

Noam Chomsky (2012) wrote in his pamphlet about the movement, *Occupy,* 'I think, if you investigate the Occupy movements and you ask them what are their demands, they are reticent to answer and rightly so, because they are essentially crafting a point of view from many disparate sources' (*JG*: 56).

In *Jack Glass,* this plurality is shown as silence, just as the Occupy movement's lack of a cohesive political programme was experienced as silence by the political and financial elites. However, this silence is a powerful resistance due to the interplay between silence and servility in the text and its intertexts. Part 3 of the novel, 'The Impossible Gun', sees Jack Glass, Diana Argent, and her once-servant Sapho arrive at the Sump where they seek someone who can access information from a droid that they have in their possession. The droid has witnessed a murder which the group believe to be recorded in its memory, if only they can access it. Since Karl Čapek's 1920 play *R. U. R.* first coined the word 'robot' (from 'robota', the Czech word for 'forced labour'),[18] robots have been used in science fiction to represent the working classes, the 'trillions' of the *Jack Glass* galaxy on whose labour the capitalist system relies. Texts featuring robots have revealed a bourgeois fear of revolution in that the earliest pulp stories about robots and mechanical men often portrayed robots running amok and destroying bourgeois society. Asimov wrote that,

> By the time I was in my late teens and already a hardened science fiction reader, I had read many robot stories and found that they fell into two classes. In the first class there was the Robot-As-Menace… In the second class (a much smaller one) there was Robot-As-Pathos. In such stories the robots were lovable and were usually put upon by cruel human beings. These charmed me. (Asimov, 1995: 9)

When Asimov set out to write his first robot story he therefore aimed to write a 'Robot-As-Pathos' story:

> But something odd happened as I wrote my first story. I managed to get the dim vision of a robot as neither Menace nor Pathos. I began to think of robots as industrial products built by matter-of-fact engineers. They were built with safety features so they weren't Menaces

> and they were fashioned for certain jobs so that no Pathos was necessarily involved. (Asimov, 1995: 9–10)

Asimov's three laws of robotics famously regulated the robots, turning these stories into philosophical dilemmas about the contradictions the machines might face.[19] The robots in Asimov's fictions are programmed to be altruistic, due to the laws they are compelled to follow. This gives a safe distance between the reader and the revolutionary potential of the robot (read: proletariat). By disregarding the Robot-As-Pathos, the sympathy that we might feel for the robot and its position of exploitation by humans is also limited.

The droid in *Jack Glass* does not deviate from the Asimovian tradition insofar as it does not rebel or run amok, neither does it elicit emotion from the reader through anthropomorphic behaviour. The use of the term 'droid' immediately carries connotations of George Lucas's bleeping and friendly R2D2 from the *Star Wars* trilogy (1977–1983) and this association is extended as *Jack Glass*'s droid, like R2D2, is used to carry information. In the first *Star Wars* film, *A New Hope* (1977), R2D2 carries a message from Princess Leia. She has been captured, and recording a message in the memory of the droid is the only way for her to ask for help. *Jack Glass*'s droid is reminiscent of this, as the recording in its memory is represented as Diana's only hope; it contains a promise from a law-enforcement official that she should be allowed to escape into anonymity, in order to be safe from the power struggle that has engulfed her family and the elite of the Ulanov system. However, unlike R2D2 (who might be considered an example of the Robot-As-Pathos), Roberts's droid does not obligingly reveal its message, never mind accompany this message with friendly bleeps and whistles. The droid's silence leaves a gap in the text, and this is emphasized in the narrative, which offers no detailed description of the droid's physical characteristics. The droid is first described as, 'one of those devices for witnessing and affirming contracts' (*JG*: 264). It is defined purely in terms of its use to its human owners, with no further description of its physical presence. Glass claims that he cares for the droid's 'authenticity' (*JG*: 265), an unusual choice of words given that, presumably, the droid cannot lie and its functionality is all that one must hope for. He goes on to say that the droid will be useful but only 'if it's kosher' (*JG*: 265). The religious connotations here, again, imbue the silent and, textually, almost invisible droid with imagined religious motivations and moral connotations. Aishwarya, an associate of Glass and a mechanic, begins to examine the droid: 'she began fondling the device. It observed her with its impassive exhaustless machine patience' (*JG*: 272). It is not clear whether the droid is humanoid and literally watches her with 'eyes', or whether the narrator is describing it in anthropomorphic terms. The word 'exhaustless' acts as an adjective but serves to efface the droid further from the text as it highlights not only the droid's tirelessness, but also that the energy source of the droid is not visible; it is not run on a petrol engine and has no visible emissions. The mystery of the droid, like the mystery of the Impossible Gun itself, and the mystery stories that make up the novel, structures the text around a silence and the journey towards overcoming that silence. This silence, then, acts as another way of portraying robots beyond Menace, Pathos, and technocratic rationality; the droid does not run amok, but neither does it attempt to help its human masters in an anthropomorphic display of obeisance, or in reaction to pre-programming. It is still described as 'rogue' (*JG*: 263), even though it has not been actively hostile to the humans. It is not humanized, or even described in the text, thereby alienating the reader. Like the Occupy protesters, it refuses to answer.

The silence of the droid is a reflection of Jack Glass himself. Jack Glass's character also refuses to be captured in a unified viewpoint. His motivations change throughout the novel; he is a brutal murderer, then a servant, before he is revealed as a revolutionary. He acts on behalf of the populace throughout the book, but claims to do everything for the love of Diana in the final pages. The name 'Jack Glass' unites the three stories, as the title of the novel, but the character of that name does not tie the book together into a satisfying single narrative. As Diana observes, 'he was a different man in each environment, and none of these personas had anything in common with the deferential servant who had been so constant a presence in Dia's former life' (*JG*: 275). Jack Glass takes on the name 'Iago' while he pretends to be merely Diana's servant, a reference perhaps to his duplicitous nature, like that of Shakespeare's Iago in *Othello*. His 'real' name, Jack Glass, comes from his use of Glass as a weapon and so is equally pseudonymous. This slippage in his naming and identity is a kind of silence in that, like the droid, he does not exist as a stable character in the text, he is invisible like the clearest glass. While we do get visual descriptions of Jack Glass occasionally, he changes from story to story. In the 'The FTL Murders' Diana observes 'his old face, as creased as any druid's. His short hair, his muscular torso, his long legs' (*JG*: 110). Later, Diana accesses her bld to find a picture of Jack Glass. 'She stared at the image of his face. It looked as bland as any other face. Murderers often did' (*JG*: 142). It later transpires that his face has been 'surgically reconfigured' (*JG*: 232). The hope for revolutionary change then from the servant class, represented by the droid and by Jack Glass himself, is not represented within the text, but is present as a defined absence.

The voices and voicelessness of the servant class is a concern of the book right up to its final pages, where it is revealed that the narrative of the novel has been composed, (or, 'doctorwatsoned') by Sapho, Diana's ex-servant. Now free from the drugs that had enforced her loyalty to Diana's family, Sapho chooses to travel the galaxy with Jack Glass as his faithful companion and biographer. Once the identity of the narrator has been revealed, we can see in hindsight that Sapho's narration is confident. She sees the role of the biographer as taking control of history. In 'The Impossible Gun', she writes, 'We have to go backwards in order to understand how we got here. To trace the line from death to death ... We can join the dots' (*JG*: 275). Sapho rejects historical necessity, whether based on linear or cyclical time: she takes control of history by using the deaths that Jack Glass has left in his wake to organize her narrative.

These three portrayals of servitude – the duplicitous servant, the droid without a voice, and the servant freed from her master who takes charge of history – are key to *Jack Glass*'s success as a popular novel. By breaking from the conventions of the Golden Age, Roberts rejects cyclical time and the myth of the benevolent underclass represented by the compliant robot. The novel hints at revolutionary potential without ever consummating this potential within its pages.

This explains the popularity of the novel, as it does not dictate or over-articulate revolutionary progress, but opens up a space for it to happen in all its plurality. As Roberts puts it, 'science fiction is […] a body of work that encourages readers to take nothing for granted, to challenge all their assumptions, to think through how things might be different. It is time and again, accordingly, a revolutionary mode of writing' (*SF*: 183). *Jack Glass* achieves this by putting the reader in the position of being aware of their assumptions (including the assumption of the subgenre they are reading) before challenging those assumptions, and thinking about how things might be different if the prison of poverty and of the galaxy might be changed. This can be done by taking control of history, as Sapho does, by refusing to be bound by a cyclical or linear history, and by imagining the impossible.

Notes

1 Adam Roberts explicitly states that one of his aims is to write a story in every sub-genre of science fiction in the preface to his short story collection *Adam Robots* (*AR*: 1).

2 For an analysis of the ways in which Adam Roberts references the Golden Age of detective fiction in *Jack Glass* see Paul March-Russell, 'Rule of Law: Reiterating Genre in *Jack Glass*', in this volume.

3 This valourization of the lone technocrat at the expense of the 'mob' can be seen in Asimov's work as I will go on to show. It is also typical of John W. Campbell's short stories (see 'Twilight' and 'The Mightiest Machine'), and in Robert Heinlein's work, for example, 'The Roads Must Roll'.

4 *Jack Glass* was awarded the John W. Campbell memorial award and the BSFA prize in 2013, making it Roberts's most critically recognized and successful novel to date.

5 This classification can be found, for example, in Brian Atterby's 'The Magazine Era: 1926–1960' (2003) and in Brian Aldiss's (1973: 215–43), 'The Future on a Chipped Plate: The World of John W. Campbell's "Astounding"'.

6 Isaac Asimov would go on to add further volumes to the *Foundation* series later in his life: *Foundation's Edge* (1982), *Foundation and Earth* (1986), *Prelude to Foundation* (1988), and *Forward the Foundation* (1993). These novels, while expanding the universe that appears in the original trilogy,

are not Golden Age texts and will not be a focus of this chapter. References to 'the *Foundation* novels' refer only to the original trilogy.

7 The *Lensman* series by E. E. Smith is one of the first examples of what became known as space opera. Many of the stories, such as those later collected under the titles *Galactic Patrol* (1950) and *Gray Lensman* (1951), first appeared in *Astounding Science-Fiction* under John W. Campbell's editorship.

8 Materialism and scientific accuracy were defining characteristics of science fiction according to Hugo Gernsback. His editorial in the first edition of *Science Wonder Stories* (July 1929) stated that he would publish 'only such stories that have their basis in scientific laws as we know them, or in the logical deduction of new laws from what we know' (*SF*).

9 This is pointed out by Charles Elkins (1976) as he argues that Asimov's psycho-historical necessity is based on a misunderstanding of Marxist theory. Elkins writes: 'Behind Seldon's psychohistory lies the assumption – shared by Asimov – that mankind will not fundamentally change, that basic human drives are universal and eternal. Marx disagrees. His optimism is based on a rejection of this cyclical view of history. History sometimes may, but as a rule does not – and certainly does not have to – repeat itself" (Elkins, 1976: 33).

10 For a description of how Isaac Asimov took inspiration from Gibbons's *Decline and Fall of the Roman Empire,* see Isaac Asimov (1982). Asimov had also shown a cyclical conception of history in his short story, 'Nightfall' (1941) which depicts a planet that only experiences night once every millennium, an unexpected occurrence that destroys society in an epidemic of madness each time. His first story to be published by John W. Campbell, 'Trends' (1939) also expressed a belief in the cyclic nature of human society.

11 Elkins points out that Asimov's characters do not react to the material changes that they face, whether economic or technological: 'There is no indication in the "Foundation" stories that scientific advancement – e.g. travelling faster than light, developing atomic technology, controlling minds, etc. – has any effect on people. Man remains essentially the same; the springs of human action are unchanged' (Elkins, 1976: 27).

12 Albert I. Berger (1988) blames this elitism on the tensions between two contradictory narratives of the Golden Age: the narrative of scientific progress, and the Second Law of Thermodynamics which says that the universe must tend towards entropy, or disorder.

13 Acknowledgement of the changes made to our scientific landscape by the advent of chaos theory also appears in Roberts's fiction. In *Stone* (2002) the main character, Ae, takes part in a political debate on the future of the galactic system, the t'T: 'I contributed little; but every now and again I would drop in some most-obvious statement of truth. For instance, the more people spouted confident predictions about the future mass behaviour of people in the t'T, the more I would want to interject that "Of course chaos philosophy demonstrates how none of your predictions are worth anything at all"' (*ST*: 111).

14 As explained in *Jack Glass*'s glossary, this term refers to 'what used to be called the *lumpenproletariat*... by far the most populous element in the solar system population' (370).

15 This is not to diminish Asimov's profound influence on science fiction and, indeed, science itself. Asimov and his writing helped to form new patterns – for example, we can see Asimov's influence in robotics, once a field that only existed in his imagination. He was recognized by the United States Congress for his contribution to robotics on 9 March 2010 in House Resolution 1055.

16 For an analysis of postmodern techniques in *Jack Glass* and their effect on reader reception see John McCalmont's insightful essay, '*Jack Glass* (2012): Apply Ending to Avoid Confusion' (2012).

17 Bill Clinton, for example, said that the Occupy protesters 'need to be for something specific, and not just against something' (Walker, 2011).

18 *Oxford English Dictionary* (3rd edn) s.v. 'robot, *n.2*' http://www.oed.com/view/Entry/166641 (consulted 17 October 2013).

19 The three laws of robotics are as follows: 1) A robot may not injure a human being, or, through inaction, allow a human being to come to harm; 2) A robot must obey the orders given it by human beings except where such orders would conflict with the First Law; 3) A robot must protect its own existence as long as such protection does not conflict with the First or Second Law (Asimov, 1995).

Works Cited

Aldiss, Brian W. (1973) *Billion Year Spree: The History of Science Fiction*. London: Weidenfeld & Nicholson.

Asimov, Isaac (1995) *The Complete Robot*. London: Voyager HarperCollins.

Asimov, Isaac (1951/1994) *Foundation*. London: Voyager HarperCollins.

Asimov, Isaac (1952/1996) *Foundation & Empire*. London: Voyager HarperCollins.
Asimov, Isaac (1953/1995) *Second Foundation*. London: Voyager HarperCollins.
Asimov, Isaac (1982) 'The Story Behind the "Foundation"', *Isaac Asimov's Science Fiction Magazine* December: 30–42.
Atterby, Brian (2003) 'The Magazine Era: 1926–1960', in Edward James and Farah Mendlesohn (eds) *The Cambridge Companion to Science Fiction*, pp. 32–47. Cambridge: Cambridge University Press.
Berger, Albert I. (1988) 'Theories of History and Social Order in "Astounding Science Fiction", 1934–45', *Science Fiction Studies* 15(1): 12–35.
Carter, Angela (1983) 'Notes From the Front Line', in Michelene Wandor (ed.) *On Gender and Writing*, pp. 69–77. London: Pandora.
Chomsky, Noam (2012) *Occupy*. London: Penguin.
Elkins, Charles (1976) 'Isaac Asimov's "Foundation" Novels: Historical Materialism Distorted into Cyclical Psycho-History', *Science Fiction Studies* 3(1): 26–36.
Lucas, George (1977) *Star Wars Episode IV: A New Hope*, LucasFilm, Twentieth Century Fox Film Corporation.
McCalmont, John (2012) '*Jack Glass* (2012): Apply Ending to Avoid Confusion', *Ruthless Culture*, URL (consulted 4 November 2013): http://ruthlessculture.com/2012/12/17/jack-glass-2012-apply-story-to-end-confusion/
Marx, Karl (1852/1979) *The Eighteenth Brumaire of Louis Bonaparte, Karl Marx/Friedrich Engels Collected Works, Vol. II*. New York: International Publishers.
Smith, E. E. (1950) *Galactic Patrol*. Reading, Pennsylvania: Fantasy Press.
Smith, E. E. (1951) *Gray Lensman*. Reading, PennsylvaniaL Fantasy Press.
United States Congress (2010) 'House Resolution 1055', Library of Congress, URL (consulted 7th August 2013): https://www.congress.gov/bill/111th-congress/house-resolution/1055
Walker, Hunter (2011) 'Bill Clinton on Occupy Wall Street: They Need to be For Something Specific', *Politicker*, URL (consulted 5 September 2013):http://politicker.com/2011/10/bill-clinton-on-occupy-wall-street-they-need-to-be-for-something-specific/
Walter, Damien (2013) 'Adam Roberts: Last of the SF Writers', *Guardian*, URL (consulted 4 November 2013): http://www.theguardian.com/books/booksblog/2013/feb/15/adam-roberts-last-sci-fi-writer

On the Topic of Plenty
Sunshine and Ice-Cream Mountains in *By Light Alone*

Catherine Parry

Food has a central role in the social and ecological construction of the world in Adam Roberts's 2011 novel *By Light Alone*, as its matter, modes and symbolism operate as a trope which traces a mechanics of oppression and disenfranchisement. Throughout human history the economic power and ability of any individual or social group to flourish has been shaped by the food resources available to them. Likewise, in *By Light Alone* populations flourish or not according to the substance of their diet. However, in the novel's climate-changed future the distinction between rich and poor, previously one of inequitably distributed quantities of resources, is now a qualitative abyss. This transformation is effected by the 'Sunlight Bug', a science fictional nanotechnology which alters humans from organisms which eat organic compounds (plants and animals) to organisms which derive nutrition from inorganic sunlight through genetically engineered photosynthesizing hair. In an ecocritical reading, this chapter examines the dehumanizing discourses that the 'New Hair' engenders and the ways in which it entangles its human bearers in a new ecological condition. *By Light Alone,* interrogating perverse re-imaginings of how humans locate themselves in their environments, is a satirical thought experiment with ontological preoccupations, energized by the superficial elegance of what appears to be a utopian solution to world hunger.

No novel by Adam Roberts is amenable to straightforward encounters within comforting, genre-defined parameters. While the paragraph above implies that *By Light Alone* is a work of science fiction interested in ecojustice, to treat the text as if what it is 'about' is located entirely in its content reduces it to a clever but unsatisfying plot. Entwined with its genuinely serious consideration of inequity and environmental degradation, the novel casts a self-reflexive and questioning eye over the conventions of science fiction writing, undermining the genre's standards and tropes by visibly deconstructing them: see my estrangement, the texts says, marvel at my novum, travel home with my stranger-in-a-strange-land, watch out for my info-dumps! Roberts does not tinker only with SF's orthodoxies for among its other interests *By Light Alone* is a novel that plays with narrative and narratives, drawing attention to the part narrative forms play in how humans understand themselves and their inhabiting of the world. It populates its pages with Homeric, Rabelasian and absurd characters who overturn the meaning of traditional metaphorical structures and mock the tidy compartments of science fictional morality tales, heroes and monsters, utopias and dystopias, and technological religiosities. Lavie Tidhar remarks that 'Roberts's work engages with science fiction without, it could be argued, being of science fiction', for it seeks not to familiarize the unfamiliar, but to '*defamiliarise the unfamiliar*' (2011). In the case of *By Light Alone,* the result is a rather unlikeable and unsettling novel, for although the components of an SF novel are there, they are behaving badly.

Roberts, in his critical text *Science Fiction* (2000), argues that, 'SF does not project us into the future; it relates to us stories about our present' (*SF,* 35), and in *By Light Alone* he examines the forms of the stories – SF and otherwise – that we are currently telling ourselves, illuminating, through the absurdity of 'heroically crass' (Clarke, 2012) fat people and extravagant austerity, the narratives, equivocations and ignorance which have constructed and continue to reinforce the yawning gap between wealth and poverty in the present day. The scientifically improbable novum of photosynthesizing hair catalyses the events of the novel and is the conceit by which SF quick-fix technologies are satirized. The novum echoes a real world and utopian faith that scientific discovery will allow human life to continue as it is, untouched either by a twenty-first century failure of the imagination to connect quotidian human behaviour with natural global systems and with the life of the other, or the consequences of a traditional set of ethics inadequate to extraordinary new technological horizons.

You Are What You Eat

In what Timothy Morton describes as the 'mesh' of the world's ecological interconnectedness, food is a critical ecological substance, but not just as mundane matter. Thinking ecologically is 'a practice and process of becoming fully aware of how human beings are connected with other beings – animal, vegetable or mineral' (Morton, 2010: 7). Therefore, to think ecologically is to think about how food and wealth, racist and misogynistic oppression, geography and climate change might be connected. The existence and possible effects of global climate change, never mind whether or not it is caused by human behaviour, has inspired a divisive debate about the nature of human inhabitation of the world, and the way humans produce, distribute, consume and share food participates inextricably in this debate. Cushioned by wealth and food distribution systems which favour the developed world, many Western human consumers currently suffer no direct effects from changing climates, and it exists for them less as observable conditions demanding action, and more as a discourse sited at the intersection of multiple political, economic, social and environmental concerns and conflicting interests. For the poor of the world – those in war-torn regions or 'developing' zones, or whose lives are defined by precarious access to food resources – climate change takes the form of what Rob Nixon (2011: 2) calls the 'slow violence' of 'delayed', 'incremental and accretive' destruction, as the worst effects of environmental catastrophe and first world polluting are perpetrated on the insignificant poor. Ecocriticism is a politically motivated form of analysis which attempts to take these concerns into account in literary critical practice, and reads texts from a perspective which asserts that human activity takes place within what Timothy Clark (2011: 4) calls a '*meta-context*' – what we more commonly call 'nature' or 'the environment'. Clark argues that:

> Broad awareness of even the probability of climate change marks a moment at which a historical epoch is discerned as such, in its *closure*, rendering its intellectual structures both newly perceptible and philosophically exhausted. The epoch whose closure is at issue is that in which the finitude of the earth was ignored, discounted or forgotten. (Clark, 2010: 132–3)

By Light Alone dramatizes the final days of such a closure, and in opposing anthropocentric humans who consume almost everything with heliocentric humans who consume almost nothing, it opens an imaginative window onto the complex enmeshing of Nature and Culture.

The principle subject matter of *By Light Alone* is the subjection of a poverty-stricken majority by a wealthy elite, and an ecocritical reading, cognisant of the terms and conditions of dehumanization, reveals the ways in which the place of humans in the 'mesh' is intrinsic to our contemporary understandings of what it means to be human. Food, the critical substance of *By Light Alone,* is often a significant feature in science fiction; in *Soylent Green* (1973) food shortages are met by making food out of humans, a strategy recently repeated in, for example, Michel Faber's *Under the Skin* (2000) and the climate-changed world of David Mitchell's *Cloud Atlas* (2004). Adam Roberts has continued to think about food in *Jack Glass* (2012), in which many of Earth's renegade poor subsist precariously on 'ghunk' (*JG*: 276) in 'shanty bubbles' (*JG*: 256) in the quieter spaces of the solar system, and in *Bête* (2014), which features the butcher Graham Penhaligon in a future Britain where animal life is divided on Narnian lines of talking and thus unkillable animals, and animals which remain edible because they are speechless. In *By Light Alone* consumption traces a line between killable subhumans – the physically stunted, photosynthesizing poor – and 'real', significantly fat, wealthy humans. Their corpulent vapidity echoes the helpless grub-like people of E. M. Forster's 'The Machine Stops' (1928), and the dull-spirited, hover-chair people of Disney's *WALL-E* (2008). In foregrounding food, *By Light Alone* draws together the relations between the appropriation of resources by the developed world, environmental degradation, rising global populations, and extreme poverty; these are developed in the text through an exposure of the legitimations of massification, and a literalizing of the traditional metaphorical structures of heaviness / lightness, and dirt / purity.

The twenty-third century Earth of *By Light Alone* appears to have suffered a catastrophic combination of rising human populations and sea levels. Against this backdrop and in the consequent alterations of physical and social geography, Leah, the ten-year-old daughter of George and Marie, is kidnapped from a luxury ski resort, and eleven months later a girl who appears to be Leah is returned to her parents in New York. Meanwhile, on the other side of the world, Issa (the original Leah, who has taken the Sunlight Bug and grown long, photosynthesizing hair) escapes from rural poverty and brutal subjection, travelling on foot and by ocean-going raft to rejoin her parents and the substitute Leah during a longhair revolution in New York. This story is told in four temporally overlapping sections, each of which, narrated by a satirical external voice, is focalized through, respectively, George, substitute Leah, Marie, and finally Issa. Wealthy George is revealed by the narrator's ironic remarks and his own actions and thoughts to be an amiable buffoon, and Marie is similarly shown to be petulantly dedicated to her own comfort; their cognitive grasp of the world's problems is constricted by their limited narrative vision, a limit exceeded by the extensive impact their fashionably swollen and unconscious bodies have on the natural environment and the lives of others. Unable to comprehend anything that disturbs their beliefs, including that the child returned to them is not their daughter, George and Marie are fat, ridiculous people, estranged from their own experiences and that of the other by their narratives of privilege and entitlement. In contrast, Issa occupies the role of female hero; resilient and resourceful, her long journey home is rendered in a chapterless and allusive 'Odyssea' (*BLA*: 261). Through her questioning but unmoved 'stranger-in-a-strange-land' eyes, the world the wealthy refuse to look at is partially revealed and the story of the poor thickened and individualized.

Through the miraculous and apparently philanthropic gift of the 'Sunlight Bug' to the hungry masses in the tropical zones of the world the problem of food shortages seems to have been solved, not by producing more equitable conditions or by increasing agricultural production, but by simply removing billions of poor and hungry people from the food system and leaving the earth's remaining resources for a privileged few. The active agents of the 'Bug' are nanobots that, when the sun shines, fizz with energy in the bloodstream, converting light absorbed through long, coarse 'ink-black hair' (*BLA*: 7) into blood sugars. Through photosynthesis the 'longhairs', as they are pejoratively known, are saved from starvation, and need only drink water and take occasional trace elements found in soil and insects to supplement solar energy. Having little need to produce solid food, old social structures which circulated around its making and eating have collapsed, and ancient relationships with the land, plants and animals that once sustained the longhairs are irrelevant when all a person need do to survive is to spread their hair in the sun. But living by light alone offers only subsistence-level nutrition. Bodies nourished only by sunlight are 'enfeebled and stringy' (*BLA*: 261), children are small and 'stunted' (*BLA*: 94), and during dull days and at night longhairs are 'sluggish and underpowered' (*BLA*: 301). In a new social order, most men have become indolent lotus-eaters, while women work in order to buy the 'hard' food necessary to sustain a pregnancy and nurse a baby. They are not, however, the automatic antithesis of the wealthy, for their newly developed feudal system echoes the exploitative system of virtual slavery with which George and Marie and the class they represent employ longhairs and a desperate middle class as servants.

The wealthy enjoy well-stocked fridges at home and extravagant food in restaurants: 'blue grapes, and little spears of compressed caviar' (*BLA*: 6), 'shredded swan in yoghurt' (*BLA*: 23), 'hot lamb petals and pea-sized potatoes in the winter, cold lamb jelid and chilled pea-sized potatoes in the summer' (*BLA*: 215). There are engineered 'cherries the size of a beachballs [sic]; toast you could shelter under; sugar grains big as dice' (*BLA*: 227). The frequent lists of sometimes ludicrous or Alice-in-Wonderlandish food emphasize the absurdity of these fat, greedy people, and their corpulent grotesqueness is symbolized by a ski-slope made of ice cream. Wealthy skiers are attracted by the novelty of this mountain-sized emblem of colossal and infantile self-indulgence, but like spoiled children who want to have their ice cream and eat it, they whine about the noisy machinery and the poor quality of skiing on ice-cream that is not even 'very *tasty*' (*BLA*: 7). Comically debased by revolting table habits (Marie indulges a fad for chewing and then spitting out her food into a bucket on a restaurant table), and with apparently perpetual unfulfilment symbolized by constant eating, the wealthy become grotesqueries with insatiable Pantagruelian appetites, imperialistically and wastefully consuming mountains of resources in an unsubtle satire of twenty-first century developed world lifestyles of acquisition.

The French gourmand Jean Anthelme Brillat-Savarin (1825: 15) wrote, 'tell me what you eat: I will tell you what you are', an aphorism that, more than making direct connections between diet, class and bodily or psychological condition, articulates food as a philosophical trope and a measure of human value. In *By Light Alone,* food legitimates an ontology that defines who enjoys the privilege of personhood and humanity and who does not. Food is far more than simple nutrition for humans; diet, says food historian Maguelonne Toussaint-Samat (1987/2009: 3), is a 'social signal ... [t]he food of the strongest – like his religion, his spiritual food – is always regarded as the best': it is 'identification magic'. Jacques Derrida develops a similar theme in his theory of carno-phallogocentrism, which is to say, his theory of the Western world. For Derrida the Western subject is predicated on a conceptual machinery of 'presence to self – which implies therefore a certain interpretation of temporality; identity to self, positionality, property, personality, ego, consciousness, will, intentionality, freedom, humanity etc.' (Derrida and Nancy, 1991: 108). These predicates reveal an onto-phenomenological structure of 'difference, trace, iterability, ex-appropriation,' (Derrida and Nancy,

1991: 108) in humans, a Heideggerian 'having of world' which is lacking in stones or animals, so that their 'not having' of the world locates them in a sacrificial structure – a place maintained and left open 'for a noncriminal putting to death' (Derrida and Nancy, 1991: 112). Through the 'executions of ingestion, incorporation, or introjection of the corpse', (Derrida and Nancy, 1991: 112) the Judaeo-Christian adult male seeks not just to master and possess nature but to accept its sacrifice and eat its flesh. In *By Light Alone* a wealthy businessman, Ergaste Horner-King, embodies a carno-phallogocentric epistemology as he points out that the Sunlight Bug has changed eating: 'We don't need to do it for sustenance now ... any of us could get the hair ... so if not sustenance, then what? I'll tell you. Power is what. God is the most powerful thing in the cosmos, top of the pyramid, and *we* eat *Him*, yeah?' (*BLA*: 153). As a Catholic, Ergaste symbolically consumes the body and blood of his God every week in bread wafers and communion wine, not because he is hungry but because to him the world is predicated on a sacrificial, predator-prey structure, and he is a predatory carnivore. Eating is not mere nutrition, but ritualized 'strength and force and the wolf's delight' (*BLA*: 154), and the sheer bulk of wealthy, fat, well-nourished bodies symbolizes and makes tangible their power to consume not what they need, but what they want.

Ergaste pontificates that longhair waitresses in a hotel receive their wages in food and shelter, claiming that '[t]he women work, to build up bodyfat. *Greedy* little leafheads ... Not greedy for food, ysee,' he clarified. 'Greedy for *babbies*' (*BLA*: 8). The claim to food, which he argues is in himself a pastime and a symbol of power, is in poor women a primal response to a reproductive urge, thus misogynistically reducing them to irrational, instinctual, less-than-humans. The dehumanization of the poor, however, makes its deepest conceptual descent in the attribution to them of a vegetable identity of 'fucking leafheads' (*BLA*: 7) and 'weeds' (*BLA*: 198), excluding them even from the higher order status of mammalian life, a status longhair women seek to reclaim by eating to give birth to live young and nurse them with mammalian breasts. Photosynthesizing hair may have seemed a blessing both to the world's poverty-stricken, lifted out of starvation, and to the wealthy, relieved of a Kiplingesque Third World burden and an unmet responsibility to share the world's food, but the distinction between eaters of food and consumers of light is only the means for ushering in, as George is told, a new version of the same – 'a variation of a very old pattern' (*BLA*: 88). Ergaste's carno-phallogocentric perspective validates wealthy domination of food resources and the relative positions of rich and poor in a quasi-biological appeal to a structure of strong wolf predator eating weak lamb prey. If the wealthy eat wolf food, locating them at the top of the ideologically organized power structure that is the food chain, then the poor languish at the bottom with the other photosynthesizers, the plants. Longhairs, obliged to eschew the mastery of nature implied by the sacrifice and ingestion of actual and symbolic flesh, consume none of the substance of the world and, as the passive recipients of calories transmitted directly to their bodies by the sun, are reimagined by the wealthy as entitled to none of it.

The Perversity of Dirt

The metaphorical formant of dirt/purity informs human imaginings of how the world should be; dirtiness is spoliation, and purity is virtuous. A pristine environment is a healthy one, undamaged by pollutants, by dirt. The wealthy of *By Light Alone* invoke these structures of thought in order to legitimate the steps they must take to protect themselves from the vast, threatening populations of longhairs who, resentful of inhibited access to water, food, and economic resources, propose revolution. Greg Garrard (2012 : 6) observes, in *Ecocriticism*, that 'pollution' as an ecological problem does not refer to a substance or types of substances, 'but rather represents an implicit normative claim that too much of something is present in the environment, usually in the wrong place'. To define a plant as a weed – a self-replicating, over-running pollutant – is to make a cultural rather than a horticultural claim about how we would wish things to be (Garrard, 2012: 6), and the wealthy of *By Light Alone* connect photosynthesizing hair with polluting weeds to draw normative conclusions about the appropriate components of a healthy environment. They enact ostentatious revulsion at displays of the New Hair from serving staff, expecting 'they might tie it decently away when they come to ... us' (*BLA*: 7), but although they focus on the hair as being in itself in some way disgusting, it is what they wish the hair to symbolize that is at issue. As 'fucking leafheads' (*BLA*: 7), and 'weeds ... poisonous weeds' (*BLA*: 198), the longhairs are not only, metaphorically, mindless vegetable matter, but are polluting, invasive, spoliating, and proliferating out of control.

A reduction in the huge populations of longhairs in the only solution, but 'proper' humans cannot, morally, be reduced so the wealthy engage in a metaphorical transformation of the poor which reimagines them as qualitatively distinct enough from other humans to open them to a 'non-criminal putting to death' (Derrida and Nancy, 1991: 112). For humans, significance and value is knitted with individuality and uniqueness: in *Postmodern Ethics* (1993), Zygmunt Bauman allies perceptions of individual distinctiveness with understandings of moral consideration (Bauman, 1993: 145). We live in intimate social spacings with other beings *like us* he says, that is, we assume that our experience of ourselves and other people constitutes what is normal and natural, but these social spacings are plotted between poles of what is known and understood and what is anonymous and not understood. Anonymous humans have no personal identities, and their strangeness and the apparent threat this makes to the safe, ordered and classified world of people *like us* is neutralized by reproducing these others as a de-individuated, dehumanized and morally inconsiderable mass too different to be empathized with. Bauman (1993: 155) concludes that 'when the Other dissolves in the Many, the first thing to dissolve is the Face. The Other is now Faceless'. The connection Bauman makes between massified facelessness and dehumanization is clearly expressed in *By Light Alone* by the nature of the wealthy's unwillingness or incapacity to encounter longhairs as human individuals. They are, instead, reconceived as an unnatural and polluting problem in the generalized singular which, ergo, justifies purification.

To the wealthy, elite few the majority of longhairs are usually encountered at a visual and cognitive distance as the 'teeming' and 'swarming poor' (*BLA*: 196). Visually, they are 'too many to process numerically' (*BLA*: 53), and the universal feature of long black hair in these crowds and 'swarms' has 'the appearance of a great expanse of black seaweed at low tide' (*BLA*: 108). The sense of a faceless mass of seaweed-like hair is accentuated during an invasive action by longhairs off Florida's coast in which they are ruthlessly gunned down until 'the sea was so thick with bodies you could have walked to the beach' (*BLA*: 243). As an amorphous mass of hair the longhairs become a vast 'Frankenstein ... Monster' (*BLA*: 211) of nano-technologically mutated subhumanness which the wealthy fear will overwhelm and displace them, figuratively and literally. Viewed via the massified and seaweedlike synecdoche of their hair the poor are unrecognizable to the wealthy as people *like us*, and are instead an invasive horror which can be non-criminally mown down in the manner of weed control.

There is a certain amount of irony in the recreation of the poor as a gargantuan polluting body – an incursion of impure and dangerous matter into a 'clean' ecology – for if dirt and purity are oppositional ecological matters then the location of rich and poor along this axis is a point of struggle. Naming the Sunlight Bug with the vernacular term for a pathogen, a generalized agent of disease, reimagines it as a penetration and infection which alters the bodies of the poor from 'proper' mammalian form to queered photosynthesizing matter. The Bug analogizes the effects of pathogenic infection by leaving the poor physically underdeveloped, undernourished, and with weak immune systems, and in demonstrating their bodies to be permeable and inseparable from the external matter of the Bug's internalized nanobots the poor lack the autonomy of the 'proper' self-possessed human. The rich also carry a load of nanobots in their bloodstreams, but rather than being environmental dirty infection, 'g-whites', a technology that protects the rich from disease and age-related decay, are sited in a framework of technological language and environmental control. If the Sunlight Bug allows the poor to escape the limitations of an Earth unable to supply sufficient food, they are nevertheless embedded in the natural environment by their subjection to sunlight as an energy source over which they have no control while, in contrast, g-whites erect a nearly impermeable boundary between the wealthy human body and infecting agents in the environment. For the rich, nanotechnology enables human transcendence of the limitations of environment and body, and the final reification of human autonomy by mastery of biology and totalized estrangement from entanglements in ecology.

Rich and poor are equally cyborg, but where the Bug emerges as an internal instrument of subjection to 'nature' for the poor, g-whites are framed as an external tool that locates the rich in a culture of purity, free from many of the 'dirty' compromises and miseries of fleshy life. However, the rich are returned to the necessities of the material, entangled world by food, for they are imbricated in the natural dirt of the world by their need to grow plants and animals and by their excretion of 'dirty' waste matter. In *Rabelais and His World,* Bakhtin (1968: 317) argues that the grotesque body embodies a perpetual unfulfilment in which the bowels outgrow and transgress that body to conceive 'a new, second body'. The substitute Leah, when changed from a diet of light which generates no faecal matter to solid food which does, has no control over her bowels. She defecates in her bed and on the carpet (*BLA*: 130), and as she joins the grotesque consuming body of the wealthy, the text, in underlining the connection between environment and ingested and excreted matter, implicates all eating bodies in the outgrowth and transgression of themselves. Although the poor must drink water and, consequently, must urinate, they do not excrete solid matter, and because they grow no food require little from the matter of the world. In this sense the photosynthesizing poor represent a kind of ecological purity compatible with some aspects of philosopher Arne Naess's 'deep ecology'. Human population growth and concurrent environmental deterioration are pressing concerns in the twenty-first century, and Naess (2008: 302) contends that one of the ways for humans to flourish while also living in a less anthropocentric and more ecocentric way is for there to be 'a substantial decrease of human population'. Naess's philosophy may be interpreted anywhere along a scale between unpleasant truth and dangerously racist misanthropy, and *By Light Alone*'s photosynthesizing can be read in similar conflicted and subjective ways, for while the damage done by longhairs to the natural world is substantially reduced by their minimal imbrication with it, this is very much an echo of 'first world' discourses on what are deemed 'third world' problems.

The metaphorical structure of claims to purity and attributions of pollution are part of a wider textual project of historiographic and allusive literary satire. The relative height and density of human bodies in *By Light Alone* develops a trope of materiality which figures the ecological lightness of poverty and comparable heaviness of wealth to satirize greed, but at the same time draws attention to the part of metaphor in structuring the language and terms of evaluation. The vigorous, 'Brobdingnagian' (*BLA*: 16) bulk of the wealthy embodies the dimensions of their absorption of resources, and the weight of their consumption of matter equates to a heavy, destructive, and thus dirty ecological 'footprint'. In contrast, the weedy and infected poor, with their short undernourished bones and muscles, are comparatively ephemeral and leave only a light and thus clean ecological footprint. Complicating the traditional metaphorical structures of dirt and purity, and weaving them into contemporary metaphors of the evils of over-consumption which themselves depend on the traditional metaphors and ridiculing of obese bodies, *By Light Alone* literalizes the dirtiness of greed. Poverty is not, however, automatically allowed to occupy the opposite moral pole to wealthy greed by embodying some kind of noble austerity. Roberts's novel does not permit this kind of simplistic thinking to go undisturbed, and the deconstruction of such binaries continues into the dismantling of utopian forms.

Refrigerating Utopia

The cover-blurb of *By Light Alone* says that 'hunger is a thing of the past, but this is no utopia ... '. Neither is it, in formal terms, a dystopia, but the final section of the novel does frame and deconstruct utopianizing impulses in a comparison of two utopian idealizations, both of which depend on extremes of estrangement from the 'metacontext' of the natural world. This final section, Issa's story, follows a traditional Homeric homecoming narrative structure, but in a subversive manner; Issa is a female Odysseus, Circe is a man, the cyclops is a phallus, the oxen of the sun is a cow with photosynthesizing hair, the Sirens offer austerity, Scylla is an engineered plague, Penelope is Issa's father George, and the suitor for his affections is the interloper Leah. Some of these Odyssean adventures are located in the building, living and destruction of utopian dreams on an unseaworthy raft and in the Ithacan Paradise of New York, and food remains central to their imagining.

The Sirens of *By Light Alone* are quasi-religious sects that have arisen from the new social order engendered by sunlight food, and they sing of utopian solutions to the poverty of longhair expectations and ambitions. Ernst Bloch (1986: 3) saw utopianism as an innate human impulse that 'is not content just to accept the bad which exists, does not accept renunciation', and *By Light Alone*'s longhair utopians tempt their followers with dreams which take what is miserable about their alienated lives and remake it as something noble. In a parody of Fredric Jameson's (2004: 49) 'intelligent fantasy of a Franciscan utopia ... of scarcity and poverty', a group called the 'Siblings of Islam' couple asceticism with spiritual purity, teaching that fasting is 'an ever-shining sun of infinite virtue and invaluable soul-strength' (*BLA*: 323). The leader of an 'Aquatic' group, Maguelone, is equally utopian, but more secular. She urges her followers to 'remake' (*BLA*: 328) themselves:

> 'The future is the sea,' sang Maguelone, 'as the past was. Simple tools – a raft to sit on, a unit to turn salt to drinkwater and, every few weeks, a net or a piece of string to catch a slimy thing or a fishy thing from the water, and suck some minerals and vitamins in your mouths. What else do you need? Only your hair, the hair that defines you! Come to the sea – you will never be thirsty again, for you will be surrounded by water. Come to the sea – you will never be oppressed again, for the sea is freedom. (*BLA*: 328–9)

Both the Aquatics and the Siblings of Islam reify light as pure, clean energy, proposing carno-phallogocentric 'ingestion and incorporation' of 'hard' food as a taint – a polluting of body and spirit. Capitalizing on the metaphorical associations of sun with happiness and water with rebirth, they propose to embrace their diminished need for the material of the earth and in an idealistic sunlit world they seek to valorize their thinned connection with matter by idealizing its absence. Issa obstinately insists that their dreams lack 'practical strategy' (*BLA*: 329), for water and fragments of fish will neither sustain them for generations nor protect them from storms. Functioning as a critical eye on the act of utopianizing, she rejects the immobility of a social structure which proposes to do little more than eternal oceanic drifting, for it is structure without substance.

Issa's sojourn with the utopians reveals, moreover, that the idealized virtue of an ascetic utopia is undercut by the utopians themselves, for many of the supposed dreamers with whom she boards a fragile raft to New York are self-centred, suspicious malcontents, and her revolutionary leaders are incompetent. Asceticism as a revolutionary and utopian ideal neither causes the poor to transcend the misery of their suffering bodies, nor deletes their ordinary flawed humanness, and the idea that utopian poverty is morally superior to Rabelasian excess is deconstructed by the unromantic and ignoble lives of the poor. There is no pleasure, virtue or nobility in suffering and alienation, and shallow utopianizing which ignores the material of the world is not, according to the text, the way to solve problems located in material existence. As a friend of the substitute Leah remarks, when Leah proposes that a science fiction novel has a solution to the 'problem' of the longhairs, the ecology of the world is too complex for simple answers and maybe her science fiction book 'hadn't thought it all through' (*BLA*: 199).

Longhair ascetic utopias are predicated on the exclusion of polluting 'hard' food from social and bodily systems, and the paradisiacal perfection of New York similarly depends on a shutting out of systemic disturbance. An enormous fridge stands in George and Marie's kitchen in their New York apartment, and to the previously poor girl who replaces abducted Leah as their daughter, its eternal bounty embodies glorious, but disquieting, extravagance. She envisions the city of New York as seen from above as 'a bristling art-installation on the topic of Plenty' (*BLA*: 194); it is 'the Fridge laid on its side with the door removed, and all the bursting, thrusting fullness solidified into something permanent' (*BLA*: 194). The giant symbolic cornucopia of New York is in vulgar contrast to Issa's sparse living conditions on the other side of the world. The village in which she is enslaved maintains a tiny utopian projection of New York's city-sized plenitude in the shape of a single fridge, which Issa imagines as a 'god, from the old pagan days, humming to itself its holy hum, all day and all night, and all of it pure. Singing of other worlds than these' (*BLA*: 298). In these metaphorical fridges lie the principles of pure and eternal utopia.

The primary purpose of a fridge is not to chill food, but to maintain optimum conditions in the purity of cool, clean air, to arrest change and decay. Similarly, Thomas More's original Utopia depended on the maintenance of an unchanging social order. Utopia is stasis, and all threats to its eternal, perfect sameness – all its dirts and degeneracies – are exiled beyond the borders, transposed to slaves and Venalian mercenaries (More, 1965: 113). As the satirical narrative voice of *By Light Alone* asserts, '[f]or the rich, few things are as disabling as *uncertainty*' (*BLA*: 43), and New York is an essay in stasis, seeking to refrigerate its plenty and outsource change and decay. Rising sea levels are incontrovertible evidence of change, but New York has embargoed change by erecting the 'Hough Wall' around its boundaries to hold back the sea so that, safe from the gross intrusion of nature, the rich can continue their secure and certain lives. Eventually, however, the world beyond the Wall – the longhairs and the climate-changed environment – can no longer tolerate the load of dirt imposed upon it. In the revolution which reunites Issa with her parents the Hough Wall is destroyed and New York is inundated by the sea. Utopia always carries within itself the antinomy of metaphorical dirt which automatically dismantles it, and in the closure of this historical epoch marked by extremes of wealth and poverty, swept away by a biblical flood, both rich and poor find themselves confronted with the ecological entanglement from which dreams of pure utopias estranged them.

Concluding Remarks

In an interview by Christos Callow Jr., Adam Roberts remarked that:

> in some of my more recent novels especially, I have pretty much achieved everything I set out to achieve. I'm thinking particularly in *New Model Army* and *By Light Alone*: I set out to do certain things, some of which were deliberately fucked up, some of which were about engaging with the ideas and the genre and I think I did what I set out to do. (Roberts cited in Callow Jr., 2013)

By Light Alone's deliberate fucked-upness – its deconstructed metaphorical forms and narratives – leaves one wondering if what Roberts set out to do was make fun of the efforts of literary critics to theorize his writing. But if one takes seriously his satire of what is, according to his own definition of SF, the present day, the novel makes a valid comment on the inequitable distribution of wealth and its entanglements with the meta-context that is the non-human world. The trope of food in *By Light Alone* explicitly traces the dehumanizing boundaries erected by the rich to out-source poverty and dirt to less-than-humans, and posits and problematizes the polar opposites of consumption-driven and all-consuming pleasure seeking, and passive, pleasureless non-consumption to imply that it views its fictional world as *at least* latent in the real world, rather than wholly imaginary. Such literary developments of environmental conditions which may become increasingly less latent and more real are an integral part of critical conversations on the nature of our unavoidably thick entanglements.

Works Cited

Bakhtin, Mikhail (1968) *Rabelais and His World*, trans. Helen Iswolsky. Cambridge, MA: MIT.

Bauman, Zygmunt (1993) *Postmodern Ethics*. Oxford: Blackwell.

Bloch, Ernst (1986) *The Principle of Hope*. Oxford: Basil Blackwell Ltd.

Brillat-Savarin, Jean Anthelme (1825/2009) *The Physiology of Taste: Or Meditations on Transcendental Gastronomy*, trans. M. F. K. Fisher, intro. Bill Buford. New York: Alfred A. Knopf.

Callow, Christos, Jr. (2013) 'Irony, Man: An Interview with Adam Roberts', *Strange Horizons*. 25 March, URL (consulted 12 March 2014): http://www.strangehorizons.com/2013/20130325/2roberts-a.shtml

Clark, Timothy (2010) 'Some climate change ironies: deconstruction, environmental politics and the closure of ecocriticism', *The Oxford Literary Review* 32(1): 131–49.

Clark, Timothy (2011) *The Cambridge Introduction to Literature and the Environment*. Cambridge: Cambridge University Press.

Clarke, Nic (2012) 'Review: *By Light Alone*', *Strange Horizons*, 27 January, URL (consulted 12 March 2014): http://www.strangehorizons.com/reviews/2012/01/by_light_alone_.shtml

Derrida, Jacques and Jean-Luc Nancy (1991) '"Eating Well", or the Calculation of the Subject: An Interview with Jacques Derrida', trans. Peter Connor and Avital Ronell, in Eduardo Cadava, Peter Connor and Jean-Luc Nancy (eds), *Who Comes After the Subject?*, pp. 96–119. New York: Routledge.

Garrard, Greg (2012) *Ecocriticism*. London: Routledge.

Jameson, Fredric (2004) 'The Politics of Utopia', *New Left Review* Jan/Feb: 35–54.

More, Thomas (1965) *Utopia*. Middlesex: Penguin.

Morton, Timothy (2010) *The Ecological Thought*. Cambridge, MA: Harvard University Press.

Naess, Arne (2008) *The Ecology of Wisdom: Writings by Arne Naess*. Berkeley, California: Counterpoint.

Nixon, Rob (2011) *Slow Violence and the Environmentalism of the Poor*. Cambridge, MA: Harvard University Press.

Tidvar, Lavie (2011) 'Shall I tell you the problem with Adam Roberts?' 14 December, URL (consulted 12 May 2014): http:/lavietidhar.wordpress.com/2011/12/14/shall-i-tell-you-the-problem-with-adam-roberts

Toussaint-Samat, Maguelonne (1987/2009) *A History of Food*, second edition, trans. A. Bell. Chichester: Blackwell.

Nation-State 2.0

Visions of Europe in Adam Roberts's *New Model Army*

Thomas Wellmann

> Now, belatedly, they're realizing that they're not dealing with the flare-up of ancient European intra-belligerence. Or they are dealing with that, but that's not the problem. The problem is that real democracy has come back. [...]. (*NMA*: 257–8)

With these words, the narrator of Adam Roberts's near-future science fiction novel *New Model Army* (2010) enthusiastically suggests that nation-states will, in the near-future, be replaced by 'real democracies', raising questions as to where and when these were previously in existence, and whether Europe will be dominated by mercenary hive-minds – as a more pessimistic reader might deduce from the novel's conclusion (*NMA*: 275–81). Rather than buying into such hyperbolic readings, the assumption behind this analysis is that the text works as an allegory of European-style democracy. While the focus on wars among Europeans (wars of which the most well-known, like the two world wars, were declared between nations) places the novel's main concerns within a European tradition of imagining the nation-state, the text also poses questions concerning a paradoxical situation of the modern individual, namely one's sense of identity while simultaneously feeling part of a certain group. How do modern Europeans imagine themselves both as unique and as belonging to a community? While no ready-made answer to this problem is available today, several approaches can be drawn from the context of continental philosophy, to which *New Model Army* constantly alludes. The 'real' democracy proposed by the narrator as a solution draws on schools of thought ranging from Athenian philosophy from 600 B.C., when real democracy was supposedly first in existence, to the science fiction of Yevgeny Zamyatin, which details the 'transparency' such democracy requires (*NMA*: 1–8).[1]

The novel's narrator is a soldier named Block who serves in one of the titular 'new model armies' (or 'NMAs') of wirelessly connected mercenaries (*NMA*: 1). Beyond the name and the arguable aspiration of serving as a model, these NMAs sport few actual similarities to their historical antetype, an English army from the seventeenth century. For example, when the real New Model Army was created it had soldiers, officers and ranks, and was 'run by Parliament's administrative committees' (Kishlansky, 1979: 28), none of which apply to Roberts's NMAs. Yet the historical allusion is not meaningless, as the novel playfully picks up on the last item on Kishlansky's list: the premise of the NMAs is their being organized along radically democratic principles. The fictional armies accomplish this by working with a wiki instead of ranks or hierarchy. Each NMA soldier is equipped with a kit that includes not just a weapon, but also a smartphone-like device that allows him or her to access and edit information on this wiki, as well as to communicate with other soldiers via a chat function. The troops make strategic decisions via online voting on this wiki system, which is described as being protected digitally by firewalls, so that the NMA members can safely use it to determine the best course of action during operations (instead of just following pre-determined mission parameters).

The overall objectives of the organization are determined by online voting as well. The soldiers might, for example, elect to accept a mission for their army from another party interested in hiring mercenaries in exchange for adequate compensation, like the narrator's NMA signing a deal with the Scottish Parliament (*NMA*: 67). In effect, the NMAs are a parody of actual visions of democracy and by extension, an allegory for hypothetical models of a national or transnational Europe. The text uses the NMAs to illustrate how social processes lead to the genesis of institutions with an agenda beyond that of their individual members. In the face of the growing alienation of the people from politics in Europe – and the on-going questioning of the democratic legitimization of (quasi)-governmental institutions like the EU – these are hardly abstract or theoretical topics.

New Model Army: Between Military and Democracy

The novel consists of three parts. The first, named 'Pantegral' just like the NMA in which the narrator serves, documents that specific NMA's history and its exploits in the UK. Throughout the plot, the text proceeds to reveal more and more information on the setting, zooming out from England step-by-step. Following the turning point of a detonation of a nuclear weapon in London, the narrator is captured and debriefed by a US colonel, so that even worldwide events are included. Only when this colonel recruits the narrator to work as a double agent for the US army at the start of the novel's second part (named 'Schäferhund'), the narrative zooms back in to Europe to focus on the narrator's first and only mission which is supposed to be directed against another NMA operating in Alsace.[2] The transnational history of the region frames Block's discussion of Europe-wide events and scenes, mostly with other soldiers (both regular and NMA).

The third part ('I, Giant') continues this focus on Europe as a whole by replacing the first-person narrator, Block, with what is, in effect, the group-mind of Pantegral. Comparing itself to the giant Pantagruel for whom it is named, the NMA group mind's elevated perspective indeed seems to encompass all of Europe. Its name fits, because Pantagruel is a character in the works of Rabelais, the sixteenth century French author who can be grouped with the Christian humanists (Screech, 1979: 14), and whose republic of letters spanned the continent like the hive mind's neural network (*NMA*: 277). Both networks are also associated with processes forming new types of social organizations. In the historical republic of letters, philosophical foundations of the early nation-states were discussed. The genesis of nations is intimately connected to the fictional NMAs, too. Being the shortest of the three parts, 'I, Giant' is also the most philosophically dense, as the hivemind's thoughts are an associative collage of European philosophers' ideas on democracy and nationhood, though these seem to have only superficially permeated the giant's consciousness. For example, the hivemind dwells on the phonetic similarity between the name of the old German monetary currency and that of Karl Marx, who 'called for the abolition of money' (*NMA*: 276).

In order to determine whether there is a stringent concept of Europe and European nation-states found within 'the story of how [the NMA hivemind] came to speak' (*NMA*: 275), this analysis will seize this suggested principle of the tripartite order in an interrogation of structure-theme interaction.[3] First, a description of the basics of the *New Model Army*'s science-fictional setting is necessary to explain why the novel should not be reduced to a high concept piece if a 'high concept' is understood in the Hollywood sense of a simple, sensationalist story pitch. Proceeding from this supposition to the two great themes of the novel – democracy, and the paradox of individuals imagining themselves as belonging to certain communities like nations (or rather their wanting to belong or contribute to such groups) – I will discuss the thesis that the novel unites two of science fiction's key functions, allegory and literary thought experiment, in a commentary on democracy as it is found in Europe today.

Looking only at the first third of the narrative, it is tempting to think of the wars tearing through Europe in the novel as mere storytelling devices employed to show off the concept of the NMA in action. This view suggests the roles of the war in the plot can be dismissed entirely. But it ignores key parts of the text like the in-depth descriptions of the spatial setting, for instance in the narrator's impressions when he is flown out of a war-zone in Strasbourg in a helicopter:

> Europe below me, and stretching all about me in every direction; the landscape of the world. […] I felt myself to be suspended directly over the exact heart of Europe. Europe the primal giant, the first to be woken […] and shake its limbs. (*NMA*: 235)

These reflections on Europe (as both a space and a giant) continue over several pages, despite contrasting with modern Europeans' inner map of many nations and only tangentially relating to the NMA as a military concept. If these descriptions of the setting do not make clear that its topography provides more than an arena for NMA combat, the detailed political causes for the narrative's many armed conflicts do. In general, the *casus belli* (provocation of war) is an intended secession of a 'rebellious region' from an existing state. Ethno-cultural groups in these regions, implicitly those deemed small or subaltern by the state's government or majority, are hiring the newly available, cheap NMAs to fight back by (re-)conquering territory. The first part of the novel, for example, details how Pantegral, the narrator's NMA, battles a supposed imperialist enemy in the UK (namely the British Royal Army) on behalf of groups in the Celtic Fringe. The causes of this conflict are expounded on over a whole chapter (cf. *NMA*: 60–7), even though Pantegral, as a third party hired from outside, has no part in this fictional history.[4] In fact, the narrative posits them as merely the one of three mercenary companies who made the best bid to the Scottish parliament.

This elaborate back-story belies the idea of the novel discussing the military concept of the NMA through a 'bellum-ex-machina' and already hints at an exploration of the limits of (national) identity. Political and social theory are ripe with a wide variety of definitions of 'identity' ranging from simple spatial assignments (for example, in the case of national identity via the nation's territory) to complex labels (especially as far as gender is concerned). In this case, I will circumvent complex classifications of identity in favour of a more simply and stringent concept which I dub 'belonging': I take this to be the fulfilment of individual humans' desires to be part of a group by mutual, active assertion of their membership in this group, whether it is a family, tribe, or other form of community.[5]

An analysis of the novel's setting and specifically its portrayals of space(s) can show the importance the text places on questions of distinct individuals imagining themselves as one community, and especially on the manner of their mutual assertions of membership. But to show this, the analysis has to acknowledge the presence of an implied vision of Europe in the text, as well as the rather overt discussion of the nation-state.[6] This focus is different from that of many literary reviews of the novel, which debate the plausibility of the novel's perceived main premise that such New Model Armies could successfully fight wars, but also the ethical implications of this proposal (e.g. Williams, 2001). The novel was published before grand surveillance programs like PRISM became public knowledge and demonstrated that sufficiently modern and technologically apt states are well-equipped to be more than one step ahead of any possible revolutionary impulses that could organize via such structures.[7] If it only rested on the concept of the digitally organized revolt (whether resembling the fictional NMAs or even the real life protests of the type associated with the Arab spring), the novel would already be obsolete.

Yet even the narrator agrees that the wars and campaigns described in the novel have nothing to do with the philosophical notions and European ideas mentioned above, when he tells an operative from another NMA that their war is not about intra-European conflict, as the introductory quote to this chapter shows. Since the novel's plot follows two such NMAs on their campaigns, it is hardly possible to argue that this military reading of the novel is somehow wrong. It is also advocated by its author, who in a lecture on this novel stated that science fiction allows writers '[...] to stage thought experiments [and] to explore the dramatic potential of ideas' (Roberts, 2012). Then again, by calling his work a 'novel of democracy', Roberts (2013) also implies that it is more than a simple thought experiment in military technology.

Looking at the text itself, it is clear that rather than fully exploring the text's potential, a singular focus on the NMA as a military strategy will result in an over-simplified interpretation. The novel's setting especially is not just an arena for combat of the eponymous new model armies, but also plays an important role in the satirical re-imagination of social processes leading to the genesis of institutions with an agenda beyond that of their individual members. A more complete analysis (including those aspects that are less easy to pitch and hence have been somewhat unfairly ignored) places the text's themes in the specific context of the European nation-state, to which the novel effectively holds up a mirror by telling the story of the NMA as an allegorical nation-state 2.0.

An analysis of the plot's structure can reveal how this happens exactly, but it requires shedding certain assumptions about the science fiction genre. A lot of traditional science fiction explores hypothetical new technologies based on expected scientific advances. In the *Oxford Dictionary of Science Fiction*'s definition of the genre, this aspect of exploration is even included as a core element of science.[8] Science fiction texts that fit this description often feature distinct action scenes depicting the technological innovations in operation, functioning as exposition for the reader at best and creating a show and tell effect at worst.[9] Note the same cannot be expected for texts that also explore the social impacts of scientific advances (and most texts will not distinguish between these two categories of consequences) and certainly not about *New Model Army*. The novel plays with the idea of the weaponized smartphone, but makes this part of its allegorical point of democracy.

The text goes even further in foregoing the conventions which are assumed to be typical of the genre according to the *Oxford Dictionary of Science Fiction* entry cited above, as the examples of the action scenes make clear. Though there is action in *New Model Army* (wars are fought), it makes no sense to distinguish between fight scenes and non-action scenes off the battlefield in *New Model Army* because the text does not render them as separate, due to the NMAs' overall modus operandi. As they are not foreigners to the countries where they fight, the NMA soldiers avoid open combat by merging into the regular population, only to reappear later. For instance, a key scene has Pantegral explode an atomic device in London in what is principally a militant flash-mob (*NMA*: 107). These fast-paced changes between rest and battle make, at best, for combat and non-combat sentences, but not entire scenes. Note that this experimental break with convention does not mean *New Model Army* is not a science fiction novel. Storytelling experiments like these are typical of texts of science fiction and fantasy.[10]

Belonging to the NMA as a (Military) Group

Focusing on portrayals of space can reveal a different form of structuring in the text, namely the spatial effect of zooming out. The second part of the novel reveals that the first part's events in the UK serve as only a small-scale reflection of the NMAs' global effects. Europe and the USA are also breaking apart. The factions competing for territory have made the Western nation-state with an established government and fixed borders obsolete. The EU especially has once again fallen into a state of what an American character in the novel calls 'civil war' (*NMA*: 210). Yet the existing political institutions are not replaced by new separatist governments, but by something else entirely. These parallels illustrate how the structure of zooming in and out ties into the portrayal of belonging, which in contemporary imagination usually remains linked to nationality and, by extension, to the raison d'être of warriors and soldiers. 'I, I, I [...] am most myself when fighting [...]', the giant says (*NMA*: 279).

The structure of the novel reflects its deconstruction of the nation-state by breaking the spatial constraints of national territories. Yet when Pantegral's members say they fight for 'our NMA' (*NMA*: 191), they assert their membership in a form of community that in many ways resembles a nation, most importantly because the soldiers behave similarly to the populace of a nation-state in imagining their NMA as a community. The term 'nation-state' here delineates the socio-cultural phenomenon that rests on the residents of a territory settling on shared objectives through historically established practices (for example the exercise of democracy). Usually, this involves the nation-state's members not only visibly committing to these goals (for instance, by subjecting themselves to military drafts in times of war), but also public punishment of those who do not act in accordance with these objectives. The result is a clear demarcation of who belongs to the nation and who does not.

Instead of a physical place on the map, the NMA essentially has its territory in cyber-space. The NMA's territory is not a Newtonian box or space, meaning it cannot be depicted as a geometric shape on a map or even as a three-dimensional object. The NMA's territory exists in a relational space created by the constant interaction of the NMA's members.[11] As a result, the established nation-states have no frame of reference that lets them even perceive its existence, whereas Block and his comrades seem unable to sense without the NMA. Tellingly, when Block's arm is injured, the hand feels numb and only starts tingling when he straps his wiki screen to it (*NMA*: 149).

This cyberspace is not some Otherworld to get lost in, but very acutely pervades normal space, as omnipresent social media already does today. The novel provides a text-immanent perspective on these territorial processes, which can be traced by shifting from literal geographic places in Europe to figurative spaces. The narrator's portrayal of the NMA as a utopia is especially interesting. In many ways an NMA only exists because its members create in it a place where they feel at home. The NMA functions like a territory for the community to which its members imagine themselves as belonging in the sense defined above. After all, they in no way represent the nations for whom, and on whose territory, they fight. A reporter interviewing some of Pantegral's soldiers is shocked to find out that they are 'fighting for the Scots' despite being English (*NMA*: 191ff.). The reason the NMAs do not disband without a national superstructure is that their members identify as soldiers, as the narrator explicitly confirms throughout with statements like 'I'm a soldier', 'this is where I belong' or 'this NMA is where I belong' (*NMA*: 192).

This idea of 'soldier' being not just a full-time job, but a mutually confirmed membership in a special group, is another rare similarity of the NMAs to the historical New Model Army from the English civil war era,[12] which actually fought in Scotland in the name of English powers (Gentles, 1992: 385) – an inversion that exemplifies the type of ironic cruelty widespread in this novel. By declaring each other to be warriors, members create what might be called a 'spirit of camaraderie' within the NMA, at least if this phrase is clear to be devoid of any sexual connotation. Chapters 16 and 17 demonstrate why, by treating the reader to a stark contrast between two subsequent experiences of the narrator; first the heartfelt loss of a comrade, then a sexually-charged encounter with his former partner at home that ultimately remains meaningless for the narrator (*NMA*: 122–177). For the narrator, belonging to the warrior group completely transcends both gender and sex. At best, the NMAs' attractiveness is in their lack of interest in these factors. Gender also plays no role in joining: an almost equal amount of male and female soldiers found their place in various NMAs, at least as far as the speaking, named characters in the novel are concerned.

The NMA does not completely erase previous identities like actual nationality, but supersedes the belonging of individuals to the associated groups. This again is especially obvious in the narrator: Block still thinks of himself as English (*NMA*: 191), despite his German father who gave him the name (*NMA*: 79) and despite the fight against the Royal Army, which together probably make him the ultimate traitor to a British nation. But the narrator feels 'something is missing' (15) – like the philosopher Bloch, best known for his work *The Principle of Hope* (1954–9), and as a celebrated utopian theorist. Block also shares the actual theorist's family name, until the narrator's father changed it 'to sound more English' (*NMA*: 79). Block's missing something is merely in a different place. The real Bloch sought his missing something in a utopia that can only be reached in hopeful works of fiction, but in practice remains a state of mind. The fictional Block, however, feels completed when he finds his place in the awakened NMA.

Do the parallels described above mean that the NMA is the nation-state 2.0? It allows for individuals to engage and identify with a group in a more efficient way and to a greater degree, but at the same time it is more inclusive: many soldiers are said to have served in multiple NMAs, illustrating how arbitrary these are in composition. Traits like these make the concept an update of older concepts of the nation and build on existing ideas like Anderson's (2006: 207) description of nations as imagined communities. But the novel presents a society more complex than traditional utopian visions. Shifting emphasis away from the cultural dimensions of belonging to this or that present or historical group is not the same as foregrounding individuality over ancient concepts of state and nation. Still, the narrator likes to compare the NMAs to 'Ancient Greece [and the] Spartan story' (*NMA*: 88), especially when speaking to non-NMA soldiers:

> There hadn't been a society like ours in the world since Ancient Greece. And ours was more perfect then theirs, because we were open to men and women, to Greeks and barbarians, to atheists and religious types [...]. You had to be prepared to stand and fight, but how could you be a human being and respect yourself if you're not prepared to stand and fight? (*NMA*: 176)

The novel's new model of an army claims an idealized version of Ancient Greece as a founding myth, making it not very new after all. Historical Greek city-states, like Athens and Sparta in the Classical period, indeed lacked long chains of representation in democracy or chains of hierarchy in the military. It was 'common knowledge' that anyone (or rather any eligible young man) who wanted to be part of the polis also was willing to serve in its army, as Josiah Ober (2008: 178–9) writes in *Democracy and Knowledge*. This overlap of membership made the two effectively the same. All members could participate, debate and thus draft a social contract that set down the general will of the polis, which was then to be enforced by the army. This is what the novel's narrator describes as real democracy, and non-fictional historians like Ober, whose work Roberts recommends in the novel's acknowledgments (*NMA*: 282), would agree that 'a time travelling Athenian democrat would condemn contemporary [...] practice, on the grounds that it wilfully ignores popular knowledge' (Ober, 2008: 1).

Interestingly, NMA soldiers seek out tasks within their NMAs for the sake of being involved in a group, but not with other individuals of the group (many of whom they only know via their kit's chat functionality). Neither national nor gender identity count in the NMA, but the NMA does not sport an integration policy. It rather weaves the individual into the collective and its efforts. Thereby, a greater meaning seems to be assigned to the toils of its members, though each of them is de facto made more replaceable. While special experts for certain tasks still exist, specialization is not connected to improved status in a hierarchy, in particular as expertise and expert knowledge can easily be drawn from the wiki. Thus, the individual becomes involved in a group and even an aim, but the involvement comes at a cost.

The NMA as an Allegory of Democracy

In its third part, the novel culminates in an account narrated by a 'giant', an awakened NMA hivemind (*NMA*: 275–276).[13] The group mind's use of the first person pronoun in repetition, 'I, I, I […] did this', echoes its nature as a collective intelligence composed of many individuals, but also its own powerful will (*NMA*: 277). More interesting is the giant's deliberate comparison of its birth to the formation of nations in Europe. Roberts has it cite relevant continental philosophers like Marx and Nietzsche (*NMA*: 276–278). Block had similarly compared his NMA to the famous picture of Hobbes' *Leviathan* (*NMA*: 241), expounding on his earlier observations: 'The European landscape, howsoever scribbled over with motorways and the cellular growth of concrete buildings, was still, in its essence, a medieval landscape' (*NMA*: 234). But if the NMA is a European democracy, it is one that is always at war and thus in a permanent state of exception. This is interesting because states of exception and emergency have long been a subject of debate. For example, Carl Schmitt's definition of sovereignty as the power to initiate a state of emergency has been criticized by Giorgio Agamben, who argued that the mechanism of the state of emergency is inherently oppressive (Agamben, 2005: 1).

If applied to the NMA's constant war, this means that sovereignty does not lie with its members, but with the giant. This corresponds to the problems of the Greek founding myth of the fictional NMAs, which is the same as that underlying our real-world democracies. Especially in Europe, modern concepts of a nation-state also rest on the idea of a general will. But the social contract is now usually seen as a metaphor, not a literal understanding of everyone within the community. Conversely, the fictional NMAs take it at face value and punish any person who does not act in accordance with the contract like we would punish breaking any other agreement; mainly by avoiding the person who did so. The narrator, too, describes dissenters merely as 'leaving' the NMA (*NMA*: 88). But given the text's war setting (the state of exception), this implies those choosing not to go along with the majority of the constantly moving NMA are left behind to face abandonment on the battlefield: 'No human being can live long outside the walls of the polis' (*NMA*: 89). Within the walls of the army/state hybrid caught in a constant state of war, the NMA defaults to a political theory indifferent to the dire consequences of insubordination to the majority. The legitimization of this policy through the option of not joining in the first place (*NMA*: 88) is why the supposed nation-state 2.0 can be used as a parody of modern visions of Europe.

Once an NMA has been institutionalized, that is, once its members have internalized their belonging within an imagined NMA community, the institution begins to develop an agenda beyond that of its individual members. The NMA offers to join, fight and likely die, but as those who do not join are hardly considered human at all and likely end as casualties, there is really no other option. This situation mimics that of being born into a nation-state and into a certain nationality. A real-life echo of the NMA's non-choice is casting the option of 'emigration' as the choice not to comply with the social treaty in order to validate the wilfulness of a nation's members (which would be a prerequisite for an actual, non-metaphorical contract). In reality, just like NMA members are forced to rely on each other for survival, being without a national citizenship is hardly an option. One nation-state may be exchanged for another, but the constraint of nationality is always present in some form. In other words, there already are structures, called nation-states, which restrict the individual's exercise of their personalities in the name of the common good.

New Model Army holds up a mirror to these by letting similar structures gain self-awareness: the complex language games the NMA members play in order to reach consent on their wiki (*NMA*: 15) may serve as an example here. Even in the NMA's direct democracy, individual personalities and wishes will occasionally conflict with the 'general' will of the NMA's collective intelligence. For instance, social rules within the cyberspace direct anyone who introduced a motion that was subsequently rejected to be the first to acknowledge this rejection via chat. But the offline discussions between the soldiers prove they sometimes regret the singular results of the preceding multiplicity of discourse, despite the constant online-polling. Even Pantegral still sets one course determined by majority-voting as a whole, mocking all the polyvocality, 'temporary suspension of rank and hierachy' and resulting 'frank and free speech' which Bakhtin (1984: 10) might see in the namesake text by Rabelais. In effect, the anarchist New Model Army from fiction is no more likely to provide a home for its own members, or even the Irish and Scottish who hired it to fight, than was the rigidly structured parliamentary army from actual history.

Visions of Europe

The NMA does not solve the problem of translating a general will into a collective effort: Simic, Block's friend in the NMA, disapproves of the choices Pantegral has made (*NMA*: 119). In the end, the only solution to this conflict that occurs to Block is the awakening of the giant which culminates in the total transfer of power to the collective consciousness, resulting in the complete removal of any meaning or value of its replaceable parts. These individual parts, that is, the human members of the NMA, are literally instrumentalized as 'component elements' (*NMA*: 279). With this finale, *New Model Army* showcases not only the technical (and technological) problems of efficient participation that are highly relevant to questions of power, especially in contemporary (real-life) democracies, but also connects to the relevant issue of the myth of the possible homogenization of a group of separate individuals underlying modern nation-states. This mythos leads *New Model Army* to celebrate the efficiency of direct democracy.

But the image of the polis as an idealized nation-state also creates dystopian impulses in the text – at least, they are dystopian in the sense that they oppose the suggested utopia and taint the beautiful allegory by overthinking it with problems of reality. This quasi-realism results in an ambiguity that is exemplified in *New Model Army* by the ease with which the name Bloch is translated to Block and a philosophy of hope becomes synonymous with control. If Block's utopian vision is read as a parody of Europe divided into warring states and nations, the narration offered can easily extend this parody to transnational visions of a united Europe. Still, this makes the novel part of the group of rare texts that offer post-national visions of Europe at all. The legitimacy of the concept of nation-states and the associated spatial construction of identity have been taken for granted throughout most of (European) modernity. People from a given territory are assigned a nationality specific to the locale. The idea of a nation-state rests on the assumption that individuals belong in a certain place and the place belongs to them. Subsequently, individuals without an immediate connection to a nation's territory are perceived as a threat. The novel avoids jumping to this conclusion, in part by re-imagining Rabelais, who preceded the modern nation-state, but also by introducing a post-national discourse: for example, it assumes that currencies have become irrevocably transnational – even British NMA soldiers are paid in Euro.

An example of this post-national discourse is introduced in the debate between the narrator and the US colonel who interrogates him and, unsurprisingly, finds the NMA's claim to be more democratic than regular nation-states questionable (*NMA*: 118). Though the text only provides Block's account of the exchange, the rhetoric the two use in their respective defences of direct and representative democracy – and the way both fail to connect their ideological arguments to pragmatic solutions for any specific problems – seems like a mocking imitation of the real life debate about the lack of democratic legitimization of the EU's (quasi)-governmental institutions summarized by Jensen (2009). Especially, the suggested remedy of returning to stronger nation-states is mirrored by the novel's setting. Most of the NMAs rise against a federated Europe and operate on the territory of 'France-EU' and 'Germany-EU' (*NMA*: 236).

An analysis of the setting cannot finally resolve the novel's many contradictions, but it is possible to summarize them in a description of how exactly its setting 'differs from our own world' and how, in typical science-fictional manner, 'the difference is explained (implicitly or explicitly) in scientific or rational terms' (Prucher, 2007: 130). If one compared the NMA's world to ours, one would find non-fictional large scale intra-European belligerence to be less ancient than we like to believe. The EU still legitimates itself as a force for peace, which necessarily implies that there is a threat. The acknowledgement of Europe's destructive past is one of the strengths of the novel.

The text deliberately leaves the reader to decide whether smartphone-wielding guerrilla gangs organized along the lines of the abstract concept of the novel's NMAs could realistically pose a more serious threat than an actual army. The concept of the NMA could work as a fictional state of exception justifying digital surveillance with Carl Schmitt's theories.[14] Instead, the text inherently advocates not to dismiss, but to go beyond the military thought experiment taking the allegory of democracy into account. Even if the novel's allegorical nature was not clear from the first section, the third and final part of the novel bring it to attention by simultaneously raising the level of allegorical abstraction and becoming more obvious, at least to those who would consider giants rampaging across Europe to be scarier than digital societies leaving dissenting voters behind on the battlefield. Either way, the novel spells out that it is not a literal prediction. It does not calculate the chance of institutions of the same type as the nation-state, with the same problems, forming in the human society found in the digital, however much some members may be idealizing their online communities.

Yet it is important to note that despite the NMAs remaining fictional, the real Europe is not a safe utopia. Misconceptions abound in the novel, not just because miscommunication is a possible precondition for war. For example, the narrator conceives the text as his attempt to set things right about the awakened NMA hivemind, but he can only earn scepticism from readers, whose viewpoint is more distanced. For them, it is possible see Block's hero in much more ambivalent colours then he does in his own vision of the awakened giant. Similarly, *New Model Army* invites us to call two visions of modern Europe into question that have become institutionalized in real-life: the narrative of the peaceful (and ever closer) union, and the war-inducing concept of the nation-state. This leaves the conclusion that the novel is far from a simple thought experiment conducted in guerrilla warfare, but a highly relevant and sceptical treatment of two fundamental principles of modernity.

Notes

1 The allusion is to the novel *We*, which describes a city of glass that works in a fashion similar to a panopticon, meaning social control is exercised by the masses instead of a single leader (Zamyatin, 1924).

2 It thus gives the second part its name. In German, one of the languages spoken in the Alsace, 'Schäferhund' (literally a shepherd's dog) is the name of the dog breed called Alsatian in English. Even the narrator notes this pun is somewhat belaboured (*NMA*: 208–209).

3 My own delineation of the nation-state concept echoes that of the *Oxford English Dictionary*, especially the last sentence. A (political, independent) nation-state is 'formed from a people who share a common national identity (historically, culturally, or ethnically). [...] A nation-state may be distinguished from states which comprise two or more historically distinct peoples, or which comprise only part of a historical people. However, such distinctions are frequently problematic' (*OED*, 2003).

4 It is also the only chapter which portrays an NMA not as a community, but a mercenary organization, a company in both the commercial and military sense of the word.

5 In other words, it can be what Anderson calls an imagined community in that the members do not need to know each other personally as long as the others also perceive themselves as part of the same group – Anderson (2006: 6–7) himself acknowledges that this definition is not just limited to nations. Of course, nations and NMAs may have more in common than is immediately obvious.

6 One especially striking example is the narrator's description of coming home to the NMA: 'Had you asked me back then, as an individual, "what is home to you?" I would have said UK-EU. Nowadays, of course, I have a different answer' (*NMA*: 5). The phrase 'as an individual' in this early passage already foreshadows the events of the novel's third part.

7 PRISM was a secret program of the NSA, which involved accessing personal digital communication in order to monitor persons within and out-

side of the US, even without reasonable suspicion (Gellmann and Poitras, 2013). When details of the program were leaked by a whistleblower, the US intelligence agency justified the program as a means to prevent acts of terrorism.

8 According to this delineation of the genre, science fiction is defined by its setting, which is different from the real world in a specific way: '[T]he difference is based on extrapolations made from one or more changes or suppositions; hence, [science fiction is a] genre in which the difference is explained (explicitly or implicitly) in scientific or rational, as opposed to supernatural, terms' (Prucher, 2007: 130).

9 The terminology of action scenes and fight scenes which I use here is, of course, borrowed from film studies for simplicity. The explication could be rephrased with terms that are not tied to any specific medium, like those provided by the *Living Handbook of Narratology*: changes of state between battle and downtime in *New Model Army* are characterized by a different type of 'eventfulness' (Hühn, 2013) than expected in science fiction if going by the given definition of the genre – namely, they are not presentation events like, for example, the awakening of the hive mind between the second and third part of the novel.

10 Attebery and Hollinger (2013: vii) compare science fiction to 'jazzlike improvisation': musicians can interpret established musical pieces or elements in new ways, giving old notes new meaning. Some of science fiction's 'settings, characters and actions' also lend themselves to being constantly redefined, for example by being repeated in new combinations.

11 For more details on these topographical and topological distinctions, see Günzel (2009: 231). Topology creates not necessarily physical, but also cultural or social spaces through Deleuzian (de-)territorialization, while topography represents objects of traditional physical spaces.

12 Gentles's (1992: 2) book continues to be relevant and gives room to both, descriptions of the New Model Army as organized along 'conservative military principles' as well as the opposing view of it being 'socially representative of the English people [and] characterized by freedom of organization and discussion'. Gentles (1992: 3) himself connects 'the army's morale or *esprit de corps* and its religion'.

13 Group minds are not a new idea: the *Oxford Dictionary of Science Fiction* has citations of the concept dating back to the 1930s (Prucher, 2007: 86).

14 This works at least if Schmitt is interpreted with Agamben, who criticizes Schmitt's description of a state of exception: according to Agamben, Schmitt discusses a situation of need in which 'state [here referring to the institution] and law reveal their irreconcilable differences' (*NMA*: 31). This means that a threat (in this fictional example the threat to people and property posed by the NMA) could be actions (e.g digital surveillance) that enforce an order that diverges from the order envisioned by the law (which protects privacy). This concept would make for a narrative different from the story in Roberts's novel, which does not endorse surveillance.

Works Cited

Agamben, Giorgio (2005) *State of Exception*. Chicago: University of Chicago Press.

Anderson, Benedict (2006) *Imagined Communities. New Edition*. London: Verso.

Attebery, Brian, and Veronica Hollinger (2013) *Parabolas of Science Fiction*. Middletown: Wesleyan University Press.

Bakhtin, Mikail (1984) *Rabelais and His World*, trans. Hélène Iswolsky. Bloomington: Indiana University Press.

Gellmann, Barton and Laura Poitras (2013) 'U.S., British intelligence mining data from nine U.S. Internet companies in broad secret program', *The Washington Post*, 6 June, URL (consulted 8 June): https://www.washingtonpost.com/investigations/us-intelligence-mining-data-from-nine-us-internet-companies-in-broad-secret-program/2013/06/06/3a0c0da8-cebf-11e2-8845-d970ccb04497_story.html

Gentles, Ian (1992) *The New Model Army: In England, Scotland and Ireland, 1645–1653*. Oxford: Blackwell.

Günzel, Stephan (2008) 'Spatial turn - topographical turn - topological turn. Über die Unterschiede zwischen Raumparadigmen', in Jörg Döring und Tristan Thielmann (eds) *Spatial Turn. Das Raumparadigma in den Kultur- und Sozialwissenschaften*, pp. 219–37. Bielefeld: Transcript.

Hühn, Peter (2013) 'Event and Eventfulness', in Peter Hühn, John Pier, Wolf Schmid and Jörg Schönert (eds) *The Living Handbook of Narratology*. Hamburg: Hamburg University. URL (consulted 29 January 2014): http://www.lhn.uni-hamburg.de/article/event-and-eventfulness

Jensen, Thomas (2009) 'The Democratic Deficit of the European Union', *Living Reviews in Democracy* 1, URL (consulted 30 January 2014): https://www.lrd.ethz.ch/index.php/lrd/article/view/lrd-2009-2/9

Kishlansky, Mark (1979) *The Rise of the New Model Army*. London: Cambridge University Press.
Ober, Josiah (2008) *Democracy and Knowledge. Innovation and Learning in Classical Athens*. Princeton: Princeton University Press.
Oxford English Dictionary Online (2013) 'nation-state, n.', December, URL (consulted 20 January 2014): http://www.oed.com/view/Entry/255438
Prucher, Jeff (2007) *Brave New Worlds. Oxford Dictionary of Science Fiction*. Oxford: Oxford University Press.
Roberts, Adam (2012) 'Science Fiction as Poetry', *TedXHull,* 22 Septemper, URL (consulted 22 October 2013): http://www.youtube.com/watch?v=y5OvsS3uwFM
Roberts, Adam (2013) 'New Model Armies - A New Kind of Democracy', *TedXHousesofParliament,* 3 July, URL (consulted 22 October 2013): http://www.youtube.com/watch?v=A28C9604320
Screech, M.A. (1979) *Rabelais*. London: Duckworth.
Williams, Mark (2011) 'Imagining War: The Ethical and Stylistic Issues in Using Real-Life War Zones as a Basis for Contemporary Fiction', *Werewolf* 25, August, URL (consulted 30 January 2014): http://werewolf.co.nz/2011/09/imagining-war/
Zamyatin, Yevgeny (1991) *We,* trans. Alex Miller. Moscow: Raduga.

Part III

Ludic Authorship

New Model Authors?
Authority, Authordom, Anarchism and the Atomized Text in a Networked World

Paul Graham Raven

Origin Stories

Before beginning this unusual chapter, it behoves me to explain – or perhaps excuse – its genesis. Around the time that the editors began commissioning chapters of the volume which you are currently reading, my attention was directed via some social media channel or another – I forget which, or exactly when – to what looked to be an experimental piece of critical writing on the Adam Roberts novel *New Model Army* (2010), a book in which I myself have a considerable critical interest. In keeping with my usually meticulous online reading habits, I uploaded a copy of the two pertinent webpages to an online clippings-archive service, so that I might return to them when the luxury of time presented itself, then sent an email to the editors of this volume suggesting that they approach the work's author for a contribution. Time remained scarce for a few months following, and

I confess I didn't think of it again until I received an email from the editors of this volume, asking me why I'd emailed them an enthusiastic quick-skim description of what sounded like an interesting (if unusual) piece of Adam Roberts criticism, only to accompany it with a link to an invalid URL?

In the months since I'd first seen them, someone – presumably the author, but not necessarily – had not simply deleted the two webpages in question, but also expunged all pertinent registration details from the databases of ICANN, the organization in charge of registering dot-com domains. Not only had the work itself vanished, but all hope of finding out anything more about it than what it had to say for itself, let alone anything more about its ostensible author. My clippings archive holds copies of the two webpages – the piece itself, and another short page of what looked to be explanatory notes – as they were rendered by the browser I was using when I clipped them, and as raw files of text with HTML mark-up. Having no record of the IP address at which said site was hosted, I have no way of knowing whether the server on which it was stored is storing it still. Having enquired around the genre fiction criticism community, it seems no one else read the piece, nor even saw it in anything more than passing. The copies in my clippings archive, I must then assume, are the last copies of this work that exist. I duly informed the editors of this volume as such, with all apologies for my scholarly sloppiness.

A reply followed a few days later, asking if I might copy and forward the work to them. Had they asked immediately, I might have simply complied, but by this point – having been reminded of its existence, and also being frustrated with my lack of progress on an intractable research question in another discipline entirely – I had been reading the clipped pages, becoming a little more familiar with what they seemed to claim to be, and testing those claims as far as I was able. The more I learned of its nature, the more obvious it became that – for reasons to be explained, and regardless of the quality or otherwise of the criticism contained within the text – it was fundamentally unsuited to publication in a scholarly anthology; I was unwilling to release the text to anyone until its 'author' could be tracked down, and certain pertinent questions answered to the satisfaction of both academic standards of behaviour, and of a specialist in copyright law.

This response was, perhaps unsurprisingly, not satisfying to the editors of this volume, who had counted on including the lost work in their table of contents, and pitched to the publisher accordingly. They remonstrated with me for some time, but I was resolute: while I am no friend to the legal fiction of intellectual property, I am (for my sins) a scholar in a world where that legal fiction exerts power over my work and my career, and I dare not risk staining my hands while passing on the folly of another. Reputations have been ruined by less.

But I am no arrogant ivory-towerist, either, nor entirely selfish – or so I would like to think. And as deadlines began to loom on this volume's horizon, I took pity on the desperate plight of its editors and offered the closest compromise I could: I would not provide them with the text (for ethical reasons already rehearsed) but I would happily provide them with a critical evaluation of it, written by myself. With the terse brevity which I have always assumed to indicate an editor who has happily concluded a negotiation to their greatest satisfaction, they accepted my offer.

And so, here we are. With explanations made, I shall go on to first describe the work in question, and to analyse its composition. I will then put its titular argument to the test, before engaging in an interpretive discussion of its methodology, and what it has to say about both Roberts's novel, and about the status and stability of texts in an era of ubiquitous digital media. Due to constraints of space, I am obliged to assume the reader's basic familiarity with *New Model Army*, the novel, and refrain from summary or synopsis thereof; a thorough review by Nader Elhefnawy (2010) is recommended for any reader as yet unfamiliar with the book.[1] Furthermore, due to constraints of a different nature (which shall be explained in more detail), I am obliged also to refrain from quoting the work in question, for which I apologize; sometimes one who would shine a light must obscure another's to let their own be seen.

Anatomy of an Oddity

According to the scant metadata saved by my clippings service, the two pages comprising the text were both available under the root directory of the *thunder-and-consolation.com* web domain, but regrettably there are no remaining records associated with that domain name which would permit one to confirm or deny such a claim. The two pages used a simple one-column layout with no images and minimal stylesheeting; each followed the format of a bold heading in 34-point Arial Dark (marked up with <h1> HTML tags) at the top of the page, followed by a hyperlink in 14-point Arial to whichever of the two pages was not the one at which you were looking, followed by a longer body of text. The title of the shorter page is simply 'REAGENTS' (capitalized in original), while the title of the longer page – something close to 3,000 words, perhaps, allowing for the unusual use of whitespace – is 'Thunder & Consolation: Adam Roberts's *New Model Army* as ephemeral anarchist utopia' (Crowe, 2013; hereafter referred to as 'Thunder & Consolation', for the sake of both brevity and convenience).

The body-text of the REAGENTS page comprises a four-item bullet point list (formatted with standard nested <li> and <ul> HTML tags) of text titles, each item of which is hyperlinked either to an online source of the text in question, where available, or to the product page of a well-known online retail website named after a river, where a copy of the list item might be purchased. In order of appearance, the listed texts are as follows:[2]

- *New Model Army*, the novel (Roberts, 2010);
- *Thunder & Consolation*, an early album by the British folk-punk refusenik band New Model Army (Sullivan and Heaton, 1989);
- 'The Agreement of the People of England, and the places therewith incorporated, for a secure and present peace, upon grounds of common right, freedom and safety' (Rushworth et al., 1648–9; hereafter 'The Agreement'), being the version of the manifesto of that name which was presented by Oliver Cromwell to the Rump Parliament of January 1649; and
- Hakim Bey's *T.A.Z.: The Temporary Autonomous Zone, Ontological Anarchy, Poetic Terrorism* (Bey, 1991).

The list is followed by the epigram 'Damned if you do, damned if you don't', which is attributed to one Barthes Simpson.

The last line of text on the page, justified to the right – which, duplicated as it is at the foot of 'Thunder & Consolation', I have taken to be the authorial signature – contains only the name *Graeme P. Crowe*. Crowe's name does not appear in any bibliographical database or catalogue to which I have access, nor in any fandom periodical or website of which I am aware.[3]

The 'Thunder & Consolation' piece defies easy categorization. While its verbose title suggests a critical essay, the text is closer to free-form poetry than to any form of prose with which I am familiar, and lacks any formal rehearsal of the argument that the title proposes. There is no consistent form, rhyme scheme or meter to be discerned, though an evolving eight-line 'chorus' section iterates itself by way of word substitutions and Mondegreen misspellings, reappearing at random-seeming intervals throughout the main flow, manifesting a new mutation for each of its 23 instances. The shape, voice and style of the 'verse' material is wildly heterogeneous, moving from terse, tight buckshot groupings of words to margin-to-margin walls of unpunctuated (and sometimes incomprehensible) text, and through every possibility in between. If there is a meter or structure to be discerned, it must be found at the purely visual level: with one's eyes blurred so as to reduce characters to fuzzy dots of darkness on one's monitor, and one's mouse-hand slowly scrolling down through the rendered pages, one gets a sense of tributaries seen from far above, struggling their way across complicated topographies to join, gradually but inexorably, into a mighty torrent… only for it to finally fragment into a delta where dozens of channels shift and slide across a widening floodplain, before finally meeting and merging in the melting-pot singularity of ocean.

The Sound and the Sorrow

'Thunder & Consolation' is reminiscent in form of the concrete poetry of Edwin Morgan, an effect achieved by the extensive (and doubtless painstaking) use of HTML whitespace characters to scatter paragraphs, sentence fragments and (sometimes) single words of text all across the full width of the main content <div> section, as if in stubborn defiance of the crude block-level alignment options to which the less patient Internet-native poet would be obliged to restrict themselves. While it tells us little in narrative terms, this code-level trace of craft and process betrays a considerable expense of time and effort, and a substantial degree of human curation involved in shaping the final piece. This is worthy of note primarily because 'Thunder & Consolation' is, as far as I can tell, a cut-up exercise – one in which the 'input' texts are those listed on the REAGENTS page.

My own exhaustive quantitative analysis of 'Thunder & Consolation' supports this theory: it contains no word that cannot be located in one or more of the source texts, using the same spelling, capitalization or trailing punctuation. However, the granularity of the cuttings from the original texts – the length, in words, of the fragments extracted before being reassembled – seems to vary to the same extent as the arrangement of the resulting assemblages on the page (although not necessarily in sympathy with it). For instance, Crowe repeatedly uses certain phrases and lines as Greek-chorus refrains or riffs throughout the piece; he leans particularly heavily on lines from the songs contained on the *Thunder & Consolation* album (Sullivan and Heaton, 1989) for this purpose (especially, and naturally enough, from the choruses), but deploys a few choice cuts from Bey (1991) and Roberts's novel as well. The end result conjures a ragged but rabble-rousing sense of backstreets oratory a-marching through the text, like chants half-misheard through the babble of an unusually coherent political protest happening a few hundred yards away.

But in many cases Crowe appears to build up his lines and sentences from individual words, shorn from the context of the sentences or phrases in which they were originally deployed. So while his lexicon is theoretically constrained, in the manner of an Oulipo-esque exercise, his expression is little limited by that constraint: witness whole lines that repeat single words, or repeatedly juxtapose related or oppositional terms one after another, or follow allusive or alliterative chains of meaning; witness fragments of coherent-seeming statements or sentences which cannot be located in any of the source texts, but whose word-level components are all traceable to one or more of the sources.

There is no narrative to 'Thunder & Consolation' that I can discern, but the *affect* of the piece – its poetic vibe, if you like – is inescapable: the unresolved tensions between determination and fear, between the individual and the state, between violence and freedom, all tumble through the text like brawling conjoined siblings. But such a reading is somewhat in conflict with the full title of the piece which, with its assertive argument, clearly invites the reader to interpret it as a work of criticism; furthermore, the reagents list invites the reader to consider in addition the method and materials in play.

By both exposing his method (with the reagents list) and destabilizing the framing of the text (with the title), Crowe invites us to look for meaning beyond the narrative level, and to shape our interpretation using the lens of his titular argument. Exposing his methods and materials to scrutiny is so deliberate a move that it is hard not to indulge in the intentional fallacy, even after Crowe's waggish reference to Barthes on the reagents page: it strongly implies that *he wants us to know how he did it,* which in turn implies that the reader's awareness of the method is, at least in part, the purpose of the piece; he wants us to know *how,* because then – perhaps – we'll ask *why*.

As such, I shall go on to offer my own interpretation of Crowe's method, and of the methodological structures it further implies. But first we must do him the dignity of assessing the eponymous argument of his piece, namely that *New Model Army* is an 'ephemeral anarchist utopia'.

From Nowhere to Anywhere

In the process of testing Crowe's apparent critical argument, I am going to assume that the anarchistic character of Pantegral's social structure is sufficiently apparent to be a given: hierarchy emerges from time to time, in response to tactical requirements, but it is ad hoc, temporary and contingent – at least up to the point of Pantegral's transcendence into a higher order of collective organization at the end of the novel. This is a classic science fictional narrative slingshot which wryly echoes the eschatological promise of the Singularity, that profoundly science-fictional myth of techno-mediated collectivist Rapture which is so paradoxically longed for by the otherwise staunchly individualist Silicon Valley libertarian set.[4]

So the framings of Crowe's with which I am here concerned are those of ephemerality and utopianism, and I shall deal with the latter first. Writing on the history of the utopian form in science fiction, Edward James (2003: 219) contends that the SF utopia has 'mutated [...] into something very different from the classic utopia', due to 'the profound way in which utopianism has permeated SF'; this resulted in the subgenre of 'technological utopianism', in which the formation of the utopian society is achieved partly or totally through technological or scientific means, as opposed to the predominantly political; these utopias are defined less by a static, perfected society than a 'continued struggle and progress' (James, 2003: 222). Meanwhile Ken MacLeod (2003: 238), in a survey of political forms in science fiction taken from the same volume, observes that 'the closest analogy for a functioning anarchy is the internet', a model whose attractiveness is rooted in the way in which it 'vastly extends both private initiative and public space' (MacLeod, 2003: 239). While the basic analogy still holds, however, technological progress has (perhaps counterintuitively) undermined the latter of the two extensional powers MacLeod ascribes to it.

In 2003, when MacLeod's essay was first published, the Internet was in many respects a simpler place, because it did indeed appear to extend public space into theoretically limitless non-Cartesian realms, where geography no longer applied; it was an *elsewhere,* another dimension which could only be accessed through the static portal of a distinctly non-portable desktop computer and modem. Much has changed since then, starting with then-President Clinton's ordering of the deactivation, on 1 May 2001, of the degraded-for-public-use 'Selective Availability' feature of the United States military's Global Positioning System (GPS), and the concomitant fall in price (and increasing ubiquity) of GPS hardware in portable consumer electronics, no longer the exclusive domain of expensive and restricted military tech. As a result, to paraphrase a character from William Gibson's *Spook Country* (2007) – a novel which dramatizes this recent shift in relationship between the Internet and the 'real', physical world – 'cyberspace has everted [sic]' (Gibson, 2007: 21); no longer outside reality, cyberspace now envelops and permeates it. But MacLeod's aforementioned extension of private initiative still holds firm, and with the benefit of hindsight Roberts's novel pre-empts – though not by much, nor controversially so – such contemporary global techno-political phenomena as the *soi disant* Arab Spring or the Occupy movement, retrospectively allowing Roberts to both have his concretized political metaphor and eat it.

Jennifer Rodgers (2005: 181) opens her lyrical examination of what is arguably the canonical anarchist utopia in science fiction, Ursula K. Le Guin's *The Dispossessed*, by saying that the novel 'provides the reader with a working model for utopia as evolution – not a place, but a process of becoming'; this sense of a functional anarchy as a system which is *by ideological necessity* in perpetual flux, constantly forming and reforming its ad hoc hierarchies in order to avoid ossifying into exactly the sort of oppressive apparatus to which it defines itself in opposition, is also apparent in Roberts's *New Model Army*. However, Le Guin's ability to model utopia as 'not a place, but a process' (Rodgers, 2005: 181) is limited by her choice (much in line with the classic utopian form) of spatially separating her revolutionary community, the moon of Annares, from its political antithesis, the planet Urras; her utopia is indeed a process, but it is also to some extent a place. Roberts, on the other hand, frees his utopia from the constraints of place entirely, with Pantegral's portable wireless communications devices making of it a moveable feast. As such, one might even argue – as perhaps Crowe is trying to do – that *New Model Army* is in fact the only *true* technological utopia which has ever been written, in that it is the only one that fulfils the literal meaning of the original Greek, *οὐ τόπος*: '*no place*'. Pantegral and the NMAs embody a cybernetic revolution, but not a cyberspatial revolution. As its name is always trying to remind us, the *Inter*net is *between* things, not outside of things: the revolution is not everywhere but anywhere, not nowhere but somewhere.

Tearing up the Text

> [E]very interpreter labors [sic] under the handicap of an inevitable circularity: All his internal evidence tends to support his hypothesis because much of it was constituted by his hypothesis. (Hirsch, 1967: 166)

And so much for that: Crowe's titular theory stands, but it is hardly thoroughly explored, nor of any great literary novelty or insight in and of itself. And it would surely be fair to say that, on the level of poetics, the altar of experimentation may have demanded rather more aesthetic sacrifices than is conducive to popular appeal – or basic readability, for that matter. Why go to such effort to seemingly say so little, we might well ask? But Crowe is twicefold shot with Barthes's bullets, in that his authordom is dead and his identity obscured; he cannot speak to the text at all, let alone with authority. And the hand that held the gun is Crowe's own; he has proudly left us his fingerprints on the weapon, right there on the REAGENTS page! Not only are we left to make our own reading of the text without any recourse to authority, we are *invited* to do so, enticed to solve the cypher's-suicide crime scene of Crowe's epistemological puzzle-box – always in the knowledge that we can never know the 'true' answer, even assuming there is one to find. Crowe invites us to construct his argument on his behalf, using his text as our reference … and as such, I shall oblige.

The closest precedent of which I am aware for Crowe's project would be Jeff Noon's *Cobralingus* (2001), which is not just a collection of concrete poems and fictions, but also a playfully rigorous methodological enquiry into the use of technoscientific metaphors for shaping the methods and materials of concrete, cut-up and remix approaches to poetry; this is much in keeping with Noon-as-novelist's habit of turning metafiction inside out and on its head, and transmuting literary-theoretical ideas into ontological problems for his diegesis. *Cobralingus* is not simply a text, it is an argument about what can be done to an existing text or texts in order to make a new text. By not just drawing attention to his process but actively explicating it (even if only metaphorically), Noon's metanarrative speaks of the total plasticity of the text as mediated by technology, whether literally (via the editing facilities of wordprocessing software) or metaphorically (as in Noon's flowcharts, process diagrams and 'modules').

Noon's interest in technological mediation flows from his closeness to the British rave culture of the late 1980s and 1990s, a scene wherein technology – whether manifest in the illegal designer pharmacology of Ecstasy, in the huge sound systems and lighting rigs used at raves, or in the electronic textures of the music played at them – was both symbol and tool of a revolutionary cross-class cultural emancipation. Indeed, we might look at the organizational logistics of the M25-based 'Orbital' rave scene of the late 1980s – which involved party organizers exploiting premium-rate phone lines, faxes and pagers, the cutting edge of consumer communications technology at the time, in order to keep their would-be customers in the know without tipping off the police – as something like an early rehearsal for the technologically mediated collective action of the NMAs in Roberts's novel. Indeed, Matthew Collin (1998: 4–5) writes of the rave scene's 'relentless dynamism, [and] its perpetual self-reinvention', describing it as 'a culture with options instead of rules', before suggesting that the spatial reterritorializations of the early free-party scene fulfilled (albeit ephemerally) the promise of Hakim Bey's Temporary Autonomous Zones: hyperlocal and temporary pocket-irruptions of lawlessness and anarchy embedded within the normal hierarchical spatial order, as described in the book of the same name which we find in Crowe's reagents list (Bey, 1991).[5] Noon's often anarchic practice, in *Cobralingus* as well as his novels, consciously mirrors the reappropriative logics of rave culture: he samples and remixes, he deterritorializes old narratives and reoccupies them, even *reauthors* them (as in his metafictional remixing of Lewis Carroll's Alice stories, *Automated Alice* [Noon, 1997]). For Noon, the map is always open to being redrawn, sliced up and rearranged like Guy Debord and Asger Jorn's Situationist replottings of Paris.[6] Indeed, this well-used theoretical metaphor is concretized afresh in *Pollen* (Noon, 1996/2013), when the X-Cabs company is revealed to have been using its networked taxi-maps to reterritorialize Noon's remixed Manchester.

The poststructuralist plasticity of text and territory is an interest that Noon could be said to share in common with Roberts, himself no stranger to the literary affordances of postmodern theory – unreliable narrators, pastiche, spoof and homage, to name but a few of his clear favourites – and actively engaged, by his own admission, with the possibilities of science fiction as an ontological genre (Kincaid, 2013). As such, both are direct literary descendants of Borges – a link that both authors have foregrounded in their own work, whether it is in the form of the knowing yet self-deprecating wink to Noon's critics which is 'PIXEL DUB JUICE (sublimerix Remix)' (Noon, 1998/2012), or Roberts's flirtations with such Borgesian forms as the review of (or excerpts from) the imaginary or fictional text (Roberts, 2009a, b, 2013).

Crowe's 'Thunder & Consolation' is likewise a work of metafictional deconstruction, but instead of deconstructing authordom at the level of narrative per Borges, Noon and Roberts, Crowe attempts to do so at the microstructural level. Crowe's choice of the networked digital medium of HTML is also telling in and of itself, and might be seen as a continuation of the developmental arc of cut-up praxis, moving ever closer to total textual atomization and manipulation: from the starting point of Gysin, through Burroughs's fully manual typewriter-newsprint-and-scissors method (Knickerbocker and Burroughs, 1982), to Noon's metaphorical ink-on-paper conflation of the word processor with the modern digital audio-visual production studio, and on to Crowe's complete migration of both method and text into the digital domain.

Language is, of course, a symbolic system of representation, and the cut-up work of Burroughs and Noon is deconstructive of originality and authordom by foregrounding the interchangeability of words and phrases by means of processes – technological or otherwise – that possess some random or serendipitous component, as opposed to the deliberate, unmediated and conscious drafting or editing of the 'traditional' author. But Crowe's method also foregrounds the double encoding of language when it is manipulated in the digital domain. Language itself encodes ideas by the use of symbols (letters and punctuation arranged according to a system of syntactical rules), but in order to store and manipulate human language digitally, the symbols of language are re-encoded by software into strings of binary digits. The meaning of any given chunk of language so encoded does not inhere in the binary digits themselves, but in the software processes involved in retrieving, decoding and displaying them to a user. What this means is that in the digital domain, language may be manipulated and/or processed *without necessarily being parsed*; the algorithmic instructions of computer systems only gain meaning by being developed and put to use by human intent. As far as the computer is concerned, all phrases, words and even individual characters are meaningless and interchangeable; their origins are indistinguishable. A word cut from a handwritten manuscript, while capable of being transposed into a cut-up work, literally embodies a trace of its author; a typewritten page, meanwhile, will betray the make and model and year of the typewriter, leave forensic clues as to whence it came; even a print-out of a digital file can contain sufficient material characteristics to allow it to be traced to a specific printer or computer. But once a text is represented by strings of binary digits somewhere within the Chinese Room (Searle, 1980) of a computer's hardware, devoid of meaning until it is reimposed upon them by an output device, those words have become untraceable, shorn of origin; as anonymous, replaceable and interchangeable as Lego components. Perhaps next you might email the resulting digital file across the planet, strip or mangle or rewrite any metadata associated with it, open it again on a different machine, stir the contents with editing tools ... and whose words are they, now? Who is the author of the resulting collage of text?

The Revolution is being Digitized

Other novelists have engaged in methods that deliberately transgress into this no-man's-land between authordom and plagiarism. Kathy Acker's novel *Empire of the Senseless* (1988), for instance, appropriates chunks of William Gibson's *Neuromancer* (1984/1995) and remixes them in order to conflate computer code with the female body. But we can also read Acker's methodology as a border provocation against authordom, and (by implication) against (male, militaristic) authority: Gibson's words implicitly do not belong to Gibson any more once Acker has cut them up and reworked them into a text over which she asserts her own authordom (House, 2005); likewise, Crowe's reagents are combined into a text over which he asserts authorship. What is different is that Crowe openly confesses his sources – an act of almost-citation that chimes with his framing of the piece by its title as a work of criticism, as previously discussed. He uses the same Burroughsian tools as Acker, and he deconstructs authordom in a similar way, but he invites us to treat him as a scholar, as a critic, rather than as the concrete poet his text might otherwise portray him as. He occupies no-man's-land, thus rendering himself no-man, shot by both sides; his inhabitation of the paradox draws our attention to its (im)possibility.

In one sense, of course, these problems of authordom are abstract, theoretical, relevant only to the rarefied discourse of literary academia. But they are also concrete problems in a world where texts are increasingly created, shared, duplicated, cited, (mis)quoted, paraphrased, summarized, lampooned, misunderstood, misrepresented and (occasionally) ignored via predominantly digital media; to be blunt, it has never been quicker or easier to locate, duplicate, cut-up, remix and re-disseminate a written document than ever before. This is problematic in the economic sphere, where authordom is all about who gets paid for their work, but also in the political sphere, where authordom is about who has access (or not) to the channels which will allow her to assert her authordom of a work – or, more simply, who gets to speak (or write), and who does not.[7]

There exists plentiful contemporary real-world evidence for the instability of authordom. For instance, at the time of writing, Hollywood actor Shia LeBeouf is at the centre of a bizarre challenge to authordom that saw him first plagiarize the work of comics writer Daniel Clowes and pass it off as his own (Pulver, 2013), and then issue a string of apologies which were themselves plagiarisms of other people's apologies (Beaumont-Thomas, 2014). LeBeouf may well transpire to have been publicly having some sort of mental health crisis, or to simply have over-internalized the 'information wants to be free!' rhetorics of the cyberlibertarians, but his celebrity brings an otherwise inside-baseball debate on intellectual property into the peanut-gallery debating halls of social media, whose verdicts upon any given accused are under little or no obligation to follow any legal precedent, let alone rational debate. No matter how the pending legal dispute pans out, there will almost certainly be people who side with LeBeouf, even if only because he's LeBeouf … but then LeBeouf might retort that that's no different to people siding with Clowes because he's 'the author' and therefore 'owns' those words or ideas.

Similar issues attended the public shamings of Jonah Lehrer, whose acts of self-plagiarism might have gained a pass on public opinion if he had not also been fingered for the fabrication of quotes (Bosman, 2012), and Johan Hari, who also fell foul of building compound quotes from other sources and passing them off as original interview material (Deans and Kiss, 2011). The water is muddier here, because both Lehrer and Hari's transgressions were more partial and subtle than LeBoeuf's. Rather than passing off another author's work as their own, they attempted to pass off their own *idealizations* of what certain individuals had previously said on record, whether to them or others. All citation suggests a certain degree of interpretation on the part of the citee, of course – and it is clear, I'm sure, that this chapter is not in any way intended to defend, promote or validate unethical writerly practice – but the cases of Lehrer and Hari highlight the fact that, for better or for worse, the borders between plagiarism, outright fabrication and earnest scholarship are subjective, contested and contextual.

Worse still, certain well-known ebook marketplaces have had periodical problems with procedurally-generated and procedurally-published titles, books compiled from text located and collected from the Internet by the crude semantic engines of web-crawler software (Hoffelder, 2012) in a manner not at all unlike Crowe's methodology for 'Thunder & Consolation'. Which is to say that not only is the abstract property of authordom an unstable social construct; *concrete* authordom – the status of being publicly recognized as the author of a *specific* text – is also socially constructed, and increasingly unstable thanks to the ubiquity of networked digital media. This, again, is the paradoxical zone which Crowe's 'Thunder & Consolation' inhabits: a technologically mediated soup of text-fragments masquerading as a work of scholarship in which the exact provenance (or the lack thereof) of any and all material used is effectively untraceable.[8]

As such, Crowe's piece echoes and critiques Roberts's novel on multiple levels, simultaneously. For instance, at the level of words and phrases, the technologically-mediated atomization of authordom in 'Thunder & Consolation' reflects the technologically-mediated atomization of authority which makes the NMAs possible; like the words and phrases of Crowe's piece, the members of Pantegral are excised from their previous positions in the social hierarchy of the state, dislodged from the matrices of authority, then recombined into fluid and tactical ad hoc structures in order to combat said hierarchy. At the methodological level, meanwhile, Crowe's choice of reagents both broadens and collapses the historical allusion of Roberts's title: by conflating three very different historically- and culturally-situated appropriations of the signifier 'New Model Army', Crowe erases the *specific* political causes it might imply in order to reveal the basic essence of a lived anarchism, namely the perpetual struggle against being reabsorbed into the oppressive hierarchical state, or against ossifying into a separate hierarchical system-within-the-system.

Finally, the paradox at the heart of Crowe's methodology is the same as the paradox at the heart of the NMAs, namely the dialectical tug-of-war between individual autonomy and collective authority: it is only the collective action of the NMAs that allows their soldiers to assert their individual autonomy, but it is only their autonomy which makes their collective action possible. This, then, is the engine of struggle in any lived anarchism: the necessity for a perpetual reconstitution of the body politic, the endless spontaneous remapping of the territory. The power of the hierarchical state lies in its privileged access to and control of high-bandwidth channels of communication; the peer-to-peer capabilities of the networked technologies enabling the NMAs, meanwhile, allow individuals to circumvent state-dominated media and organize effective collective action against the state, and – possibly, as Roberts's slingshot ending implies – transcend to a higher order of collectivity: the paradoxical *post-geographical* state, an atomized collective to whom borders are mere fictions, false maps superimposed upon the one, true, free territory.

Exit Music

Crowe's 'Thunder & Consolation' is an odd literary fish – made all the more odd, I freely admit, by its unusual provenance, and by the circumstances in which I find myself writing of it. In my discussions above, I have shown that not only Crowe's text, but the methods, materials and methodologies he has enrolled into the creation thereof, all have a number of oblique points to make about the techno-politics of Roberts's novel, and about the world for which the novel is a concrete metaphor. The affect and poetics of the piece draw upon and sustain the novel's motifs of confusion, conflicted loyalty and struggle (internal and external alike). Meanwhile, Crowe's choice of reagents both collapses the historical allusion of Roberts's title in order to make a more ahistorical point about the essence of revolutionary struggle, and sets the stage for his digitally-mediated cut-up approach to atomize the authordom of his materials, in imitation of the technologically mediated sociopolitical atomization experienced by the soldiers of Pantegral. Furthermore, Crowe destabilizes expectations around not only the formal characteristics of a work of ostensible critical scholarship, but around the very possibility of authorship (and hence authority) itself in a world where all texts are, as if in mockery of Marx's infamous indictment of capitalism, dissolving into thin air.

It is of course regrettable that we could not have simply printed Crowe's work, or otherwise made it available to the public. My attempts above to capture the sheer ambition of the piece in mere description are, perforce, inadequate, and only in the text itself can one hope to observe the broad (if somewhat handwave-y) unity of theme that attends every aspect of Crowe's project, and appreciate the way in which it appears part of that project is to critique the very possibility of critique itself. Would that he dared come out of the woodwork, if only so we might enquire of him as to his true motivations! But in his continuing absence, it is my hope that, by attempting herein to interpret his singular and deeply conflicted text, I have at least bagged a transgressive technique from beyond the literary pale and dragged it into the scholarly light; perhaps, if authority and authordom continue to collapse in upon themselves, we might even come to find it useful.

Notes

1 The reader is also advised to consider Thomas Wellmann's reading of *New Model Army* in this volume, 'Nation State 2.0: Visions of Europe in Adam Roberts's *New Model Army*'.

2 I have used the URLs from these hyperlinks in the references section to accompany the citations of the texts in question, should a reader wish to check the original sources.

3 Some of those with whom I have discussed this matter have taken a certain unbecoming delight in suggesting that Crowe is in fact an allusion to myself, whether made by myself or by whichever otherwise anonymous literary joker put it together. While I am obviously unable to refute either suggestion with substantive evidence – how exactly could one go about proving one was *not* the author of an anonymous or pseudonymous text? – I can and hereby do swear upon the fullness of my reputation as a scholar and person of fair dealings that the former suggestion is false. It certainly would not hold up in a court of law, or so I am reliably informed – and as such I hope this declaration will end any such speculations before it becomes necessary to take recourse to the law, which is never a wise strategy, let alone a cheap or enjoyable one.

4 See Shaviro (2009) for a vigorous Marxian skewering of Singularitarianism, a topic too richly freighted with paradox and irony to explore further within the confines of this chapter.

5 It is worth noting that Bey's theory of the Temporary Autonomous Zone is not without controversy, though not due to its appropriation by rave culture so much as to Bey's public status as both an anarchist and an apologist for paedophilia – one of the very rare cases where 'anarchist' is not the most publicly damning truth one might have held against one. It should go without saying, but it is possible to discuss the spatial deterritorialization implied by Bey's theory without in any way implicitly defending or promoting the sexual abuse of minors – a practice which, to be totally clear, I condemn without quarter.

6 In what may not be a coincidence, the favoured Situationist practice known as *détournement* also owed a great deal to the cut-up techniques of Burroughs and Gysin, involving as it did cutting up and recombining found media in order to subvert, mock or queer the original intended messages (Sadler, 1999).

7 Indeed, one might read Acker's project with *Empire of the Senseless* to have been, at least in part, a deliberate attempt to provoke as many as possible of the standard attacks upon female authordom listed in Joanna Russ's *How To Suppress Women's Writing* (1989), with only a single published piece.

8 Interestingly, the software systems used to check scholarly works for plagiarism, such as TurnItIn, do so by exposing both the subject text and an ever-growing number of source texts to exactly the same sort of algorithmic fragmentation and comparative analysis implied by Crowe's method; as such, the processes of plagiarism and of policing plagiarism are shown to be functionally related, and it is the purpose to which the functions are put that determines whether they are considered ethical or not.

Works Cited

Acker, Kathy (1988) *Empire of the Senseless.* New York: Grove.

Beaumont-Thomas, Ben (2014) 'Shia LaBeouf Escalates Plagiarism Row with Daniel Clowes via Bizarre Tweets', *Guardian,* 8 January, URL (consulted on 12 February 2014): http://www.theguardian.com/film/2014/jan/08/shia-labeouf-daniel-clowes-plagiarism-twitter-row

Bosman, Julie (2012) 'Jonah Lehrer Resigns From The New Yorker After Making Up Dylan Quotes for His Book', *New York Times* (Media Decoder), 30th July, URL (consulted on 12 February 2014): http://mediadecoder.blogs.nytimes.com/2012/07/30/jonah-lehrer-resigns-from-new-yorker-after-making-up-dylan-quotes-for-his-book/

Bey, Hakim (1991) *T.A.Z.: The Temporary Autonomous Zone, Ontological Anarchy, Poetic Terrorism.* Brooklyn, NY: Autonomedia. URL (consulted September 2014): http://hermetic.com/bey/taz_cont.html

Collin, Matthew (1998) *Altered State: The Story of Ecstasy Culture and Acid House.* London: Serpent's Tail.

Crowe, Graeme P (2013) 'Thunder & Consolation: Adam Roberts's *New Model Army* as Ephemeral Anarchist Utopia', *www.thunder-and-consolation.com,* consulted approx. March, URL no longer available.

Deans, Jason and Jemima Kiss (2011) 'Johann Hari suspended from the *Independent* following plagiarism row', *Guardian,* 12 July, URL (consulted on 31 July 2013): http://www.guardian.co.uk/media/2011/jul/12/johann-hari-suspended-independent

Elhefnawy, Nader (2010) 'New Model Army by Adam Roberts', *Strange Horizons,* 30 June, URL (consulted February 2014): http://www.strangehorizons.com/reviews/2010/06/new_model_army_.shtml

Gibson, William (1995) *Neuromancer*. Norstedts: Pan.

Gibson, William (2007) *Spook Country*. London: Penguin.

Hirsch, E. D. (1967) *Validity in Interpretation*. New Haven: Yale University Press.

Hoffelder, Nate (2012) 'Amazon Banning Junk & PD EBooks From The Kindle Store – What, Again?', *The Digital Reader,* 24 May, URL (consulted on 12 February 2014): http://www.the-digital-reader.com/2012/05/24/amazon-banning-junk-pd-ebooks-from-the-kindle-store-what-again/

House, Richard (2005) 'Informational Inheritance in Kathy Acker's *Empire of the Senseless*', *Contemporary Literature* 46(3): 450–82.

James, Edward (2003) 'Utopias and Anti-Utopias' in Edward James and Farah Mendlesohn (eds) *The Cambridge Companion to Science Fiction,* pp. 219–29. Cambridge: Cambridge University Press.

, Paul (2013) 'Interview with Adam Roberts', *Through the Dark Labyrinth,* 1 December, URL (consulted on 12 February 2014): http://ttdlabyrinth.wordpress.com/2013/12/01/interview-with-adam-roberts/

Knickerbocker, Conrad and William S. Burroughs (1982) 'The Paris Review Interview with William S. Burroughs', in John Calder (ed.) *A Williams Burroughs Reader,* p. 236. London: Picador.

MacLeod, Ken (2003) 'Politics and science fiction', in Edward James and Farah Mendlesohn (eds) *The Cambridge Companion to Science Fiction,* pp. 230–40. Cambridge: Cambridge University Press.

Noon, Jeff (1996/2013) *Pollen*. London: Ringpull.

Noon, Jeff (1997) *Automated Alice*. London: Corgi.

Noon, Jeff (1998/2012) 'PIXEL DUB JUICE (sublimerix Remix)', in *Pixel Juice: Stories from the Avant Pulp*. Brighton: Jeff Noon. Ebook.

Noon, Jeff (2001) *Cobralingus: Metamorphiction*. Hove: Codex.

Pulver, Andrew (2013) 'Shia LaBeouf Apologises for Short Film That Copied Daniel Clowes Story', *Guardian,* 17 December, URL (consulted 12 February 2014): http://www.theguardian.com/film/2013/dec/17/shia-labeouf-film-daniel-clowes-howard-cantour

Roberts, Adam (2009a) 'Nietzsche on Science Fiction', *Futurismic.com*, 15 July, URL (consulted 12 February 2014): http://futurismic.com/2009/07/15/nietzsche-on-science-fiction/

Roberts, Adam (2009b) 'Book Review: Kramer Wand – *Me:topia*', *Futurismic.com*, 9 September, URL (consulted 12 February 2014): http://futurismic.com/2009/09/09/book-review-kramer-wand-metopia/

Roberts, Adam (2013) 'Review: Thomas Hodgkin, Denis Bayle, a Life', in *Adam Robots: Short Stories*, pp. 98–106. London: Gollancz.

Rodgers, Jennifer (2005) 'Fulfillment as a Function of Time, or The Ambiguous Process of Utopia', in Laurence Davis and Peter Stillman (eds) *The New Utopian Politics of Ursula K. Le Guin's The Dispossessed*, pp. 181–94. Lanham, MD: Lexington.

Rushworth, John et al. (1648–9) 'The Agreement of the People of England, and the places therewith incorporated, for a secure and present peace, upon grounds of common right, freedom and safety', *Old Parliamentary History*, URL (consulted 15 January 2014): http://www.constitution.org/eng/conpur081.htm

Russ, Joanna (1989) *How to Suppress Women's Writing*. Austin: University of Texas Press.

Sadler, Simon (1999) *The Situationist City*. Cambridge, MA: MIT.

Searle, John (1980) 'Minds, Brains and Programs', *Behavioral and Brain Sciences* 3(3): 417–57.

Shaviro, Steven (2009) 'The Singularity Is Here', in Mark Bould and China Miéville (eds) *Red Planets: Marxism and Science Fiction*, pp. 103–17. London: Pluto.

Sullivan, Justin, and Robert Heaton (1989) *Thunder & Consolation*, New Model Army. EMI. Audio CD.

Splinter Swiftly

The Hermeneuting Parallax of Adam Roberts's Generic Auteurship

Andrew M. Butler

Introduction: Basic Training in Genre

There is a moment in a book by John G. Cawelti when he explains some of the pleasures of genre:

> Audiences find satisfaction and a basic emotional security in a familiar form; in addition, the audience's past experience with a formula gives it a sense of what to expect in new individual examples, thereby increasing its capacity for understanding and enjoying the details of a work. (Cawelti, 1976: 9)

In a world that is increasingly swift, splintered and dominated by the machinations of postindustrial capitalism, genre formulae provide a recognizable set of patterns that both reassure and provide ways of escape from the estranging mundane. The armies of genre provide a space for resistance to dominant ideology while – paradoxically – being precisely the product of the standardization and mass production of the dominant culture. However, through repeated exposure to the well-established narrative or thematic patterns, the reader is trained to distinguish between the different examples of a specific genre. In high culture, a connoisseur is able to differentiate early-, mid- and late-nineteenth century operas or different vintages of wine made from the same grape variety in precisely the same way as the seventy-two-year-old grandmother can identify which of the several hundred Mills and Boon novels on a secondhand market book stall she would like and which she would not. It is easy to patronize such readers, as one of Adam Roberts's characters does in *Yellow Blue Tibia* (2009): 'Science fiction is for adolescent boys and people who make models of aircraft from plastic and glue. I am a mature woman, which is to say, the opposite of a science fiction fan' (*YBT*: 222). Despite the sharpness of the reading skills of genre fans, dominant culture attempts to discredit them by dismissing the choice of reading text. Individual author names may be a factor in identifying texts and defining their genres – the author is a cog in the international money machine of a publisher such as Gollancz, currently an imprint of Orion Publishing Group that is part of Hachette Livre that is in turn part of Lagardère – but the army is made up of individual foot soldiers. These two, together, operate as a totality – a head and a distant set of bodies.

Fully defining genre would take a book at least as long as this one, but it could be seen as a series of texts grouped by family resemblances, in the same way that the Habsburg jaw is recognizable across different generations of a dynasty despite distances of time and space. Alternatively, genre texts fit a number of recognizable rules that define the sort of characters, narratives and themes the author may use. Such rules allow the regulation of genre boundaries by an army of critics; as Jacques Derrida (1992: 229) notes 'a code should provide an identifiable trait and one which is identifiable to itself, authorizing us to adjudicate whether a given text belongs to this genre or perhaps to that genre'. Through repeated exposures to individual texts we are trained to read them and hone our senses of the territorial distinctions being asserted and skirmished over.

The film critic Rick Altman identified two categories of genre, the semantic and the syntactic, as a means of understanding the classification of specific genres. The former is based on iconography and content: what are the signifiers or props that need to be spotted before a text can be appropriately pigeon-holed (the mid-nineteenth century, desert towns, horses, pistols; the 1930s, American cities, Ford motorcars, machine guns)? The latter is based on narrative and form: what is the syntax or structure that needs to be spotted before a text can be appropriately pigeon-holed (a body on the floor in the library whose murder must be solved; a man and woman who hate each other but fall in love)?

Samuel R. Delany, a leading writer and critic of science fiction, suggests that genre-based reading strategies interpret a given text in a particular way. In mimetic fiction, for example, the phrase 'her world exploded' would indicate that a character was having a bad day and that they were undergoing some kind of social or economic crisis threatening their routine. In a work of science fiction, on the other hand, the phrase would mean that a character was having a *really* bad day, along with presumably several billion members of her species. As a character observes in *Yellow Blue Tibia* 'A realist writer might break his protagonist's leg or kill his fiancée, but a science fiction writer will immolate whole planets' (*YBT*: 15). The sentence 'She gave up her heart quite willingly' can be read differently according to each genre protocol – in a story called 'The Bridge Party' it would mean something quite different from one called 'The Transplant Surgeon', 'The Love Affair' or (its actual source) 'Aztecs'.[1] The problem with genre – one of the problems with genre – is how we know which reading protocol to adopt.[2]

Basic Protocol: Recceeing the Terrain

What protocols should we be using when we come to Adam Roberts? Best known as a science-fiction writer and academic, it is the former role that is our focus for this volume. But, as I will indicate, he has far wider significance. In addition to a number of science-fiction novels, he has written the Routledge New Critical Idiom *Science Fiction* (2000), the Palgrave *History of Science Fiction* (2006), numerous reviews and articles and co-edited, with Mark Bould, Andrew M. Butler and Sherryl Vint, *The Routledge Companion to Science Fiction* (2009) and *Fifty Key Figures in Science Fiction* (2010).[3] He thus brings an intimate knowledge to what is one of the most successful of genres.

Curiously, in *Adventure, Mystery and Romance,* Cawelti largely neglects some of the largest formula types – horror, SF and fantasy – although he discusses the escapism of horror and the 'profound experience of self-transcendence' (Cawelti, 1976: 47) it engenders. SF, for Cawelti, offers 'the fantasy of knowing the unknowable through objectification' and 'various forms of transcendent, quasi-religious experiences in works [...] like those of Arthur Clark [sic] and C. S. Lewis' (Cawelti, 1976: 49). These are genres with predominantly younger audiences, as he suggests that 'older, educated people probably learn more sophisticated modes of self-transcendence' (Cawelti, 1976: 48). This is at odds with Cawelti's argument that the genre reader automatically has a sophisticated taste. And Roberts is not someone who could be accused of not being a sophisticate.

Yellow Blue Tibia offers several characterizations of the genre: 'science fiction is a kind of conceptual distortion of the familiar' (*YBT*: 74) and 'science fiction is the Olympic Games of the imaginatively fit' (*YBT*: 115). The realist writer merely corrals the world as it is in her fictional narrative, where the writer of the fantastic has to supplement reality with an internally self-consistent simulacrum of the real. This is not merely an act of escapism – 'The worlds created by a science fictional writer do not deny the real world,' says one of Roberts's characters, 'they antithesise it' (*YBT*: 147). And, in positing an alternative to the doxa of naturalist representation, the reader is enabled to imagine alternatives to the given world:

> Science fiction is the literature of the future. Science fiction *imagines* the future. It seeks not to reproduce the world as have all hitherto existing literatures, but to *change* it. It is the communism of literary forms. It is the literature of proletarian possibilities' (*YBT*: 195).

For Roberts, or at least for Roberts's protagonists, science fiction is a revolutionary form.

As academic and writer, Roberts's output crosses the traditionally separate spheres of art and science. He argues, in his introduction to a British Academy pamphlet, *Past, Present and Future: The Public Value of the Humanities and Social Sciences*: '[W]e move increasingly beyond the sterile and outdated notion of a society of "two cultures", [and] the mutual dependencies of "hard" science and the humanities and social sciences have become ever clearer' (Roberts, 2010b: 5). Some boundaries no longer require an army to police them, and SF has been at the vanguard of this liberalization. In his position as President of the British Academy, Roberts was well-placed to ensure such a rapprochement; additionally as an Emeritus Professor of International Relations,[4] he has an intimate knowledge of war and history.

Books such as *Nations in Arms: The Theory and Practice of Territorial Defence* (1976/1986), *Civil Resistance in the East European and Soviet Revolutions* (1991) and *United Nations, Divided World* (Roberts and Kingsbury, 1993) would repay greater wordage than there is space here to be read against the wars as represented in his many novels. As historian of military strategy, he can on occasions indulge his science-fiction impulses, as in his analysis of Sweden's defence plans:

> Would a hypothetical future war in Sweden in fact remain limited and localized? [... It is] possible that any opponent, once involved in Sweden and faced with strong resistance, would try to gain a physical hold over the 'brain' of the country, Stockholm; and its military heart, the large central area of Sweden from which forces and equipment might be deployed either northwards or southwards. (Roberts, 1976/1986: 113).

This analysis, which continues with 'the guerrilla or para-guerrilla element in Swedish defence plans' (Roberts, 1976/1986: 115) is a clear precursor to *New Model Army* (2010). Roberts's expertise in SF has aided his comprehension of history and vice versa: as one of his characters observes 'It is a condition of science fiction [...] that each reality is shadowed by alternate realities, every history has a variant alternate history' (*YBT*: 251). History requires the mastering of the narrative of events, policing the counternarratives nestled within it.

Roberts is both a man of letters and a man of action, which is why he reaches for the Olympic Games metaphor. He played as a midfielder for Macclesfield Town, close to his native Manchester, before being loaned to Leek Town. His lack of progress through the upper English football leagues is science fiction's gain. Perhaps this explains why at some point he took out Canadian nationality and briefly raced with Yamaha motorcycle team.[5] This identifies Roberts as a risk-taker. His avatar in *Yellow Blue Tibia* may claim, 'I'm not a warrior. I'm a science fiction writer' (*YBT*: 190), but Roberts clearly fights with the rest of the genre. War is a recurrent plot motif within Roberts's oeuvre, despite that character's assertion that 'The truth is the war bashed the science fiction out of me' (*YBT*: 115). Roberts keeps returning obsessively to war and the pity of war.

It is but a short hop across the strongly policed forty-second parallel from Canada south to the United States, where Roberts took iconic photographs of the Plains, the West, Colorado and other places, including Sweden, presumably during his research for *Nations in Arms*. The landscape photographer Frank Gohlke compares his own work to Roberts's, describing Roberts's photographs in *The New West: Landscapes Along the Colorado Front Range* (1974) as ones in which '"damage and grace are inextricably intertwined"' (cited in Cheng, 2011: 156), while Cheng notes in Roberts and Gohlke's photographs 'unremitting attempts to find lyricism in the mundane' (Cheng, 2011: 155). Roberts's engravings and architecture demonstrate his creativity, although none of his buildings survive – although the wall in *On* (2001) and the vast constructions of *Gradisil* (2006) are suggestive.[6] Roberts is a true Renaissance Man.[7]

Tactics of Attacks: Artist vs. Hack

It is with the words of a poem, 'Bright Eyes' (1978), inspired by one of his novels, *Watership Down* (1972), in mind that I turn back to his oeuvre:[8]

Is it a kind of a dream
Floating out on the tide
Following the river of death downstream
Oh, is it a dream?

Roberts is one of the most prolific contemporary writers, with some eighteen novels in the Horseclans series (1975–88) alone. How do you begin to comprehend the marvel that is the fiction of Adam Roberts as something that resembles itself within a wider assemblage of generic texts? What is the relationship of the texts that are Adam Roberts's – perhaps we should write Adam Robertses's? – to that assemblage of science fiction? What tactics should our army employ?

In understanding the current battle lines of genres, the origins of the genre need to be examined – or rather the origin myth that that genre constructs about itself needs to be analysed. Science fiction has Mary Shelley, Edgar Allan Poe or Jules Verne as its parents, their relative contributions weighed according to whether the historian is British, American or French; later candidates may include H. G. Wells or Hugo Gernsback. Roberts offers an origin myth by selecting John Milton's *Paradise Lost* (1667), which pushes SF back towards the beginning of the Baconian scientific method. But none of these authors consciously wrote science fiction, whereas Roberts is consciously within part of a genre tradition even as he questions that genre. A work which belonged in one genre in one age may be reread as being part of a different genre in another. Equally, a work may have the syntactic structure of one genre, whilst displaying the semantic content of another. Genre is never pure and a text never belongs to just one genre.

And yet genre, somehow, is considered vulgar, with literary prizes, for example, shying away from it. Weekend broadsheet reviewers proudly reject it as being beneath their dignity unless as the guilty pleasure of a holiday read. Genre is associated with the sections of a book shop (as if Literary Fiction were not in itself a category), with particular forms of publication (as if Dickens had not appeared in magazines) and with – in Robert A. Heinlein's words – competing for the reader's beer money. Stanisław Lem states:

> marketing prospects or official approval or similar concerns have no place intruding in that narrow gap between the author's eyes and the blank page. That the muse cannot be pursued over a bottle of beer goes without saying. In short, honest literature can never conform to external pressures or exigencies. (Lem, 1977: 128)

The muse of literature apparently cannot extend to the landlady's unpaid bill. Writing as genre, as product, is seen as being repetitive and formulaic trash, whereas the author who has literary merit displays artistic unity, his vision ensuring that each book has an identical theme. On the other hand, a literary writer who does not repeat herself is regarded as versatile, whereas the hack writer is unfocused and muddled, unable to express a coherent worldview. The decks are stacked against the genre writer by the old literary army.

On which side of this divide should we place Professor Roberts? Is he artist or hack? On the one hand, as I have already demonstrated his great versatility, on the other his career risks looking uneven and unfocused. *Yellow Blue Tibia* might include the assertion on its cover from Kim Stanley Robinson that it 'should have won the 2009 Booker Prize', which instead went to the determinedly non-generic (although historical) novel *Wolf Hall* (2009) by Hilary Mantel.[9] An author as artist is *sui generis,* a singular genius. The focus on the individual author is an Enlightenment product. Notions of originality and ownership of texts have changed over the centuries. When in 2004 the BBC adapted *The Canterbury Tales* for television, they updated the narratives to the present, jettisoning almost everything that was Chaucerian. Instead they were adapting writers such as Ovid and Boccaccio. Equally, the sacrosanct William Shakespeare borrowed from Ovid, Chaucer, Plutarch and historical chronicles as well as other playwrights. The author in such cases is hardly the authority of the text associated with their name, instead being the latest custodian of the narrative.

With the growth of a literate public with sufficient leisure time to read, texts became commodities that needed to be protected from piracy and incorporated into the machinery of industrial capitalism. Copyright legislation defended the publisher's right to copy a manuscript and distribute it, as much as it protected the author's income; note the uneven balance between the royalty granted to the author and the profit taken by the publisher. The author becomes an asset to be exploited as a marketing device; as Michel Foucault (1984: 107) argues, '[An author's name] performs a certain role with regard to narrative discourse, assuring a classificatory function. Such a name permits one to group together a certain number of texts, define them, differentiate them from and contrast them to others'. The study of a given work as the product of a specific author might look for particular icons, the nature of his identificatory characters and antagonists or for specific narrative structures, kinds of climax and the hermeneutics of its characters' problem-solving, as well as themes and intertextuality with other works by its author.

Foucault (1984: 107) suggests, 'the author's name serves to characterize a certain mode of being of discourse'. We use it to recognize the work of the author and through the work of the author we recognize the author's name. We bring the biographical facts of Roberts's life – his writing, academic career, artistic endeavours, football playing and motorcycling – and use them as a hermeneutic tool to interpret the texts. Equally, his life is a sales pitch for the work. The author, despite the assertion of his or her moral rights, is a trademark in international capitalism. Roberts™ asserts that, 'once a book is written it doesn't belong to the author any more' (*LOTH*: 231); it goes out to take its chances with readers.

Counterattack: The Paradox of Parody

With an oeuvre as wide and varied as Roberts™'s – the novels, lyrics, historical essays, reviews, parodies, engravings, blog entries, tweets – it is hard to define what is his work and not his work, or play. Foucault (1984: 103) reminds us that, 'even when an individual has been accepted as an author, we must still ask whether everything that he wrote, said, or left behind is part of his work'. Even focusing just on the post-2000 novels, we have an author who hardly repeats himself – but does repeat the works of others. In *On* there are debts to Hal

Clements's *Mission of Gravity* (1954), Christopher Priest's *Inverted World* (1974), Keith Roberts's *Kiteworld* (1985) and the film *Full Metal Jacket* (1987). In *Stone* (2002), Roberts draws on Alfred Bester, William Gibson, Iain M. Banks, the epistolary novel and, as Greg L. Johnson notes, 'the final chapter amounts to a drawing-room scene where All Is Explained' (2002). Lavie Tidhar (2011) notices the metanarratological nature of the work: 'the nature of the narration – addressed to the eponymous stone of the title – works to undermine our suspension-of-disbelief, to remind us of the nature of text as artefact, as artifice'. *Gradisil* is inspired by the future history, Robert A. Heinlein, Arthur C. Clarke, libertarian ideas, The Oresteia and Rose Tyler from *Doctor Who.*

His technique is most visible in *Swiftly: A Novel* (2007) and *Splinter: A Voyages Extraordinaire* (2008). The title of *Swiftly* points towards the author Jonathan Swift, whose *Gulliver's Travels* (1726) is both a savage work of eighteenth-century satire and a work of proto-science fiction, depending on the patrolling of the genre boundaries. Swift draws upon earlier travel literature. In the first of his voyages, Lemuel Gulliver visits Lilliput, where the inhabitants are much smaller than him, and in the second this is reversed by visiting a land of giants, Brobdingnag. Gulliver thus moves from consequential to inconsequential, from God to gnat. In the third voyage, the most overtly science fictional, the lands of Laputa and Lagado offer spaces to parody science and impractical ideas. Finally, the country of the Houyhnhnms is a land of intelligent, talking horses.[10] Rather than a straightforward continuation of the novel – the continuing voyages of Gulliver – Roberts™ depicts an England a century or more after Gulliver's return,[11] when some of the inhabitants of those imaginary lands have been brought to Europe. As Roberts™ notes, 'almost everything I write is in dialogue with the backlist' (Callow Jr., 2013). He ups the stakes by drawing on other incipits, Voltaire's 'Micromégas' (1752) and H. G. Wells's *The War of the Worlds* (1898). Voltaire's story gives Roberts™ the opportunity to move further up the scale – a 6,000 foot tall Saturnian and the even bigger Micromégas, from Sirius, inspire him to scale up from the Brobdingnagians and down from the Lilliputians. This furnishes Roberts™ with an intelligent analogue for the bacteria that unwittingly thwart the Martian invasion in Wells's novel. But rather than situating a Martian invasion some fifty years earlier than the original, Roberts™ initially seems to reverse the cultural imperatives under which Wells was operating – the invasion fears expressed in British fiction from 1870 onwards – to depict a French invasion of Britain as metaphor for alien invasion. As in so many of his novels, Roberts™ shows an invaded Britain, fragmented and occupied, but a Britain at the height of the industrial revolution with imperial tentacles attached.

Having engaged with several fathers of science fiction in *Swiftly,*[12] Roberts™ responds to Jules Verne in *Splinter,* reimagining *Off on a Comet/Hector Servadac* (1877). In the original, a comet strikes the Earth, splintering off a fragment of Gibraltar. The protagonist Servadac and thirty-five others survive there for two years, until the trajectory of the comet brings them full circle back to Earth. Roberts™ displaces the French narrative of a British enclave in Spain to an American location, writing within the 'American School of Updike and Roth and DeLillo' (Roberts™, 2008: 235). This translation marks the trajectory of the genre, whilst also using the very British form of the cosy catastrophe. This was a subgenre first identified by Brian Aldiss, underestimating the works of writers such as John Wyndham and John Christopher. The cosy catastrophe features an end of the world that liberates its heroes from the rigidity of good form – they have 'a girl, free suites at the Savoy, automobiles for the taking' (Roberts™, 2008: 294). Christopher Priest, whose own dialogue with SF is more ambivalent than Roberts™'s, argues that 'Wyndham is the master of the middle-class catastrophe; his characters are of the bourgeoisie, and the books lament the collapse of law and order, the failure of communications, the looting of shopping precincts and the absence of the daily newspaper' (Priest, 1979: 194). For Priest, the protagonist of the cosy catastrophe has been somewhat put out, and would write a stuffy letter of complaint to *The Times* (if there were still a postal service). Survivors tend to be middle class, white, journalists, doctors or other white-collar professionals, and work toward reconstruction of the lost society freed from the masses. The reimagining by Roberts™ isolates its international but middle-class characters in California as part of a doomsday cult. In translating the cosiness from one context to another, Roberts™ hardly challenges and perhaps reinforces the assumptions of the form.

Rally: The Paradox of Paratext

Roberts™'s afterwords for *Swiftly* and *Splinter* admit to his incipits, but also attempt to police their hermeneutic framework. The question is how seriously we are to take these pronouncements. Dora B. Master (2012: 21) warns that 'You'll get nothing out of the man or woman behind whichever book you're holding. It's exactly like talking to a corpse'. Roberts™ himself nods to Roland Barthes's 'The Death of the Author', which concludes 'The key to a text is not to be found in its "origin" but in its "destination". The birth of the reader must be at the cost of the death of the Author' (Barthes, 1977: 148). The author's copyright and moral rights over the text can act as a straightjacket of interpretation, as we are expected to decode the patterns that the author has carefully hidden for us, to say clearly what they have said obscurely. When the author explicitly states her aims, it closes down scope for interpretation. If we recognize her incipits – say, Swift, Updike, Verne, Wells, Wyndham – then our interpretations are correct, but if we read the text in terms of an author the writer did not have in mind, then she may insist we are wrong.

Roberts™ as author is a frame that is inside/outside the text that allows us to organize our responses or resistances to the novel. Gérard Genette would argue that such frames are part of the paratext, a range of written materials which surround and present the text itself: 'we are dealing in this case with a *threshold* […] between the inside and the outside, itself without rigorous limits, either towards the interior (the text) or towards the exterior (the discourse of the world on the text)' (Genette, 1991: 261). This is similar to Derrida's (1987: 9) examination of paintings, which at first sight have clear insides and outsides, but turn out to have what he dubs *parergons*, 'neither work (*ergon*) not outside the work [*hors d'oeuvre*], neither inside nor outside, neither above nor below'. The signature, which would legitimate a canvas or a text, is both a guarantee of authenticity and a mark of authorial absence – 'the actual or empirical nonpresence of the signer' (Derrida, 1988: 20). If the signature is on the inside of the text, it is open to the same possibilities for deconstruction in meaning; if it is on the outside of the text it is an assertion of meaning rather than a truth act. Indeed, an author's statements on her own work are not innocent and naked, but may be more of a strip tease or a rodeo clown using a flag to distract us from the bull.

Tidhar (2011) has called Roberts™ 'both the Fool and Knave of science fiction'; at times it is not so much that Roberts™ is writing SF – the cosy catastrophe, the invasion, the planetary romance – but rather writing a *parody* of SF. He might be on the boundaries of the genre or central to defining it. It is not easy to draw a distinct line between the operation of genre and parody. To parody is to reproduce the elements of another text so that they are recognized by the consumer, in such a way that the incipits are being commented on: 'The collective weight of parodic practice suggests a redefinition of parody as a repetition with critical distance that allows ironic signalling of difference at the very heart of similarity' (Hutcheon, 1985: 26). Again there is a sense of the connoisseur – the audience familiar with the originary text can more fully appreciate the parodist's subtle distinctions and alterations. Just as a text may share syntactic or semantic similarities to texts within the same genre, so a parody may choose to copy structure or content. Genette (1997: 24) defines four kinds of parody: pure pastiche in which style has been imitated; strict parody that permits itself as little substitution for and difference from the original as possible; the travesty which retains the subject matter but modifies the style with which it is approached and the satiric pastiche which imitates the style of the original but introduces more vulgar or inappropriate content. In practice, individual works of parody slide between the four types of parody.

The assumption is perhaps that the parodist is holding the original up to ridicule, by drawing attention to its shortcoming, with more affectionate tributes being categorized as homage. Fredric Jameson (1991: 13) distinguishes between parody as attack and pastiche as a more neutral translation of an original: 'Pastiche is, like parody, the imitation of a peculiar or unique, idiosyncratic style, the wearing of a linguistic mask, speech in a dead language. But it is a neutral practice of such mimicry, without any of parody's ulterior motives, amputated of the satiric impulse, devoid of laughter'. It is to subsume one's own identity in that of the originary author – herself an organizing principle who is part of a wider genre.

Whatever the intentions of the parodist, homager or pasticher, the original is not destroyed, in fact it may become more significant as a result of the dialogue. The attempt to kill the father grants him more power; the Fool may threaten but never fatally undermines the king. Tidhar (2011) notes that '[Roberts™] is not so much a science fiction writer as a writer engaging with – and skewering – science fiction as a mode, as a construct. In that he is both brave and, no doubt, from a commercial perspective, foolish'. Such skewering – that insertion of a metal pole into the body of the genre – may act to strengthen and support the genre. Roberts™ states that his work is 'about engaging ironically with a source or text' (Callow Jr., 2013), but irony demands an oscillating dialectic of intention and counterintention, the assertion and undermining of difference at the heart of similarity and similarity at the heart of difference. Roberts™ may come to praise rather than to bury.

Alongside his serious works, Roberts™ has produced a series of explicit parodies – *The Soddit* (2003), *The McAtrix Derided* (2004), *The Sellamillion* (2004), *Star Warped* (2005), *The Va Dinci Cod* (2005), *Doctor Whom: E. T. Shoots and Leaves* (2006), *I am Scrooge: A Zombie Story for Christmas* (2009) and *The Dragon with the Girl Tattoo* (2010a). Such works serve to reinforce the centrality of parody to his work, precisely because of the acts of disavowal that they offer – 'See! This is what parody really looks like! Those other works are not parodic!'. This is to also disguise the acts of parody (pastiche, homage) that are central to anyone who is working within – or against – the rules of a genre: to write the same thing again, to write the same thing in a different way, to write the same way about something different or to introduce something different and inappropriate into the genre. Equally, to maintain an identity as an author, even an Author™, is to self-parody, to write like oneself or to write not like oneself, to be similarly different or differently similar.

Conclusion: Insurgencies

To offer a conclusion for the future role of the new genre army is to confront the uncertainty being poised between keynote and plenary. A keynote comes at the head, establishing an underlying theme and setting an agenda; it allows the speaker (or writer) to assert her authority and her meaning. This chapter asserts that Roberts™ means *x* or *y*, and attempts to marshal the genre boundaries and the acts of interpretation. This may well be at the cost of the death of the author – uncannily, awkwardly, problematically also among us. I parody/pastiche/homage his ideas. On the other hand, a plenary is much more of a body coming together to act as a collective, to achieve consensus, with connotations of fullness and community. This, too, can be a wake, as we remember his life – his experiences as footballer and motorcyclist, his backgrounds in politics, sciences, photography and architecture, and we attempt to ascertain how this produced the works he has left behind him.

The keynote/plenary parallax is appropriate in this ongoing collision of author/genre and incipit/parody within the capitalistic economy of contemporary publishing. It is a struggle for power between head and body, between father and children, hierarchy and network. Note all those novels by Roberts™ in which fathers are killed (or appear to be killed) and note the impact that has on the offspring – usually a son. The death of the father, even if misperceived, becomes the motivating factor; the offspring acts as a parody of the parent, similar and different. Note the title of *The Land of the Headless* (2007), which explores a Swiftian sense of the body. Note the anarchistic, leaderless structure of the *New Model Army*. Not for nothing does Roberts™ point us to Gilles Deleuze in the afterword to *Splinter* (244, 246), that most rhizomic and branching and networking of theorists. Note how far Roberts™'s birth as an author is at the cost of the death of the genre's authors, a score of Banquos at the feast. *My* role as first-among-equals, *our* role as the New Genre Army is to fight those border skirmishes. We also must hold Roberts™ to account, to say clearly, what Roberts™ says obscurely,[13] to hold the body of the work against the head of the work. The Author as God is to be held to account and challenged. This is another decapitation and regicide, another act of blasphemy and patricide.

The birth of the critic must be at the cost of the death of the author. Roberts™ is dead. Long live Roberts™.

Notes

1 Vonda N. McIntyre's novella features a faster-than-light space pilot, Laenea, who like others in her trade has had to have her heart replaced with a mechanical one. 'Aztec' is a name given to such pilots on the model of the central Mexican civilisation which sacrificed their captives' hearts. Laenea denies it was a sacrifice because she chose to do so. The title oscillates between being figurative and literal, leading to a refined reading protocol as a romance narrative emerges within the technological framework.

2 For example, having watched two romantic comedies starring Cary Grant and Irene Dunne, *The Awful Truth* (Leo McCarey, 1937) and *My Favourite Wife* (Leo McCarey, 1940), I then watched *Penny Serenade* (George Stevens, 1941) in the same vein, even though it seemed much darker, especially when the Dunne's character miscarries. Eventually I realized I was using the wrong protocol.

3 If this volume has a fault, it may be the lack of a chapter on Roberts. If a second edition is compiled, it perhaps could be renamed *Fifty-One Key Figures*. The existence of the book that you are reading now is evidence that he is a key figure.

4 Note to editor from AMB: is this right? Emeritus means retired, yes? Perhaps he retired to write his SF?

5 Note to editor from AMB: have you commissioned a chapter on the Canadianness of Adam Roberts?

6 For Adam Roberts as architect see, for example, Gerson (1981) and Fensom (1984). His designs seem not to have been published.

7 Note to editor from AMB: literally, it would appear. One encyclopedia has his dates as 1540–95! How embarrassing to make such an error.

8 If that novel had been shortlisted for the Arthur C. Clarke Award, Christopher Priest might have been moved to opine: 'it is a quest saga and it has talking rabbits and a talking gull', having objected to Sheri S. Tepper's *The Waters Rising* (2010) thus: 'For fuck's sake, it is a quest saga and it has a talking horse' (Priest, 2012).

9 To claim that the Booker Prize does not go to genre books is to redefine what genre is. It has gone to Bildungsromans, travelogues, fictionalized biography and, above all, literary fiction. Such genre markers allow the novel to be sold – even literary novelists do not want to *not* sell books. The Booker Prize tends – with rare exceptions – to boost sales, being used as an advertising tool. The poorest seller in the history of the Booker appears to be Keri Hulme's *The Bone People* (1985). The almost annual controversy of the Booker either going to a readable or an unreadable book, or a too long or a too short novel, says more about the news cycle of the chatterati than any serious literary matters.

10 *Gulliver's Travels*, despite its title, is not necessarily a quest saga and so it has not been dismissed by Priest, even though it has talking horses, the Houyhnhnms. Roberts borrows these for the sapient cavalry of *Swiftly*.

11 The blurb says and diary entries in the text say 1848 (e.g., 1, 23), but the statement that '"Sir William Herschel discovered the furthest planet in the solar system fifty years ago, sir. He named it Ouranos"' (*SW*: 170) would place the action as roughly 1830, Herschel in our world having observed it in 1781. Even Homer nods.

12 I am not aware that he has engaged with the mother of science fiction, Mary Shelley, in his fiction.

13 The allusion here is to Emmanuel Levinas (1987: 1): 'Is not to interpret Mallarmé to betray him? Is not to interpret his work faithfully to suppress it? To say clearly what he says obscurely is to reveal the vanity of his obscure speech'. Levinas (1987: 2) defines the critic 'as the one that still has something to say when everything has been said, that can say about the work something else than that work'.

Works Cited

Aldiss, Brian (1973) *Billion Year Spree: The History of Science Fiction*. New York: Doubleday.

Altman, Rick (1999) *Film/Genre*. London: BFI.

Barthes, Roland (1977) 'The Death of the Author', in *Image – Music – Text*, trans. Stephen Heath, pp. 142–8. London: Fontana.

Bould, Mark, Andrew M. Butler, Adam Roberts and Sherryl Vint(eds) (2009) *The Routledge Companion to Science Fiction*. London: Routledge.

Bould, Mark, Andrew M. Butler, Adam Roberts and Sherryl Vint (eds) (2010) *Fifty Key Figures in Science Fiction*. London: Routledge.

Callow, Christos, Jr. (2013) 'Irony, Man: An Interview with Adam Roberts', *Strange Horizons*, 23 March, URL (consulted December 2013): http://www.strangehorizons.com/2013/20130325/2roberts-a.shtml

Cawelti, John G. (1976) *Adventure, Mystery and Romance: Formula Stories as Art and Popular Culture*. Chicago, IL: University of Chicago Press.

Cheng, Wendy (2011) '"New Topographics": Locating Epistemological Concerns in the American Landscape', *American Quarterly* 63(1): 151–62.

Clements, Hal (1954) *Mission of Gravity*. Garden City, NY: Doubleday.

Delany, Samuel R. (1977) *The Jewel-Hinged Jaw: Notes on the Language of Science Fiction*. Elizabeth Town, NY: Dragon Press.

Derrida, Jacques (1987) *The Truth in Painting*, trans. Geoff Bennington and Ian McLeod. Chicago, IL: The University of Chicago Press.

Derrida, Jacques (1988) 'Signature Event Context', *Limited Inc.*, trans. Samuel Weber and Jeffrey Mehlman, pp. 1–24. Evanston, IL: Northwestern University Press, 1988.

Derrida, Jacques (1992) 'The Law of Genre', in Derek Attridge (ed.) *Acts of Literature*, pp. 221–52. London: Routledge.

Fensom, David (1984) 'Geometric Form in Adam Architecture?' *RACAR: revue d'art canadienne / Canadian Art Review* 11(1/2): 97–109.

Foucault, Michel (1984) 'What is an Author?', in Paul Rabinow (ed.) *The Foucault Reader*, pp. 101–120. Harmondsworth: Penguin.

Genette, Gérard (1991) 'Introduction to the Paratext', *New Literary History* 22(2): 261–72.

Genette, Gérard (1997) *Palimpsests: Literature in the Second Degree*, trans. Claude Doubinsky and Channa Newman. Lincoln, NA: University of Nebraska Press.

Gerson, Martha Blythe (1981) 'A Glossary of Robert Adam's Neo-Classical Ornament', *Architectural History* 24: 59–82.

Hulme, Keri (1985) *The Bone People*. Auckland: Spiral.

Hutcheon, Linda (1985) *A Theory of Parody: The Teachings of Twentieth-Century Art Forms*. New York and London: Methuen.

Jameson, Fredric (1991) *Postmodernism or the Cultural Logic of Late Capitalism*. London and Durham, NC: Duke University Press.

Johnson, Greg L. (2002) 'The SF Site Featured Review: *Stone*', *SF Site*, URL (consulted December 2013): http://www.sfsite.com/11b/st140.htm

Lem, Stanisław (1977) 'Looking Down on Science Fiction', *Science Fiction Studies* 4(2): 127–8.

Levinas, Emmanuel (1987) 'Reality and its Shadow', in *Collected Philosophical Papers*, trans. Alphonso Lingis, pp. 1–14. Dordrecht: Martinus Nijhoff Publishers.

Mantel, Hilary (2009) *Wolf Hall*. London: Fourth Estate.

Master, Dora B. (2007) 'Motive and Opportunity: Post Mortem Authorial Morbidity', *The Journal of Authorial Studies* 12(3): 219–26.

McIntyre, Vonda N. (1987) 'Aztecs', in *Fireflood and Other Stories*, pp. 196–256. London: Pan.

Priest, Christopher (1974) *Inverted World*. London: Faber and Faber.

Priest, Christopher (1979) 'British Science Fiction', in Patrick Parrinder (ed.) *Science Fiction: A Critical Guide*, pp. 187–202. London and New York: Longman.

Priest, Christopher (2012) 'Hull 0, Scunthorpe 3', *Christopher Priest*, 28 March, URL (consulted December 2013): http://www.christopher-priest.co.uk/journal/1077/hull-0-scunthorpe-3

Roberts, A. R. R. R. (2003) *The Soddit*. London: Gollancz.

Roberts, A. R. R. R. (2004) *The Sellamillion*. London: Gollancz.

Roberts, A. R. R. R. (2005) *The Va Dinci Cod*. London: Gollancz.

Roberts, A. R. R. R. (2006) *Doctor Whom: E. T. Shoots and Leaves*. London: Gollancz.

Roberts, A3R (2005) *Star Warped*. London: Gollancz.

Roberts, Adam (1972) *Watership Down*. London: Rex Collins.

Roberts, Adam (1974) *The New West: Landscapes Along the Colorado Front Range*. Boulder, CO: Colorado Associated University Press,

Roberts, Adam (1976) *Nations in Arms: The Theory and Practice of Territorial Defence*. London: Chatto and Windus.

Roberts, Adam (1991) *Civil Resistance in the East European and Soviet Revolutions* Cambridge MA: Albert Einstein Institution.

Roberts, Adam (2008) 'Splinter Thoughts', in *Splinter*, pp. 229–52. Nottingham: Solaris.

Roberts, Adam (2009) *I am Scrooge: A Zombie Story for Christmas*. London: Gollancz.

Roberts, Adam (2010a) *The Dragon with the Girl Tattoo*. London: Gollancz.

Roberts, Adam (2010b) 'Introduction', in *Past Present and Future: The Public Value of the Humanities and Social Sciences,* pp. 2–6. *London*: British Academy.

Roberts, Adam and Kingsbury, Benedict (1993) *United Nations, Divided World: The UN's Roles in International Relations* Oxford: Clarendon Press.

Roberts, Keith (1985) *Kiteworld*. London: Penguin.

Robertsi Brothers (2004) *The McAtrix Derided*. London: Gollancz.

Tepper, Sheri S. (2011) *The Waters Rising*. London: Gollancz.

Tidhar, Lavie (2011) 'Shall I Tell You the Problem With Adam Roberts?', *Lavie Tidhar,* 14 December, URL (consulted December 2013): http://lavietidhar.wordpress.com/2011/12/14/shall-i-tell-you-the-problem-with-adam-roberts

Part IV

Intertextual Networks

Beyond Brobdingnagians and Bolsheviks
Extra-Textual Readings of *Swiftly* and *Yellow Blue Tibia*

Glyn Morgan

This chapter seeks to offer an extra-textual reading of novels from the most recent half of the writing career of Adam Roberts. It will propose that Roberts's novels, more than those by most authors, are not only fascinating subjects for extra-textual reading but are actually constructed to demand such a technique, having been shaped by, and developed to exploit and subvert, extra-textual forces and influences. The deployment of these extra-textual forces lends Roberts's fiction special distinction above the conventional in-built inter-textuality of the science fiction genre, but also above the more consciously inter-textual examples of recursive SF. However, before beginning, it is necessary to clarify as precisely as is possible in so limited a space, exactly what I mean by 'extra-textuality' and its different forms with which this chapter is concerned.

The first, and most important, form is intertextuality. Intertextuality 'covers the range of ways in which one "text" may respond to, allude to, derive from, mimic, parody, or adapt another' (Birch, 2009:

520). Essentially, when this chapter refers to intertextuality it is attempting to uncover deliberate references to texts by other authors which Roberts is making within his novels. Metatextuality is also a prominent technique in Roberts's work and refers to the employment of metafictional techniques to draw attention to a fictitious work's fictitiousness, or to remind the reader that they are reading a novel by making explicit references to novelistic and authorial devices. Intertextuality, combined with metatextuality and – a subset of both – paratextuality (which I will deal with in due course) form the branches of extra-textuality with which this chapter will engage.

In analysing some of the many intertextual and metatextual devices at work in Roberts's novels, this chapter will dig beneath the surface of his fiction and expose something of the mechanisms employed, particularly in his most recent – and successful – phase of novel writing. This chapter will thus be making explicit details that are implicit in Roberts's novels, drawing connections and comparisons with other works which have influenced him and highlighting fruitful avenues for more detailed examinations of specific texts in future studies.

There are numerous problems and risks with adopting such an approach to assess a body of work, not least that the author in question has in the past expressed his distaste for 'structuralist nonsense'; albeit in the informal, and combative, environment of the comments section of a blog:

> I do think that reading lots of books in a genre one loves, and spotting patterns, is a relatively easy thing to do; [...] doing something one loves is no chore, and that pattern recognition is hardwired into the human brain, we do it all the time from an early age. (Roberts, 2010)

Such comments would seem to directly undermine the fate of this study, and yet the fact remains that Roberts's fiction, particularly his most recent work, draws on his wide reading base and on techniques that push at the boundaries of what we might consider to be the text. They do so by either consciously referencing, drawing upon, parodying, or mimicking the actions of other texts, or by exploring the idea of the text itself by drawing attention to it or expanding it beyond the limits of the narrative. This chapter exposes some of these moments in Roberts's fiction, although this is by no means an exhaustive survey – such is the extent of Roberts's extra-textuality that an entire book-length study would be required on this topic alone. The intention is not to suggest any hypocrisy on the author's part, instead, I intend to propose that Roberts's fiction is double-coded and adheres to the model of postmodernism sketched by Linda Hutcheon in that it 'works within the very systems it attempts to subvert' (Hutcheon, 1988: 4). More precisely, Roberts's fiction is an extension of his personality and he is at heart an ironist as a recent interview with Christos Callow Jr. (2013), knowingly entitled 'Irony Man', suggests. At one point he expresses his respect for the form of parody, calling it 'a very important and actually underappreciated strand of Western art', and when questioned about puns, of which he is a serial instigator, Roberts remarks that 'they are rarely funny, except in a very meta-way' (Callow Jr., 2013). It would be disingenuous to claim that the same can be said of Roberts's novels, which are frequently funny, but nonetheless they do often operate in a very meta- and intertextual way.

The greatest danger in this chapter, then, is that it might commit the most terrible *faux-pas* of the ironist and kill a joke by explaining it. However, Roberts's recent novels exceed the sum of their parts and contain far more to entertain, intrigue and provoke than their extra-textualities alone; they are capable of surviving the process more-or-less unscathed due to a depth of narrative and meta-narrative not found in his parodies and rarer in his early novels. These later works will, indeed, benefit from a reading which prises open the lid, if only slightly, on the rich heritage and progressive narratives common to much science fiction which, by virtue of its nature, is a highly intertextual genre, but which Roberts consciously utilizes in his novels to an exceptional degree.

Travels into Several Remote Nations …

Adam Roberts's *Swiftly: A Novel* (2008) is a delayed sequel to the book by Jonathan Swift best known as *Gulliver's Travels* (1726, 1735).[1]

Delayed because *Swiftly* inhabits the same Universe as the original text but is set some 122 years later and as such features no common characters but instead extrapolates concepts outlined by Swift and examines their repercussions on the events of the nineteenth century. It is far from the first of Roberts's works of fiction to foreground its extra-textuality. Even putting aside the works published under Roberts's pseudonym A. R. R. R. Roberts which, being parodies, rely on intertextuality to an exceptional degree, an awareness of genre and a continuity of ideas can be found in most, if not all, of his work.

Nonetheless, *Swiftly* takes its intertextuality to a new level. Being a sequel, it is necessarily reliant on *Gulliver's Travels,* although the reader's familiarity with the ancestral text need only be the bare minimum. None of the plot is required, only the world building: the existence of peoples both larger and smaller than us, civilized horses, and floating isles. The title is of course a play on the earlier text's author, but Roberts also makes references of varying degrees to works by Beatrix Potter, Voltaire, Jules Verne and H. G. Wells among others. For example, Paul Kincaid asserts that the opening pages, demonstrating the little people at work, 'owes more to Beatrix Potter's *The Tailor of Gloucester* (1903) than it does to anything in Swift' (Harrison et al., 2008). Indeed, the descriptions Roberts provides of the worker 'wearing yellow silk trousers, a close-woven blue waistcoat [...] spectacles that shone like dewdrops' (1) and the explanation of the fine work they perform carries echoes of Potter's descriptions of clothing in that story, particularly the waistcoats produced by the mice which make the Tailor rich:

> ... the most wonderful waistcoats for all the rich merchants of Gloucester, and for all the fine gentlemen of the country round.
>
> Never were seen such ruffles, or such embroidered cuffs and lappets! But his button-holes were the greatest triumph of it all.
>
> The stitches of those button-holes were so neat – *so* neat – I wonder how they could be stitched by an old man in spectacles, with crooked old fingers, and a tailor's thimble.
>
> The stitches of those button-holes were so small – *so* small – they looked as if they had been made by little mice! (Potter, 1987: 56–7)[2]

By extension Roberts is also referencing the tale recorded by the Grimm brothers of 'The Shoemaker and the Elves', a probable source of inspiration for Potter's own tale. Roberts makes explicit allusions to this tale with factory foreman Pannell's remark that he 'never tires of watching them [his diminutive labourers] work, […] Pixies. Fairies! Creatures from childhood story' (*SW*: 1).

Such allusions are sewn throughout the fabric of the novel, and it is not my intention to expose each one, nor comment extensively on the quality of its stitching. However, a careful analysis of some selected cases reveals the extent to which Roberts is dependent on intertextuality, or rather how his literary awareness colours and informs his fiction. It has already been remarked above that an awareness of *Gulliver's Travels* is helpful but not necessary to read *Swiftly* and this theory is tested on the second page when we are informed that the little workers are not Lilliputians but 'from the neighbouring island, Blefuscu.' Blefuscans are believed 'to be better workers. They are less prone to disaffection […] they work harder and are more loyal' (*SW*: 2). By selecting the lesser known tribe of miniature humans, Roberts is at once paying homage to the Swiftian source material, while also signalling that *Swiftly* is not a standard sequel which panders to expectations of continuity; he is being faithful while also subverting the most familiar episode in the original book: Blefuscans are inhabitants of the next island along from Lilliput and at the time of Gulliver's visit they are amassing a navy to attack. Part of the contract with Gulliver 'the Man-Mountain' laid out by the Lilliputian Emperor states that: 'He shall be our Ally against our Enemies in the Island of Blefuscu, and do his utmost to destroy their Fleet, which is now preparing to invade Us' (Swift, 1726/2008: 38). For those unfamiliar with the reference the sleight of hand does not distract from the commencing narrative as they are simply being told that these little men are not of one fantasy race with a strange name, they are of another. Meanwhile those readers with a knowledge of the original appreciate the attention to detail Roberts employs (a lazier author, or one less familiar with Swift, may have just used Lilliputians after all), they also become complicit in binding Swift's world-building to Roberts's. In the unique manner of the shared-universe metatext, for those readers the world of *Swiftly* becomes deeper, more nuanced, and more expansive with every reference.

It would, however, be a mistake to assume that the Swiftian elements of the novel begin and end with the fantastical beings, and thus that to rename them – to call them pixies and giants, for example – would dissolve the connection to the earlier work. In fact, Roberts has tied *Swiftly* to *Gulliver's Travels* on a much more fundamental level, aping Swift stylistically and thematically at several junctures. A notable example of this is the continuation of Swift's fondness for scatological humour. In *Gulliver's Travels,* Gulliver extinguishes a fire in the royal quarters of Lilliput by urinating upon it (Swift, 1726/2008: 50). His descriptions of the difficulties of 'discharging [his] Body of that uneasy Load' (Swift, 1726/2008: 24) while temporarily the prisoner of the Lilliputians (a load which had to be taken away in wheelbarrows) is only the first of several references to excrement in the novel: another is Gulliver's accidental running jump into a massive cowpat in the land of the gigantic Brobdingnagians (Swift, 1726/2008: 112), or the scientists at the Academy of Lagado attempting to turn faeces back into sustenance (Swift, 1726/2008: 167). The abundance of scatology in Swift is not limited to *Gulliver's Travels*; it is a common motif in his other works as well, so common that it prompted Aldous Huxley to write:

> That the hatred of bowels should have been the major premiss [sic] of his philosophy when Swift was fifteen is comprehensible, but that it should have remained the major premiss when he was forty requires some explanation. (Huxley, 1929: 104–5)

By way of explanation, Huxley goes on to propose a sexual element to the fascination, reporting that Swift was incapable of 'making love in the ordinary, the all too human manner' and creating a (sometimes tenuous) connection between Swift's scatological obsession and an erotic fetishization bordering on the masochistic. While Huxley seems unable to convince even himself that this is completely the case, Roberts duly incorporates these elements into the novel, under the pretext of pestilence symptoms. Whatever the psychological motivations for Swift's fascination with the scatological, there is no denying that he also uses such moments for humorous, often satirical effect, and Roberts follows suit. The exasperatingly self-conscious Bates is the first character to succumb to the sickness and Roberts pulls him from a fog-like delirium just long enough to describe the necessary bodily functions:

> He felt a griping in his guts and knew that a flux of the bowels was upon him. It was a task to get the door open, fumbling and panicky as he was, but he managed it and half-stepped, half-slid down to the ground. His breeches came free and he pulled them down just in time before the mess spewed from his rear. He was squatting next to the great wheel of the carriage, and he clasped one of the wooden spokes to steady himself. It was a position compounded of physical discomfort and indignity.
>
> [...] Once again the flux of the bowels overcame Bates; he hurried outside and clung precariously to the carriage wheel as he squatted to empty himself. It was humiliating. The flow seemed never to come to an end. (*SW*: 165–6)

To subject a character of Bates's temperament to such treatment is a near-perfect embodiment of Frontain's (1992: 301) assertion that 'nothing deflates human pretensions to grandeur more quickly ... than the satirist's insistence upon biological processes'. Yet Roberts finds a way to inflict even greater trauma upon the character by then having the same affliction befall his travelling companion (and subject of barely hidden adoration) Mrs. Eleanor Burton; Bates finds himself 'extraordinarily upset by this development. He was almost unmanned by how upset this simple fact made him' (*SW*: 178). Roberts seems to revel in pushing Bates from the state of being 'almost unmanned' into something approaching a genuine breakdown as, over ten pages, he describes Bates well-meaning, but often ill thought out, attempts to clean Eleanor up so that she can awaken from her fever without the knowledge of what has befallen her. The episode enters the territory of farce deriving much humour from the deflation of Bates as he – Basil Fawlty-esque – makes the situation worse the more he tries to fix things.

Roberts further develops the scatological motif, tapping into Huxley's proposed sexual underpinnings for Swift's fascination (or abhorrence) for all things faecal, by cultivating between the pair a fetishization of the scatological. *Swiftly* follows a double helical spiral structure with plot elements winding outwards to a vast scale as the novel progresses, while at the same time they wind inwards towards the minute. So it is that after the Lilliputian/Blefuscans and Brobdingnagians are made familiar, we are exposed to things far smaller, and larger, than they. The scatological elements of the novel follow the same route, resulting in two extremes by the end of the novel in the epilogue-like fifth chapter 'The Gift'. Thus 'Bates and the other men who had survived had been obliged to build boats, like Phoenicians, ... And on these unlovely constructions they had oared their way across the valley through a faecal sea, until they broached clean turf and could disembark' (*SW*: 354–5). While the same chapter can contain a moment of intimacy in which Eleanor gifts him 'a small mahogany box from her handbag' which contains 'a perfectly tapered, delicate turd' (*SW*: 356).[3] The starting point of both of these strands, the arms of the spiral which wind outwards and inwards from a common point is that created by the original *Gulliver's Travels*. It is the norm for sequels to elaborate on their predecessors and, true to form, Roberts's novel extrapolates from this point in both directions.

Travels into Several Remote Histories ...

Swiftly's intertextual sources, and the mining of Roberts's extensive knowledge of speculative fiction, continues in one of the novel's central Macguffins: a French-built Babbage computational device. While Charles Babbage and his successors designed and worked on so called Difference and Analytical Engines throughout the nineteenth century of our own history, the difficulty in manufacturing a mechanical machine with the precision required for the designs proved either too expensive or beyond the capabilities of his patrons; Benjamin Disraeli in his capacity as Chancellor of the Exchequer labelled the engines as 'indefinitely expensive, the expenditure impossible to calculate, and its ultimate success problematical' (cited in Hyman, 1982: 230). However, with Lilliputians and Blefuscans enabling much greater precision, Bates reports that 'the French have perfected it [...] and with it they have constructed new engineering devices, and plotted new techniques of war-making' (*SW*: 16). This crucial role of the Babbage proto-computers in *Swiftly* often causes the novel to be classified as steampunk (Bidisha, 2008; Gevers, 2008), a problematic classification as any elements that could fall into this category are manipulated with only the lightest of touches by Roberts. Nonetheless, it is a term Roberts has himself, on occasion, used to describe the novel, which makes the presence of the Babbage machine significant for its association with steampunk, not least as the titular device in *The Difference Engine* (1990) by William Gibson and Bruce Sterling, a seminal novel in the subgenre. The novel is also frequently categorized as an alternate history (as indeed are many steampunk novels), even being nominated for a Sidewise Award in 2008.[4] This term is little better than steampunk as an accurate label for what Roberts achieves in the novel, although once again it is a label for which the author has himself conceded *Swiftly* 'just about qualifies'.[5] However, using the categorization does provoke some interesting ways of thinking about the novel, and about Roberts's oeuvre as a whole.

Alternate history is an intrinsically intertextual medium that relies on meta-textual connections with historical narratives. In his New Critical Idiom study, *The Historical Novel* (2010), Jerome de Groot refers to alternate histories as 'kind of historical novels squared', in that they are fictionalizations of fictionalizations of history (De Groot, 2010: 173). Famously referred to as a 'parlour game' for idle minds by historian E. H. Carr (1968: 97), on the contrary alternate histories require a complex engagement to achieve their full potential. Just as a reader who has not read Swift should be able to read *Swiftly* without worrying too much about the differences between Lilliputians and Blefuscans, so too a reader ill-informed about history should be able to read most alternate histories and enjoy them for their intrinsic worth, ignorant of the changes in the timeline being described by the author. Nonetheless, a full reading of an alternate history yields something far more complex and rewarding; for where a historical novel tries to camouflage into the narrative of history, fitting characters into the gaps and generally passing itself off as plausible, alternate history deliberately cuts across the grain. To fully appreciate this phenomenon one must retain a certain familiarity with the conventional historical narrative. In effect the reader is required to process, simultaneously, the narrative of the novel alongside the narrative of history. If we accept the narrative of history as a form of text, albeit one with very specific limitations and a unique set of problems, then we have to consider alternate history to be intrinsically intertextual.

The alternate history content of *Swiftly* is slight, discounting the presence of the little and big peoples, which – admittedly – is quite a large element to put aside. Its most significant, and possibly most easily spotted element, is the premature death of Napoleon Bonaparte. The novel begins in 1848, 27 years after Napoleon died in exile in our history but within *Swiftly*'s timeline he died much earlier as an exchange between Bates and his French handler D'Ivoi shows:

> 'And in France also?' retorted Bates. 'Did not your revolution result in the tyranny of-' But his memory wasn't sharp enough to recall the name. 'The Geralissimo, he who, during the civil war…'
>
> 'He was himself called Buonoparte,' said D'Ivoi. 'But he was no tyrant; merely a general too small to fulfil his ambition. Even had he lived, he could never have subdued a nation as vivid, as passionate as France. Do you know why? […] Because he lacked the support of the Church. Your Cromwell, he made his own Church, I believe. This was a good policy. Truly, without such support, without the Church on his side no ruler can last. Church,' D'Ivoi concluded, sententiously, 'is bigger than nation.' (*SW*: 125–6)

There are several possible motivations for killing Napoleon Bonaparte: one is purely practical, from a narrative point of view, while another possible motive is intertextual and typically subversive. In the former case, killing off Napoleon prematurely dodges his tenure as commander-in-chief of the French forces during the Napoleonic Wars, a period during which he became respected by friend and foe alike as one of the greatest generals of all time, and certainly one who would have changed history considerably with the use of tactical resources drawn from the fantastic creatures and sights described by Swift.[6] By eliminating him prematurely, Roberts is removing the possibility of Napoleon altering the timeline into too unrecognizable a form before it can reach the time period he is most interested in writing about: the mid-nineteenth century. The fact that Bates cannot remember his name, and the Frenchman misremembers it, shows how limited the impact of one of the most famous men in history has been.[7] The manipulation of the French Revolution also allows Roberts to reposition the role of the Church in French society and thus engage with theological and spiritually epistemological issues which serve as motivation for Bates initially siding with the French, among other practicalities.

From an intertextual perspective, it is also perfectly possible that Roberts alludes to the Napoleon issue, an issue he could simply have avoided with few consequences to the integrity of his narrative, as a reference to the history of alternate history literature itself: the earliest novel-length alternate histories in Western Literature are French, and they are almost exclusively concerned with Bonaparte, not least the earliest by Luis-Napoleon, *Napoléon et la Conquête du Monde, 1812–1823: Histoire de la Monarchie Universelle* [Napoleon and the Conquest of the World, 1812–1832: History of the Universal Monarchy], published in 1836.[8] As well as subverting the norm, in typical Roberts fashion, by removing the character most popular in alternate histories of the nineteenth century, and indeed among the most popular of all eras, he is also making an extra-textual statement of intent simultaneously referencing and disregarding conventions of the past.

Swiftly Moving onto Science Fiction

A considerable proportion of this chapter has been devoted to discussing *Swiftly*, not because it is Roberts's most ambitious, or most successful work in its overall scope, but because it is the most heavily intertextual of his non-A. R. R. R. Roberts works. It achieves this by combining the inherent intertextuality of being a sequel with

Roberts's own extensive knowledge of both the history of speculative fiction and eighteenth and early-nineteenth century literatures. As a key proponent of the 'long history' of science fiction, Roberts is more acutely aware than most of speculative fiction antecedents.[9]

As has already been stated, this intertextuality is present throughout Roberts's novels – *Splinter* (2007) is notable, for example, for the manner in which it pre-empts much of what Roberts would achieve with *Swiftly*. In *Splinter*, Roberts updates Jules Verne's *Off on a Comet* (Fr: *Hector Servadac*) in the manner of a 'sidequel' of sorts. Like the later Swiftian novel, *Splinter*'s debt to Verne is never denied nor veiled; indeed some versions, such as a hardback special edition published by Solaris, include Roberts's translation of Verne's original novel, using identical cover designs as if to suggest that these are two works somehow separated at birth.

While there is no space to discuss it here, another intertextually-fascinating novel is the later *Jack Glass* (2012), which is filled with references both direct and veiled to a range of detective fiction and consciously and explicitly subverts the genre in which it is written.[10] The titular character is described as both detective and murderer but, in a move which is the most deconstructive of all, in the prologue to the novel he is also revealed to be the killer in all three of the subsequent mysteries: 'In each case the murderer is the same individual – of course, Jack Glass himself. How could it be otherwise? Has there ever been a more celebrated murderer?' (*JG*: 1–2). That the genre upon which Roberts is offering a science fictional spin is so often referred to as the 'Whodunnit', the revelation at the beginning of the identity of the murderer is signal enough of the deconstructive and subversive nature of *Jack Glass*. An epistolary prologue is used to craft this effect, which only serves to further emphasize the contrasts with other epistolary detective narratives such as Conan Doyle's *Sherlock Holmes* stories, and so, while the novel makes ample use of the same form of intertext as *Swiftly*, it also invokes the second major type of extra-textuality this chapter will discuss: metatextuality.

Any excessive use of intertext is going to create a metatextual effect, as repeated reference to another work of fiction highlights the artificiality of the narrative and draws attention to the novel as a construct.

This is true of *Jack Glass* where the central character Diana makes repeated assertions as to her familiarity with murder mysteries of all sorts, but in none of Roberts's novels is this phenomenon more easily noted than in *Yellow Blue Tibia* (2009). This is a novel that intrinsically calls to attention its artificiality as a science fiction novel written by a science fiction author by being about science fiction authors and their work, albeit in the Soviet Union. It is thus the most recursive of Roberts's fictions.[11]

Cheryl Morgan identifies *Yellow Blue Tibia* as Roberts's 'Philip K. Dick novel' (2009), proposing that several of his novels can be pigeon-holed in this manner as he aims not simply to imitate a given author, but to lampoon them (as, for example, Jules Verne or Jonathan Swift). Morgan suggests Roberts is targeting Dick through the style of novel, particularly the extent to which the narrative becomes saturated in paranoia as it progresses, as well as in an explicit nod of the head through a direct reference to *The Grasshopper Lies Heavy*, the novel-within-the-novel from Dick's *The Man in the High Castle* (1962).[12] A detailed survey of the novel would turn up many more intertextual allusions and references, not least to the works of L. Ron Hubbard who looms in the shadows of the narrative through the far-from-insignificant presence of Scientology.

Where *Yellow Blue Tibia* is particularly interesting, however, is through its use of a very specific form of intertextuality, a form described at length by French literary theorist Gérard Genette as a paratext.[13] On the cover of certain editions, the novel (and it is still clearly labelled as a novel, in a similar manner to *Swiftly*) is described as 'Konstantin Skvorecky's memoir of the alien invasion of 1986/ translated by Adam Roberts'. This joke takes on an at times confusing meta-humour when we consider that Roberts genuinely did translate Verne's *Hector Servadac* alongside *Splinter*. The playfulness is carried through to the cover's reverse upon which the blurb describes the novel in a matter-of-fact tone:

> Konstantin Andreiovich Skvorecky was one of a group of Russian SF writers called together by Josef Stalin in 1946 and tasked with creating a convincing alien threat; a story of imminent disaster that would

> unite the Soviet people. [...] Skvorecky claimed (tastelessly many believe) that the Chernobyl disaster and the destruction of the Challenger space shuttle conformed to the pattern set by Stalin's scenario. Skvorecky moved to America soon afterwards and married a Scientologist. He believes the alien invasion is ongoing. (*YBT*: back cover)

While the influence of any author's artistic input into cover design and blurb-writing is doubtful in the modern commercial age, this does not preclude their inclusion in discussion of the text, as Genette himself asserts:

> ... we do not always know whether these productions are to be regarded as belonging to the text, in any case they surround it and extend it, precisely in order to *present* it, in the usual sense of this verb but also in the strongest sense: *to make present,* to ensure the text's presence in the world, its 'reception' and consumption in the form (nowadays, at least) of a book. (Genette, 1997: 1)

Even should we desire to exclude cover design and blurb content from our analysis, it must be acknowledged that these artistic choices echo a paratext authored by Roberts which purports to be the Wikipedia page on Skvorecky, including affectations which users of the online encyclopaedia would recognize such as '(Redirected from Skvorecki) / Jump to: navigation, search/ This article on a writer is a stub. You can help Wikipedia by expanding it' (*YBT*: 324). While it is artistically and semiotically interesting to mimic the fluid format of a wiki in the static medium of print, what Roberts is actually doing is giving his novel a veneer of reality. Very few readers would be knowledgeable enough about Soviet-era Russian science fiction to immediately rule out the possibility that Skvorecky was not a real author upon whom these events could be based.[14] The use of a faux-Wikipedia article contains an additional jibe from Adam Roberts the educator, highlighting the unreliability of the online encyclopedia despite its favoured status with undergraduate students.

The false memoir is a common method of narrative deconstructionism; a variation of which was used, not insignificantly, by Jonathan Swift, with *Travels into Several Remote Nations of the World* being presented as a genuine document by a real traveller, complete with paratextual information to assert this fact such as an advertisement and prefacing letter between Gulliver and his cousin Sympson (a pseudonym Swift sometimes adopted).[15] The illusion is, after all, sufficient to fool a young Jane Eyre (Brontë, 1847/2001: 17). A slightly more contemporaneous example, and one more fitting to *Yellow Blue Tibia*'s themes of conspiracy, secrecy and paranoia, would be Kurt Vonnegut's *Mother Night* (1961) which claims to be the confessional memoir of American / German (and fictitious) war-criminal and Nazi propagandist Howard W. Campbell Jr. In an 'editor's note', Vonnegut writes that his 'duties as an editor are in no sense polemic. They are simply to pass on, in the most satisfactory style, the confessions of Campbell' (Vonnegut, 1961/2000: xi).

The paratextual trimmings that adorn *Yellow Blue Tibia* parody what Jerome de Groot (2010: 63) refers to as historical novels' obsession with such devices. Since Walter Scott, English language historical novels have used paratexts to create an air of historical authenticity, rooting their novels in 'historical fact' in order to justify their fiction, and meet reader expectations about the plausibility of the narrative. In adopting such methods, *Yellow Blue Tibia* is pushing at literary and genre boundaries. While gently mocking the pretensions of historical fiction, it positions itself to be read in the guise of conspiracy fiction, or a 'secret history', a sub-genre or offshoot of alternate history. Other than hard SF novels, which can contain postscripts explaining the 'real science' behind the fiction, it is unusual for a science fiction novel to present itself in this way.

Within the novel, Skvorecky is one of a group of soviet science fiction authors recruited by Stalin to create a new enemy for the Soviet Union which would rally the nation in the same way as the battle against the Nazis had done in the Second World War, the Americans failing to serve quite the same purpose:

> 'I do not find that America *unites* the people in hostility, the same way the German threat did [...] Besides,' said Stalin with force, 'I give America five years. [...] But it is my duty to ensure that the revolutionary vigour is preserved long into the future. [...] Once the West falls, as it inevitably will, and the whole world embraces Commu-

> nism, where *then* will we find the enemies against which we can unite, against which we can test our collective heroism?' (*YBT*: 8)

Stalin's plan is for the writers to create 'the greatest science fiction story ever told' and craft the mythology of an extraterrestrial menace. While the manner in which Roberts presents this scheme has the air of authenticity, sufficient to lend credence to the idea that *Yellow Blue Tibia* is a secret history novel (at least as much as *Swiftly* is an alternate history one), it also hints at the intertextual.

As Niall Harrison (2010) observes, the plan resembles a variation of the actions performed by Adrian Veidt (aka Ozymandias) – to fool a world on the brink of nuclear war into a climb-down in the face of an external and alien threat – in Alan Moore and David Gibbons's seminal graphic novel *Watchmen* (1986). Indeed, just as the Buran program was the Soviet response to NASA's Space Shuttle, one could imagine a scenario where a Soviet genius is operating in the USSR developing plans similar to Veidt's, plans which could feasibly have resembled the events of *Yellow Blue Tibia*.[16] The metatextual significance of a work of science fiction being the central plot device of a work of science fiction cannot be understated, but Harrison takes it one step further by going on to suggest that Skvorecky is not only the protagonist/narrator, he is in fact Adam Roberts himself. Harrison points out that both are 'overly ironic, irreverent about everything, including [their] fiction' (Harrison, 2010):

> 'One thing I hate in this world and you are fucking *it*. You are an ironist.'
>
> 'An ironist?'
>
> 'Fundamentally, you take nothing seriously. You believe it is all a game. It was the same in your novels; they were never serious. They had no heart.' (*YBT*: 122)

There are further clues to support Harrison's hypothesis in the text, such as Skvorecky mentioning that he has 'rendered several English writers into Russian, Browning amongst them' (Harrison, 2010: 68). Roberts, after all, completed a PhD thesis on Robert Browning and the Classics (Callow Jr., 2013).

In inserting a facsimile of himself into his fiction (albeit an Eastern-bloc imitation of the real thing), Roberts is committing the ultimate extra-textual act. He must have known that those familiar with either his work or his personality, would recognize the similarities between Skvorecky and the author, particularly the version of himself that he presents when reviewing books.[17] In featuring a character of this type, *Yellow Blue Tibia* becomes the snake which eats its own tail; a feedback loop is created whereby Roberts blurs the boundaries between reality and fiction. This occurs in the novel through dream sequences and semi-hallucinatory encounters with 'radiation aliens', but the reader also experiences it through the metafictional and paratextual elements being deployed. Thus, Roberts turns these elements on themselves; he uses them to draw the reader into a closer affinity with Skvorecky and to immerse them in the novel, rather than pulling them out of it as such elements normally do since they draw attention to the artificiality of the system they inhabit. For these reasons *Yellow Blue Tibia* most perfectly encapsulates the double-coding this chapter has identified in Roberts's work and 'works within the very systems it attempts to subvert' (Hutcheon, 1988: 4).

Conclusion

At the time of writing it seems Roberts will continue to write in this style: *Twenty Trillion Leagues Under the Sea* (2014) follows *Splinter* as a Jules Verne 'sequel/update/metatext/doojabs' (Roberts, 2012). And why not? The increasing quality of the novels written in the latter-half of Roberts's career is as much due to him writing in a style and mode which is comfortable for him – an extra-textual mode – as it is about a writer maturing into his craft.

As Roberts has continued to write fiction, so too has he continued to mesh together genres and texts, often resulting in narratives which are more complex and multiplicitous than may initially be apparent, while still retaining a base level of accessibility to the non-academic readers. There is always the risk, inherent in this style, of creating what Paul Kincaid has referred to as 'a *jeu d'esprit*, a showing-off, a game to be played with bits and pieces from the history of SF' (2008), of attracting the same criticism once levelled at T. S. Eliot, Ezra Pound, and others, that their extensive use of allusion creates an inaccessibility that borders on elitism. However, Roberts remains the right side of obfuscation, remains accessible; if there are references which remain obscure then they are normally non-essential elements of the novel, they do not impact on meaning but instead add a richness and a knowing wink for the reader with the tools to find them. At their best, this extra-textual meshing allows the novels to achieve aims which are clearly very dear to Roberts: his novels educate us about the rich history and interconnected nature of genre, specifically SF; simultaneously, they subvert this history and, by extension, the literary criticism founded on these texts, thumbing his nose at the establishment and preconceptions of boundary and style; and they do so in a manner which entertains, which achieves serious aims in a non-serious manner. The irony is that despite Roberts's comments against 'structuralist nonsense' at the opening of this chapter, his novels encourage and indeed reward being lined up with others of their ilk, spotting in-jokes and references. But this should be expected. Roberts is, after all, first and foremost an ironist.

Notes

1 I will be using the convenient, and more familiar, shortened title but the original title is *Travels into Several Remote Nations of the World. In Four Parts. By Lemuel Gulliver, First a Surgeon, and then a Captain of Several Ships.*

2 Although, given the workers' state of forced servitude (unlike the mice), they also have something of Simpkin, the Tailor's put-upon cat, about them. Simpkin is a rare Potter animal that cannot talk except at midnight on Christmas Eve, although he walks on his hind legs, interacts with humans and sometimes wears clothes.

3 While there is humour in this gift, it is thrown into contrast by the absurd image of boats on a faecal sea. It is clearly a moment of genuine sentimentality, the end of both characters' arcs and their emotional and sexual growth. Whether Roberts intends it to be genuinely erotic (after Huxley's

reading of Swift) requires a closer examination of the erotic in Roberts's novels.

4 The Sidewise Award is for Best Long Form Alternate History (uchronia.net/sidewise).

5 Roberts makes the comments about alternate history and *Swiftly* in an interview on the book blog *Dark Wolf's Fantasy Reviews* (see Adascalitei, 2009).

6 For an example of Napoleon using fantastical creatures to change the course of the wars consider his use of dragons in Naomi Novik's *Temeraire* series, for example.

7 Although Bounoparte is closer to the Italian spelling, Buonaparte, which makes some sense given that it was in Italy that he first served as a general.

8 More details can be found on Uchronia.net, the first stop for any alternate history bibliography (Schmunk, n.d.).

9 In many ways Roberts's repeated employment of intertextuality can be read as an attempt to validate, or perhaps ratify, the ideas proposed in his works of criticism such as *The History of Science Fiction* (2005).

10 For a discussion of this intertextuality in *Jack Glass* see Anna McFarlane's 'Breaking the Cycle of the Golden Age: *Jack Glass* and Isaac Asimov's *Foundation* Trilogy' and Paul March-Russell's 'Rule of Law: Reiterating Genre in *Jack Glass*', both in this volume.

11 The *Encyclopedia of Science Fiction* (edited by John Clute) defines examples of recursive SF as those 'which treat real people, and the fictional worlds which occupy their dreams, as sharing equivalent degrees of reality'. However, it also correctly connects this phenomenon with the innately recursive nature of alternate histories and so while *Yellow Blue Tibia* is by far the most recursive of Roberts's works, it is also worth acknowledging the recursive elements of *Swiftly*.

12 In *Yellow Blue Tibia*, SF writer Nikolai Nikolaivitch has translated *The Grasshopper Lies Heavy* from English to Russian, tweaked, and passed it off as his own. He also claims *Dark Penguin* and *The Vulture is Moulting*, fictional works mentioned in Woody Allen's story 'Without Feathers' (1975) and Ayn Rand's *Atlas Shrugged* (1957) respectively. Also mentioned is *L'Homme qui peut vivre dans L'eau* [*The Man Who Could Live Underwater*] which is a real 1909 novel by French pulp author Jean de la Hire (*YBT*: 16).

13 An essential work on the nature of paratexts of all varieties is Gérard Genette, *Paratexts: Thresholds of Interpretation* (1997). To grossly simplify the matter, paratexts are items separate to a narrative but crucial in its transformation into a physical (or indeed digital) text and that can impart their own meanings should we choose to decode them. This includes cover design, titles, chapter headings, font, etc ...

14 He was not, however Roberts's starting point while constructing him could easily have been Czech author Josef Škvorecký, who dabbled in genre writing – albeit detective fiction, rather than science fiction.

15 This is noted by Claude Rawson in his introduction to *Gulliver's Travels* (Swift, 1726/2008: xx).

16 Moore/Gibbons (and likely Roberts too) are themselves playing on the idea expressed in Goldstein's book-within-a-book from George Orwell's *Nineteen Eighty-Four* which illustrates the benefits to a totalitarian regime of having an enemy with whom to be in eternal conflict.

17 For an interesting example of Roberts's reviewing style see 'We're Reading *Ender's Game and Philosophy,* edited by Kevin S. Decker' (Roberts, 2013). Alternatively, a large number of reviews (including the reviews of Robert Jordan's *Wheel of Time* series which were nominated for the 2010 BSFA Award for Best Non-Fiction) are now included in *Sibilant Fricative* (Roberts, 2014).

Works Cited

Adascalitei, Mihai (2009) 'Interview – Adam Roberts', *Dark Wolf Fantasy Reviews,* 22 June, URL (consulted September 2014): http://darkwolfs-fantasyreviews.blogspot.co.uk/2009/06/interview-adam-roberts.html

Bidisha, (2008) 'Steampunk Shenanigans in Victorian London', *Independent,* 27 July.

Birch, Dinah (ed.) (2009) *The Oxford Companion to English Literature.* Oxford: Oxford University Press.

Brontë, Charlotte (1847/2001) *Jane Eyre.* London: Norton Critical Editions.

Callow, Christos, Jr. (2013) 'Irony Man: An Interview with Adam Roberts', *Strange Horizons,* 25 March, URL (consulted September 2014): http://www.strangehorizons.com/2013/20130325/2roberts-a.shtml

Carr, E.H. (1968) *What is History?* Middlesex: Penguin.

Clute, John (ed.) (2014) *The Encyclopedia of Science Fiction,* URL (consulted September 2014): http://www.sf-encyclopedia.com

De Groot, Jerome (2010) *The Historical Novel*. Abingdon: Routledge.

Frontain, Raymond-Jean (1992) 'Scatology in the Sophomore Survey; or Teaching Swift as a Christian Swift' in Peter J. Schakel (ed.) *Critical Approaches to Teaching Swift*, pp. 297–305. New York: AMS Press.

Genette, Gérard (1997) *Paratexts: Thresholds of Interpretation*, trans., Jane E. Lewin. Cambridge: Cambridge University Press.

Gevers, Nick (2008) '*Swiftly*', *sfsite*, URL (consulted September 2014): http://www.sfsite.com/03b/sw268.htm

Harrison, Niall, Dan Hartland, Victoria Hoyle and Paul Kincaid (2008) 'A Discussion About *Swiftly*', *Torque Control* , 4 July, URL (consulted September 2014): http://vectoreditors.wordpress.com/2008/07/04/a-discussion-about-swiftly/

Harrison, Niall (2010) '*Yellow Blue Tibia*', *Torque Control*, 6 January, URL (consulted September 2014): http://vectoreditors.wordpress.com/2010/01/06/yellow-blue-tibia/

Hutcheon, Linda (1988) *A Poetics of Postmodernism: History, Theory, Fiction*. London: Routledge.

Huxley, Aldous (1929) *Do What You Will: Essays*. Chatto and Windus: London.

Hyman, Anthony (1982) *Charles Babbage: Pioneer of the Computer*. Princeton, NJ: Princeton University Press.

Moore, Alan (1987) *Watchmen*, illus. Dave Gibbons. New York: DC Comics.

Morgan, Cheryl (2009) '*Yellow Blue Tibia*', *Cheryl's Mewsings*, URL (consulted September 2014): http://www.cheryl-morgan.com/?page_id=5706

Potter, Beatrix (1987) *The Tailor of Gloucester*. London: Frederick Warne.

Roberts, Adam (2010) 'Hazard Adams, The Offense of Poetry (2007)', *Punkadiddle*, 2 January, URL (consulted September 2014): http://punkadiddle.blogspot.co.uk/2009/12/hazard-adams-offence-of-poetry-2007.html

Roberts, Adam (2012) '*20 Trillion Leagues Under the Sea*: Cover', *AdamRoberts.com*, 6 December, URL (consulted September 2014): http://www.adamroberts.com/2012/12/06/20-trillion-leagues-under-the-sea-cover/

Roberts, Adam (2013) 'We're Reading *Ender's Game and Philosophy*, edited by Kevin S. Decker', *Arcfinity*, URL (consulted September 2014): http://arcfinity.tumblr.com/post/66768002575/were-reading-enders-game-and-philosophy-edited-by

Roberts, Adam (2014) *Sibilant Fricative: Essays and Reviews* . Steel Quill Books.

Schmunk, Robert B. (n.d.) *Uchronia: The Alternate History List,* URL (consulted September 2014): http://www.uchronia.net/

Swift, Jonathan (1726/2008) *Gulliver's Travels.* Oxford: Oxford University Press.

Vonnegut, Kurt (1961/2000) *Mother Night.* London: Vintage.

Rule of Law
Reiterating Genre in *Jack Glass*

Paul March-Russell

During the past fifteen years – the period in which Adam Roberts has been a professional novelist – generic approaches to the understanding of science fiction have been rigorously challenged. In 2000, Roger Luckhurst summarized the rival definitions of Samuel R. Delany and Darko Suvin as such:

> So, for Suvin, 'it should be made clear that the sf universe of discourse ... presents possible worlds ... as totalising and thematic metaphors', whilst for Delany the focus is on 'the most basic level of sentence meaning [where] we read words differently when we read them as science fiction'. Suvin, in other words, isolates the specificity of science fiction in the rigour of its cognitive leap between levels (metaphor), whereas Delany insists that the conjunctions and disjunctions of science fiction be located as 'a specific way of reading', an abuse of 'particular syntactical rules' in the science fictional sentence (metonymy). (Luckhurst, 2000: 70)

In his own criticism, Roberts sides more closely with Suvin than Delany through a reassertion of SF as metaphor derived from a reading of Paul Ricoeur (*SF*: 143–6). Despite its influence upon SF criticism, Suvin's notion of cognitive estrangement is also severely contested. Although Carl Freedman has attempted to loosen Suvin's strictures on scientific understanding via reference to a 'cognition effect' (Freedman, 2000: 18), Suvin's account of science and science fiction is nonetheless ideological rather than historical: 'a novum is fake unless it in some way participates in and partakes of what Bloch called "the front-line of historical process"' (Suvin, 1979: 81–2). As has been observed, Suvin discards the eschatological elements from Ernst Bloch's description of the novum (Csicsery-Ronay, 2008: 49–52) so that it becomes an instrument of rational understanding 'validated by the post-Cartesian and post-Baconian scientific method' (Suvin, 1979: 64–5). By contrast, an SF story that acknowledges a metaphysical entity is no longer SF but 'committing creative suicide' (Suvin, 1979: 8). In Roberts's *Jack Glass* (2012) however, although the plot hinges upon the impossibility of breaking the universal constant at which light travels, one of the notable features is the presence of religion and of religious practice, even among the otherwise rational Argent sisters: 'After supper they prayed together, and kissed, and then they went to their separate bedrooms' (*JG*: 145). This narrative element may be symptomatic of Roberts's view that SF 'was directly the product of a specifically doctrinal-religious cultural upheaval, known to us today as "the Reformation"' (Roberts, 2012: 115). Certainly, it marks a departure from Suvin's attempt to originate SF within the utopian and satirical traditions of Lucian, Thomas More and Cyrano de Bergerac, an approach that mirrors previous exercises in grounding the genre's prehistory within canonical literature (James, 2000: 31).

More wholesale critiques of Suvin, or indeed of any premeditated attempt to define SF, have come in various guises. Following Gwyneth Jones, China Miéville has argued that the cognition effect, 'a term which grows more sinister the more the phenomenon is critically interrogated' (Miéville, 2009: 239), should be regarded as a rhetorical strategy: 'SF relies above all not on the language of science, nor on the command of that language, but on the *appearance* of that command' (Miéville, 2009: 238). Paul Kincaid, disputing the genealogical approach that underwrites any history of a given genre, borrows Ludwig Wittgenstein's notion of family resemblances to argue that SF is 'a restless, dynamic form that might head out in multiple different directions from multiple different origins, and yet still be something that we can talk about sensibly under the one heading' (Kincaid, 2003: 415). John Rieder builds upon Kincaid's description of SF 'as a network of such family resemblances' in which narrative tropes 'are braided together in an endless variety of combinations' (Kincaid, 2003: 416–7) to constitute SF within 'a system of genres' that is constantly fluctuating over time according to the changing conditions of the marketplace and readerly expectation (Rieder, 2008: 18). These non-foundational approaches to genre definition have coincided with Gary Wolfe's popularization of what he terms 'evaporating genres':

> Because of the uncertainty of these genre markers, the fantastic genres contain within themselves the seeds of their own dissolution, a nascent set of postmodern rhetorical modes that, over a period of several decades, would begin to supplant not only the notion of genre itself, but the very foundations of the modernist barricades that had long been thought to insulate literary culture from the vernacular fiction of the pulps and other forms of non-canonical expression. (Wolfe, 2011)

As already indicated, Roberts is a participant within these critical debates and his fiction can be read as both commenting upon and contributing to the fuzziness of generic boundaries and the cross-fertilization of genres. In *Jack Glass*, the accentuation of the reader's role foregrounds detective fiction's traditional reliance upon an unspoken pact between writer and reader. The moral and ethical stake invested-in by the detective genre, but often glossed-over by SF stories that are no more than exercises in problem-solving (Tom Godwin's 'The Cold Equations' [1954] is a notorious example), removes Roberts's fiction from the formal discourse in which debates of genre have been conducted. As this chapter argues, Roberts's framing of the detective genre within the SF context of *Jack Glass* works by a process of disavowal – a concept developed from Karl Marx via Sigmund Freud to Jacques Derrida – that is also integral to the doubled nature of the detective genre and in its relationship to its generic twin, science fiction. Such formulations do not explain away Roberts's practice; instead, by revealing its duplicities, Roberts not only affirms the dialectical tensions – and hence vitality – within genre but also indicates the *a priori* of such contradictions.

In the acknowledgements to *Jack Glass*, variously subtitled 'The Story of a Murderer' and 'A Golden Age Story', Roberts writes that the novel's 'impulse ... was a desire to collide together some of the conventions of "Golden Age" science fiction and "Golden Age" detective fiction, with the emphasis more on the latter than the former' (*JG*: 372). As Mike Ashley and Peter Nicholls acknowledge in *The Encyclopedia of Science Fiction* in their entry on the 'Golden Age of SF', Golden Age SF is primarily an invention of contemporaneous fans whose starting-point can be dated to John W. Campbell's ascent to the editorship of *Astounding* in October 1937. Its end-date, sometime in 1946, is harder to establish since, as Ashley and Nicholls note, it 'may have had more reality ... for devotees of *Astounding* than for SF readers in general.' Although later periods within the SF genre could justifiably be called Golden Ages, and non-Anglophone cultures and other media would have their own golden epochs, Ashley and Nicholls concede that 'for older readers ... there has been nothing since then to give quite the same adrenaline charge'. By contrast, as Stephen Knight observes, the Golden Age in detective fiction was primarily the invention of critics, first applied in 1942 to the period 1918 to 1930, subsequently antedated to 1913 (the year that E. C. Bentley published *Trent's Last Case*), but more usually attributed to the crime writing of the inter-war period. Knight side-steps these problems of periodization by drawing attention to the 'coherent set of practices which were shared, to a greater or lesser extent, by most of the writers then at work': 'a genre of crime fiction, best named for its central mechanism as the clue-puzzle ... clearly forms a recognisable entity by the mid-1920s' (Knight, 2003: 77). In the parlance of SF critics such as Damien Broderick, it would be possible to refer to Golden Age detective fiction as a 'mega-text'; Susan Rowland points to the high degree of self-referentiality within the writing of the period (Rowland, 2010: 118–20). Key practitioners of the clue-puzzle formula included the writers that Roberts cites as influences upon *Jack Glass*: Margery Allingham, Michael Innes, Ngaio Marsh and Dorothy L. Sayers.

Yet, as Knight also states: 'The date of the clue-puzzle must raise the question to what extent it is a version of modernism.' He argues 'that the plain flat style ..., the formal concerns [celebrated by such critics as Jacques Barzun, George Grella and Tzvetan Todorov], the anonymity of the authorial voice ... and especially the way in which the texts continuously expose identity to be a constructed illusion, are all aspects of modernism' (Knight, 2003: 90). It is in these terms that Alison Light reads the work of Agatha Christie as a type of popular modernism: 'a literature of convalescence' that 'set its face firmly to the future' and that addressed 'all those who identified with a younger generation stifled first by their elders and then silenced by the tragedies' of World War One (Light, 1991: 69). For Brian McHale (building upon the earlier work of William V. Spanos), the cool detachment towards violence and the unemotional attachment towards the mechanics of puzzle-setting associate Golden Age detective fiction with the epistemological concerns of modernism: each 'revolve around problems of the accessibility and circulation of knowledge, the individual mind's grappling with an elusive or occluded reality' (McHale, 1992: 147). In what is now a critical commonplace, McHale regards postmodern, anti-detective fictions such as Paul 's *New York Trilogy* (1985–7), Jorge Luis Borges's 'Death and the Compass' (1942), Italo Calvino's *If on a winter's night, a traveller* (1977), Umberto Eco's *The Name of the Rose* (1983) and Thomas Pynchon's *The Crying of Lot 49* (1967) as exposing the methodological limits of epistemology (McHale, 1992: 150–1). Patricia Merivale outlines the difference, albeit rather too neatly, by quoting G. K. Chesterton's *Father Brown*: 'What we all dread most ... is a maze with *no* centre' (Merivale, 2010: 309). By contrast, postmodernists such as Borges rejoice 'in the centerlessness of the maze, or its paradoxically empty center, or its center with something "wrong" in it' (Merivale, 2010: 309).

For McHale, the pragmatic acceptance to be found within anti-detective fiction of epistemological uncertainty is prefigured by science fiction which 'is openly and avowedly ontological in its orientation' (McHale, 1992: 12). Elana Gomel appropriates this claim to argue that there exists a sub-genre of SF – Christopher Priest's *Inverted World* (1974) is her exemplum – in which the protagonist turns detective in order to make sense not of a mystery within his/her world but the mystery that *is* the world: physical laws of nature that do not correspond with what is empirically known and which would otherwise appear to be impossible. According to Gomel, in coming to terms with the true nature of his/her reality, the protagonist experiences not pragmatic acceptance but divine revelation that radically alters the world (Gomel, 1995: 343–56). In other words, although such fictions commence as ontological quests, they reassert – in contradistinction to McHale's position on SF – an epistemological concern: it is the will to knowledge that fundamentally affects the protagonist's condition of being. By contrast, the ambiguous ending of Roberts's second novel, *On* (2001), a text that would seem – at the very least – to have surface similarities with not only Priest's work but also such philosophical puzzles as Edwin A. Abbott's *Flatland* (1884), contests Gomel's revelatory narrative and appears to reinforce the emphasis upon ontology to be found in McHale.

Consequently, in turning to *Jack Glass*, the reader might expect Roberts to reproduce the postmodern, anti-detective novel favoured by McHale and others. Although the novel prioritizes the conventions of Golden Age detective fiction, it nevertheless refracts the narrative tropes of 'a prison story', 'a regular whodunit' and 'a locked-room mystery' (*JG*: 1) through the prism of science fiction, so that the reader might expect a critique of the epistemological precepts upon which those conventions are founded. In practice, though, something far more interesting occurs. As the narrator declares at the outset, the novel is written so as 'to play fair' with the reader in keeping with one of the cardinal rules of classic detective fiction – although, in practice, the rule was either broken or evaded in the years after its formal statement in 1928 (Horsley, 2005: 40–1). Furthermore, 'playing fair' is not only a cerebral pastime, it is also embedded within moral codes of personal and social responsibility that permit Golden Age detective fiction to be read in its historical and cultural contexts (Rowland, 2010: 119–20). Part of the irony, then, of *Jack Glass* is not that its epistemological assumptions are found to be wanting in themselves but that the nostalgia, through which such assumptions are presented, reflects critically upon the novel's milieu. For, it is the futuristic, dynastic setting – familiar from Golden Age science fiction – which is revealed to be lacking in terms of moral conduct. 'Playing fair', then, is not just an intellectual game between writer and reader in *Jack Glass*: it constitutes an ethical standard by which the dispensation of the Lex Ulanova, the law of the ruling oligarchy, can be judged.

To say 'judged' emphasizes the legal – as well as the moral – background against which Golden Age detective fiction was written. Throughout the inter-war period, and up until 1965, the sentence for murder in the UK was death by hanging. In Dorothy L. Sayers's *Strong Poison* (1930), for example, Lord Peter Wimsey fights to save the murder suspect (and his future wife), Harriet Vane, from execution. Judgement, then, in the Golden Age detective novel cannot be substituted for a postmodern emphasis upon gaming or *le différend*, in which the act of judgement is indefinitely suspended. The revelation of the murderer in Golden Age novels would always, in the real world, have automatic consequences. Despite their cerebral content, the novels are often underscored by a brutal and dispassionate justice. In the last of the Miss Marple mysteries, for example, Christie's seemingly innocent detective is explicitly compared with the classical deity of moral revenge:

> 'What do you think of her, Edmund?'
>
> 'The most frightening woman I ever met,' said the Home Secretary.
>
> 'Ruthless?' asked Professor Wanstead.
>
> 'No, no, I don't mean that but – well, a very frightening woman.'
>
> 'Nemesis,' said Professor Wanstead thoughtfully. (Christie, 1974: 216)

Equally, in *Jack Glass*, judgement is not a matter of play: the imminent prospect of death is registered from the outset so that the reader, too, is constantly reminded that their act of judgement – of reading right

– is implicated in the mystery which, as Jack repeats, is played at high stakes.

The amateur detective, Diana Argent, is the figure upon which the novel's moral argument turns. A past master of virtual-reality murder mysteries, she regards the killing of her servant, Leron, as a continuation of the fictional and historical crimes that she has solved. As she explains to the professional detectives, 'An invented whodunit has the same relation to real life as a chess puzzle has to an actual game of chess' (*JG*: 113), the allusion echoing the analogy given in Edgar Allan Poe's 'Murders in the Rue Morgue' (1841): 'To observe attentively is to remember distinctly; and, so far, the concentrative chess-player will do very well at whist ... But it is in matters beyond the limits of mere rule that the skill of the analyst is evinced' (Poe, 2003: 143). Disappointed by the sight of Leron's corpse, for it lacks 'buzz, more startlement, more *thrill*' (*JG*: 107), so Diana is also bored by the mechanics of investigating the crime scene and interviewing the suspects. When Jack (disguised as Iago) reminds Diana's sister that Leron constituted 'A fully grown human being ... With all the emotional and intellectual and practical capacity that entails' (*JG*: 195), Roberts is recapitulating a moment familiar from Golden Age crime fiction, for example in Sayers's *Whose Body?* (1923), when the amateur detective is upbraided for treating the mystery only as a game; for not in other words 'playing fair':

> You want to hunt down a murderer for the sport of the thing and then shake hands with him and say, 'Well played – hard luck – you shall have your revenge tomorrow!' ... You want to be a sportsman. You can't be a sportsman. You're a responsible person. (Sayers, 1963: 123–4)

The sometimes direct or garbled citation of Golden Age detectives (Christie's Poirot becomes a verb: 'They would be *properly* Poirot'd' [*JG*: 159]) reiterates the clue-puzzle's self-knowing references to other crime fictions. This is a tendency that can be traced back to Sherlock Holmes's comparison with Poe's Auguste Dupin in *A Study in Scarlet* (1887): 'He had some analytical genius, no doubt; but he was by no means such a phenomenon as Poe appeared to imagine'

(Doyle, 2009: 24). Diana's portrayals of herself as Holmes, her tutor as Watson, and her sister as Mycroft, are self-consciously deliberate comparisons on Roberts's part. Equally, Diana's lecture to the professional police on the differences between fictional and real-life crime recalls similar meta-commentaries, for example Dr Gideon Fell's lecture on the locked-room mystery in John Dickson Carr's *The Hollow Man* (1935), while the comparatively mild uses of metafiction ('Only an idiot would think that this sordid crime constituted the first of what a crime narrator might call "The FTL Murders"' [*JG*: 129]) pale in comparison to Dickson Carr's deconstruction of character:

> 'I will now lecture,' said Dr Fell, inexorably, 'on the general mechanics and development of the situation which is known in detective fiction as the "hermetically sealed chamber." Harrumph. All those opposing can skip this chapter. Harrumph. To begin with, gentlemen! Having been improving my mind with sensational fiction for the last forty years, I can say – '
>
> 'But, if you're going to analyse impossible situations,' interrupted Pettis, 'why discuss detective fiction?'
>
> 'Because,' said the doctor, frankly, 'we're in a detective story, and we don't fool the reader by pretending we're not. Let's not invent elaborate excuses to drag in a discussion of detective stories. Let's candidly glory in the noblest pursuits possible to characters in a book.' (Dickson Carr, 2002: 152)

Ironically, in this instance, it is Dickson Carr who appears to be a more postmodern author than Roberts. Instead, for the most part, Roberts is recapitulating tendencies towards self-referentiality and meta-criticism that were already present within Golden Age detective fiction. His comparative restraint, in sharp contrast to the overt playfulness that occurs in other novels, let alone the self-declared parodies, foregrounds the political commentary of *Jack Glass*. Whilst interrogation techniques such as 'vacuumboarding' clearly echo the US government's real-world condoning of torture, Jack's deliberate setting-up of Sapho to kill Leron is designed to shock Diana out of her emotional disaffection:

> You *wanted* me ... to be angry. You wanted me to feel used, to be outraged at the disposal of a live human being into such a game. You wanted me to feel *that*, so I would confront this fact of power. That to rule means to treat people in that way. (*JG*: 242)

Crucially, although to an extent Roberts is here reiterating the charge levelled in Golden Age crime fiction against the amateur detective to play fair, he is also going much further than the moral humanism of, for example, Sayers. Jack's entrapment of Diana forces her not only into moral but also political recognition. Her epiphany echoes Gomel's model of revelation within the ontological mystery story, but Diana's insight is not divine and what she perceives is not the bending of physical laws – throughout the novel, Roberts consistently states that faster-than-light travel is impossible – but the corruption of political, social and economic structures. Although a Marxist interpretation can be performed upon Golden Age detective fiction, for instance in reading the genre against the grain of bourgeois ideology (Mandel, 1988: 209–19), Roberts consciously yokes its conventions to a political critique by refusing to allow either his protagonists or his readers to be distracted by the formal and ideological constraints of the genre.

In this respect, the paradoxical figure of Jack Glass, 'detective, teacher, protector and murderer' (*JG*: 1), is more than the eponymous hero: he is integral to the shape of the novel. As both pursuer and pursuant, he contradicts another of Ronald Knox's cardinal – albeit parodic – rules that 'The detective must not himself commit the crime' (Knox, 1988: 201). The declaration that 'in each case the murderer is ... Jack Glass himself' (*JG*: 1–2) only counters Merivale's description of the metaphysical tendency within postmodern detective fiction, by substituting the question of 'why' for 'how'. However, it also complements post-war detective novels, such as Ruth Rendell's *A Judgement in Stone* (1977), which similarly negotiate the legacy of Golden Age authors like Christie and Sayers by betraying the solution at the outset; in Rendell's case, in the opening sentence: 'Eunice Parchman killed the Coverdale family because she could not read or write' (Rendell, 1978: 1). At one point, the servant D'Arch refers to

Jack as 'the father of lawlessness': he breeds not only criminal activity but also symbolizes a mode of thinking that supplements the Lex Ulanova. When Diana expresses the 'reasonable' proposition that if Jack 'can kill anybody in the system ... why doesn't he just kill the Ulanovs', D'Arch's mental response, 'just putting the words together like that was probably a legally actionable thing' (*JG*: 171), suggests her shock does not stem from her chemically-induced obedience but from her internalization of the law embodied by the Ulanovs. Jack's criminality does not represent mere anarchy but rather an alternate symbolic code. As Jack concedes, however, to describe his abilities as 'skills' is 'tendentious': 'I'd say a skill ought to be something constructive' (*JG*: 232). Furthermore, as both John Clute and Dan Hartland indicate in their reviews of the novel, Jack's personal code supplements the ruling law but does not subvert it. For Jack, 'killing is enclosure' (*JG*: 248): a case of maintaining order in which murder is a matter of expediency rather than pleasure. As his nemesis, Ms Joad, observes: 'when he murders, now, it is only for a *very* good reason' (*JG*: 137).

Although both Clute and Hartland view Jack as an unredemptive shepherd-figure, in sharp contrast to Alan Moore's sacrificial hero of *V for Vendetta* (1990), he is ultimately redeemed by both Diana's blessing and Sapho's faithfulness. The latter outgrows her role as 'doctor-watson' documenter at the start of the narrative (*JG*: 1): she is instead a witness and interpreter, an acolyte. Her adherence to Jack bolsters both his pathos and Romantic characterization. Divorced of origins and identity ('The whole concept of real names ... isn't a terribly coherent one, I think' [*JG*: 231]), he is variously the solitary wanderer, the unacknowledged legislator and the demiurge who can make 'the impossible happen' (*JG*: 137). As W. H. Auden comments:

> Murder is negative creation, and every murderer is therefore the rebel who claims the right to be omnipotent. His pathos is his refusal to suffer. The problem for the writer is to conceal his demonic pride. (Auden, 1988: 19)

Roberts veils Jack's pride by making him largely non-descript in the first section, portraying him as reticent in the second (he is compared at one point to P. G. Wodehouse's Jeeves), and then endowing him with a gravitas that shades his less desirable views: 'human beings, who breathe and feel and hope as we do, are a resource we exploit' (*JG*: 242). But Auden's comments have their basis in Thomas De Quincey's essays on murder, in particular, 'On the Knocking at the Gate in Macbeth' (1823) and 'On Murder Considered as One of the Fine Arts' (1827). Here, as Robert Morrison suggests, De Quincey elevates the serial murderer, John Williams, to the level of an artist 'for both are interested in pleasure and power': 'both seek freedom by outstripping or subverting the social institutions they feel thwart or confine them' (Morrison, 2006: xi). Although Roberts's use of the frame-narration distances himself from Jack, his narrative hold over the reader depends largely upon the characterization as well as the mechanics of how each crime can be solved and their function within the larger political context. Consequently, the novel retains the vicarious thrill sensed by Diana ('she was the investigator! She could ask anything no matter how outrageous!' [*JG*: 173]), yet which was already a constituent part of such early detective novels as Wilkie Collins's *The Moonstone* (1868), and the contagious 'detective-fever' (Collins, 1999: 117) that spreads throughout the manor-house.

For, though Jack can be read as the Romantic murderer-artist, he can also be read as the world-weary detective who, having spent too much time close to death, has a blurred sense of morality:

> '... Death is *flow*. It is the necessary lubrication of universal motion. It is, in itself, neither praiseworthy nor blameworthy.'
>
> 'Death is always individual, though,' she objected, in a low voice. 'To the person dying.'
>
> 'You're right,' he agreed. (*JG*: 337)

The need, though, to view death both at the level of the microcosmic and the macrocosmic, the personal and the impersonal, echoes the convoluted dialectical thinking that preoccupies Collins's amateur detective and intellectual dilettante, Franklin Blake:

> Arguing in this way, from within-outwards, what do we reach? We reach the Subjective view. I defy you to controvert the Subjective

> view. Very well then – what follows? Good Heavens! The Objective-Subjective explanation follows, of course! (Collins, 1999: 163)

The 'bewildering manner' of Blake's discourse (Collins, 1999: 70) is attributed by the faithful steward, Betteredge, to 'his French side, and his German side, and his Italian side' (Collins, 1999: 47); the mixture of foreign influences acting as a contaminant: 'Here (God bless it!) was the original English foundation of him showing through all the foreign varnish at last!' (Collins, 1999: 48).

The infectious quality of detecting crime, and of how the detective can inoculate him/herself against its effects, is present in the figure of Sergeant Cuff: 'I am one of the many people in this miserable world who can't earn their money honestly and easily at the same time' (Collins, 1999: 134). It recurs in Golden Age novels such as Sayers's *Gaudy Night* (1935):

> 'Peter – I feel exactly like Judas.'
>
> 'Feeling like Judas is part of the job. No job for a gentleman, I'm afraid. Shall we wash our hands like Pilate and be thoroughly respectable?'
>
> She slid her hand under his arm.
>
> 'No; we're in for it now. We'll be degraded together.' (Sayers, 1970: 319)

The theme of moral contagion, so common throughout the detective genre, echoes what Derrida terms 'the law of the law of genre': 'a principle of contamination, a law of impurity, a parasitical economy.' Genre is riddled with its own disaffection, 'a sort of participation without belonging' (Derrida, 1992: 227), which is embodied by what Derrida calls the 're-mark' that both supplements and encodes the literary genre:

> Every text *participates* in one or several genres, there is no genreless text, there is always a genre and genres, yet such participation never amounts to belonging ... In marking itself generically, a text unmarks itself [*se démarque*]. If remarks of belonging belong without belonging, participate without belonging, then *genre-descriptions cannot be simply part of the corpus*. (Derrida, 1992: 230)

Derrida's argument turns upon the principle of disavowal introduced previously in *Glas* (1974) and borrowed from Freud's essay, 'Fetishism' (1927). Freud's usage, though, is prefigured by the operation that disavowal performs within the mechanism of commodity fetishism as described by Marx:

> The commodity-form, and the value-relation of the products of labour within which it appears, have absolutely no connection with the physical nature of the commodity and the material [*dinglich*] relations arising out of this. It is nothing but the definite social relation between men themselves which assumes here, for them, the fantastic form of a relation between things. (Marx, 1976: 165)

For Georg Lukács and the subsequent Frankfurt School, the fetish magically ascribed to the commodity reifies the material basis to its construction, effectively substituting the part for the whole. Freud appropriates this principle of substitution as the mechanism of sexual fetishism, a process that he identifies as the inability of the boy-child to acknowledge the mother's lack of a penis since such acknowledgement would precipitate fears that he too might be castrated. On the one hand, 'he has retained that belief' but, on the other hand, 'he has also given it up': 'the vicissitude of the idea' is best summed-up for Freud by the German word, *Verleugnung* ('disavowal'). The fetishist resolves his dilemma by unconsciously selecting a substitute – a shoe, for example – that stands-in for both the lost object and the horror of its castrated other, the female genitalia. He clings to the substitute as his defence against 'the threat of castration' (Freud, 1977: 353) and the repression of heterosexual desire.

Derrida, too, adopts the principle of substitution for his understanding of fetishism: 'Despite all the variations to which it can be submitted, the concept fetish includes an invariant predicate: it is a substitute – for the thing itself as centre and source of being' (Derrida, 1986: 209). In a characteristic gesture, however, Derrida regards the fetish as deconstructive of the category of truth: 'the fetish is opposed to the presence of the thing itself, to truth, signified truth for which the fetish is a substitutive signifier ... truth of a "privileged" transcendental, fundamental, central signifier, signifier of signifiers, no longer belonging to the series' (209). Disavowal, then, is what underlies not only the act of fetishism but also signification: between saying that the object is the same as its meaning (and acting in the world) and saying that it is different from its meaning (and reflecting upon the world). Such equivocation, however, potentially undermines the structuralist correspondence between signifier and signified. Julia Kristeva describes this crisis of meaning like so:

> But is not exactly language our ultimate and inseparable fetish? And language, precisely, is based on fetishist denial ('I know that, but just the same', 'the sign is not the thing, but just the same', etc.) and defines us in our essence as speaking beings. Because of its founding status, the fetishism of 'language' is perhaps the only one that is unanalyzable. (Kristeva, 1982: 37)

Yet, despite its abysmal status, the subject cleaves to language as in accordance with Jacques Lacan's proposition of the mirror stage (Lacan, 1977: 1–7). Derrida recognizes the logic of the situation when he writes: 'As soon as the thing itself, in its unveiled truth, is already found engaged, by the very unveiling, in the play of supplementary difference, the fetish no longer has any rigorously decidable status' (Derrida, 1986: 226). Disavowal becomes the rock that not only supports the classification of genre but upon which such taxonomy also founders.

Roberts embodies this principle in the figure of the lawless Jack Glass: his supplementary code not only shadows the Lex Ulanova, it also unfixes – without unseating – the genre of the novel that bears his name, a nomenclature which, as has been established, disguises a lack of identity. Yet, to read Roberts's novel exclusively as a deconstructive exercise in the categorization of genres would be too neat. In the essay, 'The Law of Genre' (1980), Derrida's source-text is an avant-garde fiction by Maurice Blanchot; he does not consider the possibility of extending his critique to popular fiction. Yet, as has been argued, such self-reflexivity was endemic to the detective genre and, via Poe, in its parallel development with the history of SF. As Laura Marcus notes, postmodern critics have tended to homogenize classic detective fiction so as to advance their own version of the anti-detective novel (Marcus, 2003: 249–53). Even Merivale's notion of the metaphysical detective story, although acknowledging Umberto Eco's claim that 'every period has its own postmodernism' (Eco, 1985: 66), remains troubled by periodization since her account of the decentred maze could describe an early modernist text, such as Joseph Conrad's *Heart of Darkness* (1899), as much as it does Borges.

Instead of the pathos ascribed to the postmodern sublime of Borges and his successors, Roberts asserts the vitality of genre fiction in the same moment as expressing the paradoxical condition of working within – and between – genres. For Roberts, it is even a lived contradiction. Like his predecessor, Michael Innes, the pseudonym of the noted Conradian scholar, J. I. M. Stewart, Roberts resides as both Professor of Nineteenth Century Literature at Royal Holloway College, London and as an increasingly feted author of science fiction. But not, so far, of detective fiction. Yet, what differentiates *Jack Glass* from Lauren Beukes's tale of a time-travelling serial killer, *The Shining Girls* (2013), short-listed for the Crime Writer's Association's Goldsboro Gold Dagger Award? Do genre markers really lie in the fuzzy gaze of the beholder... ?

Works Cited

Ashley, Mike and Peter Nicholls (2012) 'Golden Age of SF', in John Clute and David Langford (eds) *The Encyclopedia of Science Fiction*, URL (consulted March 2013): http://www.sf-encyclopedia.com/entry/golden_age_of_sf

Auden, W. H. (1988) 'The Guilty Vicarage', in R. W. Winks (ed.) *Detective Fiction: A Collection of Critical Essays*, pp. 15–24. Woodstock VT: Foul Play Press.

Christie, Agatha (1974) *Nemesis*. London: Fontana.

Clute, John (2012) 'Scores', *Strange Horizons*, URL (consulted April 2013): http://www.strangehorizons.com/2012/20120730/clute-c.shtml

Collins, Wilkie (1999) *The Moonstone*. Ware: Wordsworth.

Csicsery-Ronay, Istvan (2008) *The Seven Beauties of Science Fiction*. Middletown, CT: Wesleyan University Press.

Derrida, Jacques (1986) *Glas*. Lincoln: University of Nebraska Press.

Derrida, Jacques (1992) *Acts of Literature*. New York and London: Routledge.

Dickson Carr, John (2002) *The Hollow Man*. London: Orion.

Doyle, Arthur Conan (2009) *The Complete Sherlock Holmes*. 2nd edn. London: Penguin.

Eco, Umberto (1985) *Reflections on the Name of the Rose*. London: Secker & Warburg.

Freedman, Carl (2000) *Critical Theory and Science Fiction*. Middletown, CT: Wesleyan University Press.

Freud, Sigmund (1977) *On Sexuality*. Harmondsworth: Penguin.

Gomel, Elana (1995) 'Mystery, Apocalypse and Utopia: The Case of the Ontological Detective Story', *Science Fiction Studies* 22(3): 343–56.

Hartland, Dan (2012) '"Death is the currency of power": Adam Roberts' *Jack Glass*', 17 August, URL (consulted April 2013): http://thestoryandthetruth.wordpress.com/2012/08/17/death-is-the-currency-of-power-adam-robertss-jack-glass/

Horsley, Lee (2005) *Twentieth Century Crime Fiction*. Oxford: Oxford University Press.

James, Edward (2000) 'Before the Novum: The Prehistory of Science Fiction Criticism', in Patrick Parrinder (ed.) *Learning from Other Worlds: Estrangement, Cognition and the Politics of Science Fiction and Utopia*, pp. 19–35. Liverpool: Liverpool University Press.

Kincaid, Paul (2003) 'On the Origins of Genre.' *Extrapolation* 44(4): 409–19.

Knight, Stephen (2003) 'The Golden Age', in Martin Priestman (ed.) *The Cambridge Companion to Crime Fiction*, pp. 77–94. Cambridge: Cambridge University Press.

Knox, Ronald A. (1988) 'A Detective Story Decalogue,' in Robin W. Winks (ed.) *Detective Fiction: A Collection of Critical Essays*, pp. 200–2. Woodstock, VT: Foul Play Press.

Kristeva, Julia (1982) *Powers of Horror: An Essay on Abjection*. New York: Columbia University Press.

Lacan, Jacques (1977) *Écrits: A Selection*. London: Tavistock.

Light, Alison (1991) *Forever England: Femininity, Literature and Conservatism Between the Wars*. London: Routledge.

Luckhurst, Roger (2000) 'Vicissitudes of the Voice, Speaking Science Fiction', in Andy Sawyer and David Seed (eds) *Speaking Science Fiction*, pp. 69–81. Liverpool: Liverpool University Press.

McHale, Brian (1992) *Constructing Postmodernism*. London: Routledge.

Mandel, Ernest (1988) 'A Marxist Interpretation of the Crime Story', in Robin W. Winks (ed.) *Detective Fiction: A Collection of Critical Essays*, pp. 209–19. Woodstock, VT: Foul Play Press.

Marcus, Laura (2003) 'Detection and Literary Fiction', in Martin Priestman (ed.) *The Cambridge Companion to Crime Fiction*, pp. 245–67. Cambridge: Cambridge University Press.

Marx, Karl (1976) *Capital: A Critique of Political Economy, Volume 1*. Harmondsworth: Penguin.

Merivale, Patricia (2010) 'Postmodern and Metaphysical Detection', in C.J. Rzepka and L. Horsley (eds) *A Companion to Crime Fiction*, pp. 308–20. Chichester: Wiley-Blackwell.

Miéville, China (2009) 'Cognition as Ideology: A Dialectic of SF Theory', in Mark Bould and China Miéville (eds) *Red Planets: Marxism and Science Fiction*, pp. 231–48. London: Pluto Press.

Morrison, Robert (2006) 'Introduction', in Thomas De Quincey, *On Murder*, pp. vii–xxvii. Oxford: Oxford World's Classics.

Poe, Edgar Allan (2003) *The Fall of the House of Usher and Other Writings*. London: Penguin.

Rendell, Ruth (1978) *A Judgement in Stone*. London: Arrow.

Rieder, John (2008) *Colonialism and the Emergence of Science Fiction*. Middletown, CT: Wesleyan University Press.

Roberts, Adam (2012) 'Does God Need a Starship? Science Fiction and Religion', in Keith Brooke (ed.) *Strange Divisions and Alien Territories: The Sub-Genres of Science Fiction*, pp. 112–25. Basingstoke: Palgrave.

Rowland, Susan (2010) 'The "Classical" Model of the Golden Age', in Charles J. Rzepka and Lee Horsley (eds) *A Companion to Crime Fiction*, pp. 117–27. Chichester: Wiley-Blackwell.

Sayers, Dorothy L. (1963) *Whose Body?* London: New English Library.

Sayers, Dorothy L. (1970) *Gaudy Night*. London: New English Library.

Suvin, Darko (1979) *Metamorphoses of Science Fiction: On the Poetics and History of a Literary Genre*. New Haven, CT: Yale University Press.

Wolfe, Gene K. (2011) 'Evaporating Genres', *Strange Horizons*, URL (consulted October 2013): http://www.strangehorizons.com/2013/20130722/2wolfe-a.shtml

Notes on Contributors

Andrew M. Butler is the author of *Solar Flares: Science Fiction in the 1970s* and Pocket Essentials on Philip K. Dick, Cyberpunk, Terry Pratchett, Film Studies and Postmodernism. His article on the British SF Boom in *Science Fiction Studies* won the Pioneer Award. He is co-editor of *Extrapolation*.

Christos Callow Jr. is a Teaching Assistant at Queen Mary, University of London and an Associate Tutor at Birkbeck College where he has also completed his PhD titled 'Etherotopia, an Ideal State and a State of Mind: Utopian Philosophy as Literature and Practice'. He also has a BA in Acting and an MA in Playwriting.

Niall Harrison is Editor-in-Chief of *Strange Horizons*. His reviews and essays have appeared in *Foundation, Vector, The New York Review of Science Fiction,* and *The Los Angeles Review of Books*.

Paul March-Russell teaches Comparative Literature and Liberal Arts at the University of Kent. He edits the journal, *Foundation,* and the series, SF Storyworlds (Gylphi Press). His most recent publications include *Modernism and Science Fiction* (Palgrave, 2015). Among his current projects are relevant chapters on Modernism and SF for *The Cambridge History of Science Fiction* and *The Cambridge History of the English Short Story*.

Anna McFarlane is the research assistant for the Wellcome Trust-funded Science Fiction and the Medical Humanities project at the University of

Glasgow. Her PhD analysed the use of gestalt theory in literary criticism through a study of William Gibson's science fiction. She is the co-editor of *Vector: The Critical Journal of the British Science Fiction Association.*

Farah Mendlesohn is Head of English and Media at Anglia Ruskin University. She has written in both science fiction and fantasy but is best known for *Rhetorics of Fantasy*. She is currently working on a monograph on Robert A. Heinlein for Illinois University Press.

Glyn Morgan is a doctoral candidate and tutor at the University of Liverpool researching speculative fiction and the Holocaust. He is the co-editor of *Vector: The Critical Journal of the British Science Fiction Association* and co-founder of the annual Current Research in Speculative Fiction (CRSF) conference.

Catherine Parry is a doctoral candidate and associate lecturer at the University of Lincoln, UK. Her PhD reads animal representation in the negotiation of the human-animal divide in twenty-first century fiction. She has recently published a chapter on reflexive literary landscapes in *Interpreting Rurality: Multidisciplinary Approaches.*

Paul Graham Raven is a futures researcher, a writer and critic of science fiction, an essayist, and a reflexively constructed narrative purporting to describe a contiguous identity which in no way reflects its own subjective and self-referential experience of being-in-the-world. He is owned by a cat.

Thomas Wellmann works as a researcher at the DFG-Europa-Kolleg of the University of Münster, where he is also a PhD student at the Graduate School 'Practices of Literature'. He holds a BA and an MEd; his PhD thesis analyses how Europe is negotiated through metanarratives in the Contemporary English Novel.

Michelle K. Yost is a recent graduate of University of Liverpool, where her research focused on the nineteenth-century hollow earth narrative. She has contributed reviews to *Foundation* and helped to edit the third edition of the *Encyclopedia of Science Fiction.*

Index